THE FLOOD
IN THE LIGHT OF
THE BIBLE, GEOLOGY,
AND ARCHAEOLOGY

THE

FLOOD

IN THE LIGHT OF THE BIBLE, GEOLOGY, AND ARCHAEOLOGY

By Alfred M. Rehwinkel (†) M.A., B.D., LL.D.
Professor of Theology, Concordia Seminary
Saint Louis, Missouri

CONCORDIA PUBLISHING HOUSE · SAINT LOUIS

29 30 31 32 33 34 35 36 37   19 18 17 16 15 14 13 12 11

To my children

Dorothy, Helen and Eugene

Preface

THE material here presented in book form was originally delivered in a series of lectures before District church conventions, pastors' institutes, laymen's seminars, teachers' meetings, and in Walther League camps in many parts of the United States and Canada. The audiences which heard these lectures differed greatly in character and education, and hence it was necessary to choose the popular lecture style to find a common ground where all minds could readily meet. The original lectures were revised considerably in preparation for publication, but the popular style has been retained.

Another point to be noted is that these lectures grew over a long period of time and were not originally prepared for publication. It was therefore not always possible, when the revision was made, to indicate at all times the sources that had been consulted, but the reader is referred to a lengthy bibliography at the end of this book. All books and articles listed there have been helpful, and grateful acknowledgment is hereby made, also for the illustrations in the book.

The author has received aid and suggestions from many friends and a variety of sources. He wishes to acknowledge particularly his debt to Dr. George McCready Price, a noted geologist and author of many books on geology and Biblical subjects. Dr. Price is a brilliant champion of Biblical truths, and his searching analysis of the evolutionary theories of modern geology has been very helpful. The author also wishes to acknowledge with deep appreciation the interest shown by, and the encouragement received from, many friends who supplied him with valuable clippings and pictures of newly discovered fossils and other materials from all parts of the United States and Canada. He feels especially indebted to his wife, Bessie, nee Efner, M. D., whose interest, help, and encouragement have been constant.

The author's interest in the study of the Flood dates back to his college days, particularly to the time when he was a student of geology in the University of Alberta, under Dr. John Allan, a great teacher and one of Canada's foremost geologists. This interest was further stimulated when later he was called upon to teach a course in physical geography at Concordia College in Edmonton, Alberta. As a whole, this study has been a lifelong labor of love and a source of much genuine pleasure, because it opened up ever greater visions of God's most wonderful and omnipotent majesty manifested in the works of His creative and destructive powers. It is the author's desire to share this pleasure with many others who have not heard these lectures, by making them available in printed form. In offering this book to the reading public of the Church, he finds no better closing words for these introductory remarks than the beautiful prayer of the great Kepler, who prayed: "I thank Thee, my Creator and my Lord, that Thou hast given me this joy in Thy creation, this thrill in the works of Thy hand. I have made known Thy glory to men as far as my limited spirit can grasp Thine infinitude. If I have written something unworthy of Thee, forgive it in grace."

A. M. Rehwinkel

Concordia Seminary
St. Louis, Missouri

Contents

Illustrations

Introduction

WHY a book on the Flood in the days of Noah? Why devote time and effort to an event which lies on the very threshold of an indistinct twilight of legend and myth and which is farther removed from the present than all the most ancient peoples and empires known to us from secular history? What benefit could there be in a study so hoary in age and so far removed from the thinking of people in the world today? There are four reasons why this study was made and why the results are here presented in book form.

Next to Creation, the Flood of Noah's time is the greatest event in the history of our earth. Nothing comparable with it has happened since nor will happen until the final destruction of this universe in the fire of Judgment Day. The Flood marks the end of a world of transcendent beauty, created by God as a perfect abode for man, and the beginning of a new world, a mere shadowy replica of its original glory. In all recorded history there is no other event except the Fall which has had such a revolutionary effect upon the topography and condition of this earth and which has so profoundly affected human history and every phase of life as it now exists in its manifold forms in the world. No geologist, biologist, or student of history can afford to ignore this great catastrophe.

The second reason for this study is the fact that the Flood occupies a most prominent place in our Bible. The sacred writer devotes more space to the history of the Flood than to the story of creation. About one third of the first eleven chapters of Genesis, which deal with the first two thousand years of the world's history, are devoted to the Flood. There are repeated references to the Flood in other books of the Old Testament. Jesus and the Apostles refer to it in the New Testament and hold it up as a warning example of God's wrath against sin as well as an example of His saving mercy. What Paul wrote concerning the Old Testament Scripture most certainly applies to this section, namely: "All Scripture is given by inspiration of God and is profitable for doctrine, for reproof, for correction, for instruction in righteousness" (2 Tim. 3:16). We shall have ample opportunity to learn later that there is indeed much reproof, correction, and instruction in righteousness in the Biblical account of the Flood.

Every student of the Bible and of geology knows there exists today a seemingly irreconcilable conflict between Genesis and geology. This conflict dates back about 125 years and had its origin in the rise of evolutionary geology. Up to that time, theologians and scientists were generally in agreement with the Biblical teachings concerning Creation and the Flood. But that is no longer the case. Today textbooks prescribed for courses in physical geography and geology in American high schools and colleges no longer teach a Biblical creation of the universe in six days of twenty-four hours each by a divine fiat. Some teachers, in fact, take delight in ridiculing the Biblical creation story and rule it out of modern thinking as naive, absurd, or as mere folklore of primitive people. Now and then there are still those who try to harmonize Genesis and the theories of geology by juggling language and extending the six days of creation into six periods of unlimited time, each measured by millions, or possibly billions, of years. Still others preserve an outward reverence for the Bible and speak of Genesis patronizingly as a beautiful but poetical conception of the origin of things.

The shock received by the inexperienced young student is therefore overwhelming when he enters the classroom of such teachers and suddenly discovers to his great bewilderment that these men and women of acclaimed learning do not believe the views taught him in his early childhood days; and since the student sits at their feet day after day, it usually does not require a great deal of time until the foundation of his faith begins to crumble as stone upon stone is being removed from it by these unbelieving teachers. Only too often the results are disastrous. The young Christian becomes disturbed, confused, and bewildered. Social pressure and the weight of authority add to his difficulties. First he begins to doubt the infallibility of the Bible in matters of geology, but he will not stop there. Other difficulties arise, and before long skepticism and unbelief have taken the place of his childhood faith, and the saddest of all tragedies has happened. Once more a pious Christian youth has gained a glittering world of pseudo learning but has lost his own immortal soul.

To help these students and others like them over this difficult and dangerous period is the chief reason for this study and its publication. A careful study of the Biblical account of the Flood will prove that this fearful world catastrophe offers the most reasonable solution for most or all of the difficulties which confront the student of historical geology and which tend to disturb his faith in the truth and reliability of the Bible.

For the encouragement of young Christians who are overawed by the show of great learning of unbelieving professors it ought to be said that there always have been and still are very eminent scientists and men of great learning who retain their faith in the Bible as God's own infallible revelation to man. Everyone knows that men like Kepler,

Newton, Faraday, and others of like stature were humble Christians and believers in the Bible. Great geologists of the last century, like Hugh Miller, Pye Smith, Murcheson, Sir William Dawson, and others, remained faithful believers and defenders of the Bible. Dr. Samuel Johnson, who was well known for his profound classical scholarship, was a humble and pious man and took the Bible for his guide throughout life and leaned entirely upon its promises for comfort in the hour of death.

At a meeting of the British Association of Scientists held in 1865 a manifesto was drawn up and signed by 617 men of science, many of whom were of the highest eminence, in which they declared their belief not only in the truth and authenticity of the Holy Scriptures, but also in the harmony of Scripture with natural science. A copy of this manifesto was deposited in the Bodleian Library of Oxford. The text of this manifesto is very interesting. It reads as follows:

We, the undersigned students of the Natural Sciences, desire to express our sincere regret that researches into scientific truth are perverted by some in our own times into occasions for casting doubt upon the truth and authenticity of the Holy Scriptures.

We conceive that it is impossible for the Word of God as written in the book of Nature, and God's Word written in Holy Scripture to contradict one another, however much they may appear to differ.

We are not forgetful that physical science is not complete, but is only in a condition of progress, and that at present our finite reason enables us only to see as through a glass darkly, and we confidently believe that a time will come when the two records will be seen to agree in every particular.

We cannot but deplore that Natural Science should be looked upon with suspicion by many who do not make a study of it, merely on account of the unadvised manner in which some are placing it in opposition to Holy Writ.

We believe that it is the duty of every scientific student to investigate Nature simply for the purpose of elucidating truth, and that if he finds that some of his results appear to be in contradiction to the written Word, or rather to his own interpretation of it, which may be erroneous, he should not presumptuously affirm that his own conclusions must be right, and the statements of Scriptures wrong.

Rather leave the two side by side until it shall please God to allow us to see the manner in which they may be reconciled; and instead of insisting upon the seeming differences between Science and the Scriptures, it would be as well to rest in faith upon the points in which they agree.*

Great men of science are humble men because they best know the frailties and limitations of finite men. It is the small man, the second-rate scholar and scientist, who struts in arrogant conceit, who parades his learning to impress the uninitiated, who is intolerant and dogmatic in his pronouncements. These are well characterized by Quintilian, a Roman teacher of oratory at the time of Paul, who says: "The less ability man has, the more he tries to swell himself out as those of short stature exalt themselves on tiptoes, and the weak use most threats." †

The final reason for a study of the Flood is to remind the Christian reader that the Flood was a prototype of the Final Judgment, which will make a sudden and fearful end of the second world. The Lord says: "As the days of Noe were, so shall also the coming of the Son of Man be. For as in the days that were before the Flood they were eating and drinking, marrying and giving in marriage, until the day that Noe entered into the ark, and knew not until the Flood came and took them all away, so shall also the coming of the Son of Man be." (Matt. 24:37-39.) As the first world perished by water, so this present world shall be destroyed by fire. (2 Pet. 3:3 ff.) And as this second world emerged from the Flood stripped of its original glory, so shall emerge from the fire of Judgment a new heaven and a new earth cleansed of sin and all evil, of misery, war, and death, and restored to a perfection which shall transcend even its original glory. (2 Pet. 3:13 ff.)

A study of the Flood will prove to be extremely fascinating and rich in instruction, both spiritual and secular,

---

* Samuel Kinns, *Moses and Geology*, p. 5 f.
† *Institute of Oratory*, Book 2, Chap. 3.

for in this awful catastrophe we behold our God in His wonderful and fearful majesty as He deals in His anger and mercy with the children of men. And as we now undertake this study, we must always remain mindful of the fact that we are dealing here with a great miracle of God, though the natural forces already in the universe were employed to bring it about, and miracles, in their very nature, are supernatural acts of God and therefore contrary to the established laws of nature and incapable of explanation and complete understanding by finite man. Hence we must expect that many problems connected with the Flood will remain unsolved mysteries. The general plan of the study aims to develop the following broad outline:

I. The World Before the Flood

II. The Biblical Account of the Flood

III. Extra-Biblical Evidence for the Flood

IV. The World After the Flood

PART I

The World Before the Flood

The End of All Flesh, by Doré

CHAPTER I

The Physical World Before the Flood

THE recorded information we have concerning the physical condition of the world before the Flood is very meager. The only direct Biblical reference is found in Gen. 1:31, where we read: "And God saw everything that He had made, and, behold, it was very good." When God had finished creating, He inspected, as it were, the works of His hand, and He was delighted with the things that He had made and pronounced them very good. What God pronounces good, that is good in the absolute. God had created a perfect abode for man, the crown of His creation. It was perfect and complete in every detail. There were no thorns and thistles in that world. The earth brought forth abundantly of everything that was needful to provide for the wants, comforts, and pleasures of man. There was no need of a struggle for an existence either between man and man or between the beasts and their companions. There were no Saharas, no barren wastes, no bleak and sterile hills, no rigors of the arctic and no disease-breeding heat of the tropics. The most enchanting islands in the subtropical area of the South Seas today are but an imperfect replica of what that world was which received the verdict "very good" from its Creator.

It is true, after God had spoken these words, sin came into the world and with sin the blight and the curse of sin. And the curse which God had pronounced became effective at once, but its consequences were not immediately apparent to their fullest extent.

It was here as it was with men. God had said: "The day that thou eatest thereof thou shalt surely die," and when man ate, death was upon him and in him, but man did not die immediately. That body created unto immortality defied death for nearly a thousand years. He lived as though he would never die. And as with men, so it was with the rest of creation. Though the blight of sin was upon it, its original glory did not depart at once, and the "groaning and travailing in pain" of which St. Paul speaks (Rom. 8:22) was not yet as audible as it is now.

Even after sin and death had come into this world, it was still a world vastly superior to the world which now is. It was, as Luther says, "a veritable paradise compared with the world that followed."

In the first place, it was a world with more "living space" for the human race than the present world offers. The world of Adam and his immediate descendants contained proportionately more habitable land than the world of today. There were no enormous waste areas, such as the great deserts of Africa, Asia, America, and Australia. Nor were the land masses separated by such vast expanses of ocean water, which today constitute about seven tenths of the earth's surface.

The earth's surface is approximately 197,000,000 square miles. Of this, 139,000,000 square miles of the world today is sea, leaving 58,000,000 square miles of land, or only a little more than one fourth of the globe which is not covered with water. But not even all of this one fourth of the earth's surface is suitable for human habitation. The regions of the earth which are capable of supporting an average population by virtue of fertility of land, the abundance of natural

2

resources, and favorable climate are distinctly limited. Large areas are closed to extensive human habitation because of climatic and other conditions.

The greatest hindrance to extensive settlement in the world since the Flood are the vast desert and mountain belts which completely divide the great continents into fertile and wasteland areas. Beginning with the Sahara, the latter areas continue through the deserts of Arabia and Iran to the enormous barren plateaus of Tibet and Mongolia, ending finally with the mountain wilderness of lower Siberia. In North America a mountain belt extending from Alaska down through the entire length of the continent to the southernmost peak is likewise sparsely settled and offers living space only to comparatively few.

To these forbidding sections of our earth today must also be added the northern tundras of Canada and Siberia and the ice-covered continents of Greenland and Antarctica, the Australian desert, which comprises over half of that continent, and the lofty mountain regions of northern India and western South America.

All told, the regions of the world unsuitable for human habitation comprise about 40 per cent of its land surface. To this must be added the tropical forest lands as found in the valleys of the Amazon, the Congo, and on the equatorial islands of southeastern Asia. These regions add up to another 10 per cent or more. The actual land areas therefore suitable for habitation comprise less than one half of the land surfaces of the earth.

But this is not all. The earth after the Flood was not only reduced considerably in land area, but even in this shrunken earth the fertility of the soil and the natural resources necessary for human progress are now unequally distributed, so that the people in some areas live in plenty while others eke out a miserable existence, thus giving rise to jealousies, rivalries, and bloody wars between the nations. But the world before the Flood was not so.

3

The general contour of the antediluvian Europe was not the same as that of modern Europe. The great Sir William Dawson describes the Europe of a previous world as compared with the present as follows: "In Europe, the British Isles were connected with the mainland, and Ireland was united with England. The Rhine flowed northward to the Orkneys through a wide plain, probably wooded and swarming with great quadrupeds, now extinct or strange to Europe. The Thames and the Humber were tributaries of the Rhine. The land of France and Spain extended out to the one hundredth fathom line. The shallower parts of the Mediterranean were dry land, and that sea was divided into two parts by a land connecting Italy with Africa. Possibly, a portion of the shallower areas of the Atlantic were so elevated to connect Europe and America more closely than at present." [1]

Fossils of plants and man-made implements found in the Sahara show that this great African desert was at one time covered with luxuriant vegetation and was inhabited by man. Similar remains have been found in the Gobi Desert of China and in the great desert areas of northwestern India.

Australia and Tasmania constituted one continent, while the north and south islands of New Zealand together formed one unbroken body of land.

The Arctic and Antarctic regions of the two poles and Greenland were not always covered with mountains of ice and snow, but were habitable for both animals and man. Wallace speaks of a "rich warm temperate flora once covering what are now the icy wastes of Greenland and Spitzbergen." [2] The broken-up character of the coast of Ireland and Newfoundland, Labrador, Greenland, and Iceland, with the extensive bank of the Azores, all point to a certain amount of recent sinking of land on the outskirts of this area of great depression. [3]

The flora and fauna found in the northern part of South America and in the southern part of the United States in-

4

dicate that there was another land bridge between these two continents besides the present narrow neck of Central America. This other link connected the two continents from Florida southward by way of the islands of the Caribbean.

The sea at Bering Strait is so shallow that we may safely conclude that the continents of Asia and America were once connected, while the shallow Okhotsk, Japan, and Yellow Seas indicate a large extension of lowlands of eastern Asia.[4]

The eastern coast of North America extended much farther eastward into the Atlantic, possibly connecting with Europe in the north and by way of the mythical continent called Atlantis in the south.

The ancients had a legend concerning a vanished continent in the Atlantic Ocean which, according to tradition, had existed somewhere in the great sea west of the "Pillars of Hercules." It was the dwelling place of the gods and a great race of people, but was suddenly and mysteriously swallowed up by the ocean as a result of an earthquake. Plato tells us that Solon was the first of the Greeks to hear of this mysterious island-continent and its wonders while visiting in Egypt, where the wise men of Sais told him of its existence. Solon intended to write its history but found that he was too far advanced in years to undertake such a task. Two hundred years later, Plato decided to do what Solon had left undone. Plato's history of Atlantis is found in the unfinished dialog known as *Critias*.[5] Soundings in the Atlantic Ocean between southern Europe and America have revealed the possibility of the existence of a prehistoric continent in that area which served as a bridge between Europe, Africa, and America.

Today great mountain ranges divide the continents and smaller land masses into clearly defined climatic and biological zones. Think of the Rocky Mountains in North America, the Andes in South America, or the Himalayas in Asia, and the tremendous effect these rocky walls have had on the

5

climate in the respective continents where they are found. But this was not always so. The mountain ranges in the world of Adam were not the same high, forbidding walls as found in the world of today, but were much lower, covered with vegetation, and did not seriously interfere with the climatic condition as do the mountains of today. The English scientist Alfred Wallace, speaking about a world that has disappeared, writes: "The Alps, the Pyrenees, the Rocky Mountains, and even the Himalayas were all in early Miocene times many thousand feet lower than they are now. This is proved by the fact of Eocene and Miocene marine deposits of great thickness, which must have been formed in rather deep water, being found elevated from ten to sixteen thousand feet above the sea level. As an example, we may mention the Dent du Midi in Switzerland, where marine shells of early Miocene or late Eocene type are found at an elevation of 10,940 feet; and as this mountain must have suffered enormous denudation, these figures can only represent a portion of the rise of the land, most of which occurred during the Miocene period." [6]

Nor is it mere speculation to speak of the first world as a "veritable paradise." For though there are but meager written records concerning this first world, there is another kind of record which God has preserved for us in His wisdom. This record is reliable and true and is written in large and legible letters in the very foundation rocks of our present world. The record I refer to are the fossil remains that have been found in great abundance in every part of the globe. These fossils may be called the mummified remains of an extinct world. Fossils do not lie. Just as the pyramids of Egypt and the monuments of Greece and Rome are an evidence of the greatness of the civilization that produced them, so these fossils speak an eloquent language of the glories of a world which has passed away. These fossils have been preserved by God for a purpose. They are, as it were, the inscription on a tombstone erected to that magnificent world

6

and at the same time a warning to the world which was to follow. The fossils have stimulated the imagination of men ever since the early Greeks. The early church fathers were familiar with them. Tertullian mentions them and gives a fairly correct interpretation of them. Luther also knew of them and understood their meaning. Others since then have had very fantastic ideas about them, but to us their language is clear. A more detailed discussion of these fossils will follow in a later chapter. Here I merely wish to refer to them as evidence and conclusive proof that the physical condition of the world of Noah, the climate, animals, and plant life, was vastly different from that of our world today.

With respect to climate, the fossils show that there was a uniformly mild climate in high and in low altitudes of both the northern and the southern hemisphere. That is, there was a perfectly uniform, non-zonal, mild, and springlike climate in every part of the globe. This does not mean that the climate was of necessity the same in all parts of the earth. There were differences, but not the present extremes. Sir Henry H. Howorth, a noted geologist and competent interpreter of these fossils, says: "The flora and fauna are virtually the only thermometer with which we can test the climate of any past period. Other evidence is always sophisticated by the fact that we may be attributing to climate what is due to other causes. But the biological evidence is unmistakable; cold-blooded reptiles cannot live in icy water; semitropical plants, or plants whose habitat is the temperate zone, cannot ripen their seeds and sow themselves under arctic conditions." [7]

Or another outstanding authority, Prof. Alfred R. Wallace, says: "There is but one climate known to the ancient fossil world as revealed by the plants and animals entombed in the rocks, and the climate was a mantle of springlike loveliness which seems to have prevailed continuously over the whole globe. Just how the world could have thus been warmed all over may be a matter of conjecture; that it was so warmed effectively and continuously is a matter of fact." [8]

F. H. Knowlton, in speaking about the climate which prevailed in the region of Yellowstone National Park during the so-called Tertiary period, writes: "A final word may be added regarding the probable climate of the region during the lifetime of these fossil forests. It is obvious that the present flora of the Yellowstone National Park has comparatively little relation to the Tertiary flora and cannot be considered a descendant of it. It is also clear that climatic conditions must have greatly changed since Tertiary times. The Tertiary flora appears to have come from the south, but the present flora is evidently of a more northern origin. The climate during the Tertiary times as indicated by the vegetation was temperate or warm. Temperate, not unlike that of Virginia or the Carolinas of the present time, and the presence of numerous species of figs, a supposed breadfruit tree, cinnamons, and other southern plants indicates that it may have been almost subtropical. However, the conditions that were favorable to this seemingly subtropical growth may have been different from the conditions now necessary for the growth of similar vegetation. . . . It is certain, however, that the conditions were very different from those now prevailing in this part." [9]

Or Prof. George McCready Price writes: "It would be quite useless to go through the whole fossiliferous series in order, for there is not a single system which does not have coral limestone or other evidence of a mild climate way up north, most systems having such rock in the lands which skirt the very pole itself. The limestone and coal beds of the carboniferous period are the nearest known rocks to the North Pole. They crop out all around the polar basis; and from the dip of these beds, they must underlie the polar sea itself. But it is needless to go through the systems one after another, for they *'uniformly testify that a warm climate has in former times prevailed over the whole globe.'* " [10]

8

It is difficult for us today even to imagine a world as just described, a world in which there was neither arctic nor antarctic and no steaming jungles of the Equator. We know that our present climatic zones and seasons are the results of the changing relations of the earth to the sun, the source of the heat that warms our globe. It is, therefore, quite natural to ask at this point: How could these laws of nature have functioned in that world so as to produce conditions so different from those prevailing today, and what caused the change?

That our earth at one time in its history enjoyed a uniformly mild climate in all of its parts is a fact which can be demonstrated, as we have seen, and that a change came suddenly, in fact, very suddenly, and probably at a time of a universal flood, seems to be established beyond a doubt from the frozen mammoths found fully preserved in the flesh in the frozen tundras of northern Siberia, of which we shall hear more later. But what caused the change is not definitely known. All we can do is guess at an answer and project possible theories as to the most reasonable solution for these difficulties.

Three theories have been suggested. The first is that the earth was tilted 23½ degrees at the time of the Flood, bringing about a change in the relation of the earth to the sun and thus creating the climatic zones as they now exist.

If the earth's axis were perpendicular to the plane of its orbit, the sunlight would always extend from pole to pole, and days and nights would always be of equal length, that is, twelve hours each, and every portion of the earth's surface in the same latitude would continually receive the same amount of heat and light. In that case there would be no change of season, as is shown in the diagram on page 10.

But the axis of the earth is not perpendicular to the plane of its orbit. It inclines at about 23½ degrees. In figures A and B are shown the two portions of the earth in its orbit. In figure A the north pole on December 21 is turned away

9

from the sun, and consequently the sun's rays fall short of it by 23½ degrees. At the same time they shine upon the South Pole as shown in figure B by a like amount. By June 21 the condition is completely reversed, and the rays of the sun reach the North Pole, while they fall short of the South Pole.

The tilted position of the earth therefore accounts for the arctic and antarctic regions of the two poles and for the seasons of the year. According to this theory the tilting of the axis of the earth to the amount of 23½ degrees occurred at the time of the Flood, thereby causing a change in the climate and creating the present climatic zones, but also

The Sun

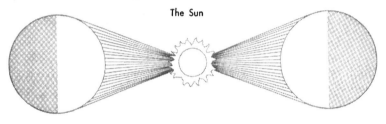

Fig. A   Fig. B

bringing about those violent cosmic revolutions on the earth which affected the entire universe and which resulted in the Flood.

According to a second theory the uniform climate of the first world was brought about by the warm ocean waters which surrounded the antediluvian continents. It is believed that the land and water segments were more equally distributed so that no portions of the existing continents were as far removed from the ocean as they are now. It is quite conceivable that a universal ocean of warm water could very well cause a uniformly mild climate in every part of the globe, but that alone could not account for the luxuriant vegetation which flourished during this period in the ancient polar regions, if the antediluvian poles like today were shrouded in darkness for six months of each year.

Another version of this same theory holds that warm ocean currents were so distributed that every portion of the existing land masses was touched and warmed by them, similar to the conditions of those parts of the world today that are affected by the Gulf Stream and the Japan Current.

Everyone is familiar with this strange phenomenon of ocean currents, that is, those remarkable rivers of warm water flowing in a sea of cold water and keeping a definite and permanent course for thousands of miles. The Gulf Stream, which derives its name from the Gulf of Mexico,

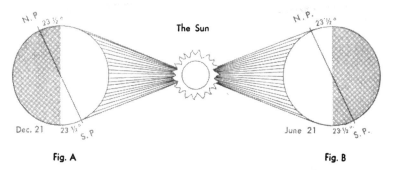

The Sun

Fig. A   Fig. B

where it seems to originate, is the best known and the most remarkable of these ocean currents. It is a stream much larger than either the Mississippi or the Amazon. It is fifty miles wide at the Straits of Florida and has an average depth of about 1,500 feet. This stream is more than 4,000 miles long, its rate of flow varying from about three to five miles an hour. The temperature of its water is warmer than the ocean at the Equator, but cools slightly as it travels northward. This Gulf Stream, with the prevailing westerly winds, is responsible for the mild climate of England and northwestern Europe and affects the climate even as far north as Spitzbergen. In southern England, which lies in about the same latitude as Edmonton, Alberta, the winters are very mild, with very little ice and snow, so that vegetables like cabbage can be left in the gardens all winter, while the

11

mercury in Edmonton at the same time might dip to fifty and occasionally even to sixty degrees below zero.

The Japan Current has the same influence on the climate of Alaska and British Columbia.

If similar currents touched all of the antediluvian continents and affected them as the Gulf Stream affects northwestern Europe and the Japan Current Alaska and British Columbia today, then it is quite conceivable that this might well account for a uniformly mild climate throughout the ancient world. But this, too, would not offer a satisfactory explanation for the rich vegetation in the polar regions.

The third theory attempting to explain the antediluvian climate is the so-called canopy theory.[11] According to this theory the earth was originally surrounded by a canopy of vapor which intercepted the direct rays of the sun. The heat which penetrated the canopy was diffused so equally over all the zones of latitude that the subtropical climate prevailed even in the high latitude. This canopy served to bring about conditions similar to those in a hothouse with a temperature of about 72° F. The chemical rays of the sun, especially those most active in the aging of living things and those that bring about decay and fermentation, were intercepted by the canopy, and as a result, men and animals lived to great ages. Storms and rain were unknown in the world of Adam, and hence the rainbow was first seen on the day that Noah left the ark. Extremes of cold and heat were not possible. In the Flood all this changed. The canopy collapsed and was the chief source of the floodwaters. The immediate effect of the removal of the canopy was a radical climatic change. Now the seasons became sharply divided, and there was from now on "a seedtime and harvest, cold and heat, summer and winter" (Gen. 8:22).

These are the three theories that have been proposed to offer a possible solution for the wonderful climatic conditions that prevailed in the world before the Flood. It is impossible, of course, to know which, if any, of these theories correctly describes the conditions. The most reasonable view would seem to be to assume that all three, or at least the first two, might have applied, that is, to assume that the earth was tilted at the time of the Flood out of its original position, thus changing the relation of the earth to the sun and creating the two polar regions, and that the temperature of the first world had been equalized by the warm ocean water or warm ocean currents. But something might even be said in favor of the canopy theory. At any rate Gen. 2:5 and Gen. 9:13 become more meaningful within the framework of this theory.

With such favorable climatic conditions prevailing everywhere, it requires no great flights of the imagination to perceive that the flora and the fauna of that world would be in harmony with their physical surroundings, and therefore far superior to the flora and fauna of the world today. And so it was, for this, too, is borne out by the records in the rocks. Beginning with the animals, we find that the fossils reveal 1) a greater distribution of the various genera and species in all parts of the earth; 2) a far greater variety of genera and species than have existed in the world since then; and 3) a distinct deterioration of the animals which have survived when compared with their antediluvian ancestors.

It is not within the scope of this study to treat any of these questions in great detail. A few examples must suffice. Everybody today has read about or seen the pictures of the dragonlike prehistoric reptiles known as the sauria. Their fossils are found in every continent, sometimes in great numbers. The dinosaurs of the Red Deer Valley in Alberta must have lived and died there by the thousands, so thickly are their skeletons scattered over the adjoining region known as the "Bad Lands." Some writers on the subject hold that they must have been as numerous as the hardy buffalo of a generation ago, but with much more variety and form of

13

species. In point of size they ranged from the size of a small dog to monsters of over eighty feet in length. In point of diversity they represent almost a world of their own. In Alberta alone twenty-six different species have been identified. There were those that lived on land, others in water, and still others in the air.

The sea that in ages past covered the regions which now constitute our own western Kansas was the headquarters of a species known as Monassaurs, and thousands of specimens have been taken from the chalk bluffs of this State, some of them in such a fine state of preservation that we are not only well acquainted with their internal structure, but with their outward appearance as well. Another species of marine reptile found in Kansas measured nearly fifty feet in length. Of the flying reptiles, one has been found with a head a yard long and with a stretch of wings of over twenty feet. Another of these prediluvian monsters was a reptile which modern paleontologists have very fittingly called Tyrannosaurus, that is, the tyrant lizard, for he was absolutely the most formidable creature that stalked the earth. A monster when standing erect, he measured eighteen feet high, with claws like an eagle's, and provided with double-edged, daggerlike teeth, two and three inches long, set in a mouth with a yard-wide gap. Brontosaurus was probably the largest of them all, in fact, we know, the largest creature that ever walked on this earth. A specimen of this prehistoric giant is found in the American Museum in New York and measures sixty-six feet, eight inches in length, and it is estimated that, when living, this animal must have weighed at least thirty-eight tons. One even larger than the New York specimen was reported found in South America, which was said to have measured 150 feet in length. Similar discoveries have been made in Russia, in different parts of the United States, Africa, and elsewhere. Only the whale in the world today compares in size with these ancient land animals.

Associated with these reptiles here in America and Eu-

Restoration of Brontosaurus, the Thunder Reptile. From the Jurassic of Medicine Bow, Wyo. Painting by Charles R. Knight

*Tylosaurus. One of the Rulers of the
Cretaceous Sea*

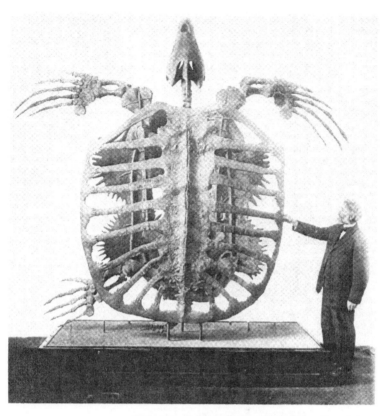

The Giant Sea Turtle Archelon. A contemporary of the Morosaurs. From the specimen in the Yale University Museum

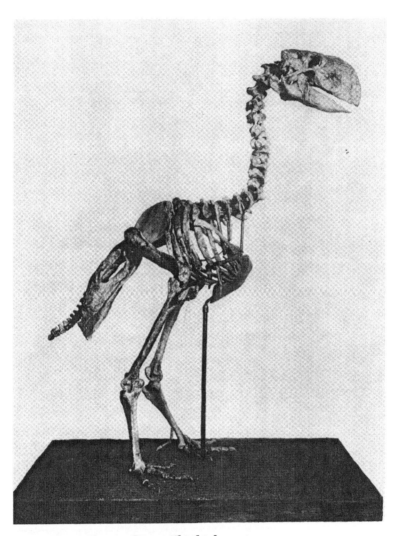

Diatryma, an Eocene Giant. This bird was ten feet tall. This unique specimen is in the American Museum of Natural History

*Jaws of the Giant Fossil Shark. The teeth are
real, but the jaws are of necessity restored. In
the American Museum of Natural History*

rope were other animals, now either extinct or found only in tropical climate, such as the elephant, lion, tiger, tapir, the camel, and others. In the frozen north of Siberia and Alaska the mammoth once roamed in immense herds, while walruses, rhinoceroses, and similar animals had their habitat within the present territory of the United States.

"The bird kingdom, too, was far greater than now. Bones of a bird have been found which indicate that this species must have stood at least ten feet high, or two feet higher than the largest ostrich." [12]

Fossil snail shells have been found measuring nearly a foot in diameter; other shells related to the pearly nautilus measured over a yard across; and straight-shelled cephalopods with shells more than a foot in diameter and fifteen feet long have been discovered.

Everyone is familiar with the modern lobster; when a specimen is found to measure a foot or more in size, it is regarded as an exceptional curiosity. But fossil crustaceans belonging to that family have been known to measure at least six feet in size. The same is true of the insects. Some of the ancient locusts had a spread of wing of more than seven inches, while some of the dragon flies had bodies nearly a foot and a half long and wings spreading over two feet from tip to tip. Monstrous amphibians belonging to the frog family were discovered, measuring six and even ten feet, with heads twenty inches long.

In 1921 the fossil remains of a prehistoric bat were found near Entwistle, Alberta, which, when living, must have had the size of an average sheep, with a head like a crocodile and with a spread of wings measuring fifteen feet. The greatest zoological gardens with their animals gathered from all the continents are poor affairs as compared with the native dwellers that once inhabited our North American continent. And what is true of North America is true of every other continent.

Professor Wallace is, therefore, quite right when he says: "It is quite clear, therefore, that we live in a zoologically impoverished world, from which all the hugest and fiercest and strangest forms have disappeared." [13]

What is true of the animals also applies to the plant kingdom of that strange world. Here, too, the rocks reveal wonders upon wonders. Not only was there a greater variety of plants, but the species still in existence were much larger and more widely distributed over the face of the earth; and there was an abundance and luxuriance of plant life in every part of the earth of which we today no longer are able to form an adequate conception. A few examples must suffice: Trees such as the oak, beech, myrtle, laurel, walnut, palms, banana trees, magnolias, breadfruit, grape vines, sequoias like those of modern California, and others like them were not only found in the northwestern States as Wyoming, Montana, and western Canada, but also in Alaska, Greenland, and up to the very polar regions. The abundance and the great varieties of plant life found in Arctic Siberia have even suggested to some that the Garden of Eden might have been in that region.

An irrefutable proof for the unparalleled luxuriance of plant life in that prehistoric world are the great coal beds found in every continent of the earth today. The recent Byrd Antarctic Expedition discovered a whole mountain of coal at the South Pole. These coal beds were God's wonderful way of preserving for future generations the magnificent trees and the plants which covered the face of the earth as this had come forth from the hands of the Creator. It has been estimated that it requires from ten to fourteen feet of vegetable matter to produce a seam of coal one foot in thickness. There are seams of coal ranging from forty to fifty feet in thickness. In a strip mine in Wyoming a seam measuring from sixty to ninety feet in thickness has been discovered. [14] This means that a solid mass of vegetation, trees, and other plants from five hundred to a thousand feet in thickness was required to make possible the creation of coal seams of such magnitude.

What a marvelous world this must have been! Our imagination is inadequate to reconstruct for ourselves a picture of the world which God had given as a possession to Adam and his descendants.

May this suffice on the subject of the physical world before the Flood. Much more could be said. What has been said is sufficient to show that the world of Adam, Methuselah, of Enoch and Noah, was a wondrous world. A world rich in plant and animal life. A world which yielded food of every kind for man and beast without any great effort on the part of either, a world which could therefore support a population many times greater than our present population. A world which was made delightful by a uniform climate of springlike loveliness like that of Paradise itself. In short, the whole world was a garden of God, or as Luther said, "a veritable paradise," compared with the world which followed. This was the golden age in the history of the earth. It was a creation of God's love, created for the enjoyment of him who was created in His own image and made to rule over it and possess it. And yet this world was destroyed by the Flood. God Himself destroyed it. In Jonah 4:10-11 we read: "Then said the Lord, Thou hast had pity on the gourd, for the which thou hast not labored, neither madest it to grow, which came up in a night and perished in a night. And should not I spare Nineveh, that great city, wherein are more than sixscore thousand persons that cannot discern between their right hand and their left hand, and also much cattle?" And Jeremiah laments over the desolated city of Jerusalem: "Is it nothing to you, all ye that pass by? Behold, and see if there be any sorrow like unto my sorrow, which is done unto me?" (Lam. 1:12.) And on entering Jerusalem and beholding the city and its future destruction, Jesus wept because she had not known what belonged to her peace. God grieved over Nineveh, He lamented and wept over Jerusalem, but what were Jerusalem and Nineveh in all their glory compared with that world which perished in the Flood!

Our God is a God of love, of tender mercies and long-suffering to them that fear and love Him and do according to His commandments; but He is a terrible Judge to those that reject His mercy. If He spared not the angels that sinned, but cast them down into hell, and if He spared not this magnificent world of His original creation, how will the ungodly and the wicked of today escape His wrath when the Day of Judgment shall dawn upon this second world?

CHAPTER II

The Duration of the First World and Its Population

THE story of the Flood is told in Chapters Six to Nine in the first book of the Bible. The story of the fall of man is found in Chapter Three. Between these two events are only two chapters, and both of these are largely devoted to genealogical tables. In our school Bible histories and Sunday school literature the account of the fall of man is usually followed by the story of Cain and Abel, and that again by the story of the Flood. As a result, children as well as adults are often found to have formed an erroneous conception concerning the duration of the first world. We usually think of that period as having been much shorter than it really was. It must be remembered, however, that the duration of the first world covered a long period of time, a period much longer than any kingdom or empire in ancient or modern times had ever flourished. We have an exact chronology of this age in Genesis 5, and that chronology is confirmed by the genealogical table found in Chronicles 1 and Luke 3. According to this chronology the Flood occurred in the year 1656 after Creation.

But to say that the first world stood for 1,656 years does not mean a great deal unless we try to visualize the length of this period by translating it into our own time. If we turn back the pages of modern history to the number of 1,656 years, we shall find ourselves in the midst of Roman history, about the time when Diocletian was ruler of that great empire and when the Roman amphitheaters and arenas were still re-echoing with the mad shouts of the spectators witnessing the gruesome slaughter of persecuted Christians. Much of the ancient, all of the medieval, and all of modern history has occurred since that time.

Such events as the Barbarian invasion, the fall of Rome, the rise of the Papacy, the establishment of the European nations, the founding and spreading of Mohammedanism, the discovery of America and Australia, the Protestant Reformation, the French Revolution, and countless wars, the invention of gunpowder, of the printing press, the steam engine and electricity, and a thousand other events which have influenced the course of history and made this modern world, have happened in the last 1,656 years. A new world, distinct from the ancient world, developed since then, and a population which numbered at most a few hundred million has grown to the enormous number of over two billion. Sixteen hundred and fifty-six years is a long time in human history. It was a long time in the first world. It was long enough for the human race to increase and expand and take possession of the earth as God had commanded.

The common view is that the population before the Flood was quite small and that its geographical distribution was limited to a comparatively small area. Or, as one learned author says: "It would be highly unreasonable to suppose that mankind had so increased before the deluge as to have penetrated to all the corners of the earth. It is indeed not probable that they had extended themselves beyond the limits of Syria and Mesopotamia." [1]

And yet, even in our age, 1,656 years is sufficient for the human race to grow to an enormous population. To this must be added that conditions then were much more favorable for propagation than in the present world. Original man was endowed with far greater vitality of body and mind than now. This can be inferred from the great age to which he lived. And from this it would also necessarily follow that the antediluvians were far more prolific than man is in his present state. Add to this the climatic conditions, the fact that food supplies were far more plentiful and accessible for all, that a world of virgin soil and unlimited riches beckoned man to take possession, and you have the most ideal conditions for the rapid growth of population.

In modern times the world has witnessed a phenomenal growth in population. During the century between 1830 and 1930 the population of the world doubled in number, that is, it increased by about 850 million within one century. Students of population ascribe this extraordinary growth to the application of steam, to transportation and industry, and to the opening up of new virgin territory in America, Australia, Africa, and elsewhere. Or, in other words, the fact that new facilities were created by which the necessities of life could be provided in greater abundance and with more ease had as a result this unparalleled increase in population.

But as already stated, conditions in the antediluvian world were far more favorable than they ever can be in the world of today, and hence it is not unreasonable to assume that the population grew more rapidly than is possible today.

Just what the population of the world of Noah might have been is, of course, entirely a matter of conjecture. But even a most conservative speculation will reveal extremely interesting possibilities.

Our life now lasts threescore years and ten, and only by virtue of strength, fourscore years, as Moses says. Only dur-

ing about thirty or thirty-five years of this perio.
more specifically, woman, is capable of reproduct.
yet in spite of this limited period of life and still more
period of reproduction, families of eight, ten, twelve
teen, or even more are not uncommon, at least, wei not
uncommon a generation or more ago. They are still quite
common among the French-Canadians in Quebec, the Mexicans in our southwestern border States, and among the
hill folk of our Southern mountain regions. Even families
of fifteen or sixteen occur occasionally. Benjamin Franklin
was the fifteenth child in a family of seventeen, and John
Wesley was one in a family of nineteen children. Recently
I met a man on Mount Petit Jean, Arkansas, who was at
that time eighty-seven years old. He had twelve children,
sixty-one grandchildren, seventy-four great-grandchildren,
and five great-great-grandchildren, making a total of 172
descendants in the lifetime of one man, and that today in
Arkansas under conditions which are far from representing
antediluvian abundance. In Clarinda, Iowa, I had the priv-
ilege of speaking to a mother of twenty living children. She
was at the time (1944) still quite youthful in appearance,
very active in the community, and a member of the local
church choir.

The *Idaho Daily State* of September 28, 1946, reported
that Mrs. Mary Jones, a Negro sixty-five years old, gave
birth to her twenty-seventh child, a baby girl, at the University Hospital of Columbus, Ohio. Twenty-one of her
children are living. Her husband is sixty years old.

Now if man, with a vitality much lower, and his age
limit reduced to a mere fraction of that of the antediluvian,
can reproduce his kind to the extent of ten to fourteen and
more to one family, it is certainly reasonable to assume that
the human race in the primeval world was capable of repro-
ducing, and did reproduce, at a much higher rate than is

possible today. If the period of reproduction in the life of a woman is nearly equal to one half of her total possible age today, it is again reasonable to assume that the same was true of the antediluvian mother. From Genesis 5 we know that men lived to an age of eight or nine hundred years and more in the first world. This would mean that the reproduction period continued over a period of at least from four hundred to five hundred years. And that this is not an unwarranted or an absurd conclusion can be established from the same fifth chapter, for in verse fifteen we read of Mahalaleel that he begat a son at the age of sixty-five, and in verse twenty-one, Enoch begat Methuselah at the age of sixty-five, and, again, in verse thirty-two we read that Noah was five hundred years old when he begat Shem, Ham, and Japheth. Here is a period of more than four hundred years during which the generation of that age was able to beget children. And, again, because of the greater antediluvian vitality and vigor, and because of the abundance of food supplies, infant mortality must have been much lower than in any succeeding age of human history. Tradition also has it that families of that age were very large. In Josephus we find such a tradition according to which Adam had fifty-six children, thirty-three sons and twenty-three daughters. The history of Cain also presupposes a population quite numerous, for he says to God: "Everyone that findeth me shall slay me." Cain would not have spoken that way if the whole human race at that time had consisted of the members of a modern family. And again we read that Cain went into the land of Nod and there built a city. A family consisting of a dozen or more children would not build a city for itself.

On the basis of what has been said, it would not be unreasonable to assume that an average family in that age might have consisted of at least eighteen to twenty living and marriageable children. All will agree that on the basis of what has been said, this is a very conservative estimate. According to Genesis 5 there were ten generations from

Adam to Noah. Taking these figures as a basis for a calculation, we obtain the following results:

First generation	2
Second generation	18
Third generation	162
Fourth generation	1,458
Fifth generation	13,122
Sixth generation	118,098
Seventh generation	1,062,882
Eighth generation	9,565,938
Ninth generation	86,093,442
Tenth generation	774,840,979

To this number must be added all surviving previous generations, which would probably number an additional hundred million. According to this calculation, the population at the time of the Flood would have been nearly nine hundred million, or about equal to the population of the world just a hundred years ago. If we assume that the average family numbered 20 children, and retain the ten generations of Genesis 5, we get the following figures:

First generation	2
Second generation	20
Third generation	200
Fourth generation	2,000
Fifth generation	20,000
Sixth generation	200,000
Seventh generation	2,000,000
Eighth generation	20,000,000
Ninth generation	200,000,000
Tenth generation	2,000,000,000

If we were to try another approach to the problem and assume that the ten generations of Genesis 5 did not apply to the entire human race, but only to the descendants of Seth, and that the average age of that generation was not the same as that of the ten patriarchs, and that, instead of ten, there were at least fifteen generations between Adam and Noah, while the average family numbered only ten children, we obtain the following results:

First generation	2
Second generation	10
Third generation	50
Fourth generation	250
Fifth generation	1,250
Sixth generation	6,250
Seventh generation	31,250
Eighth generation	151,250
Ninth generation	756,250
Tenth generation	3,781,250
Eleventh generation	18,906,250
Twelfth generation	94,531,250
Thirteenth generation	472,656,250
Fourteenth generation	2,368,281,250
Fifteenth generation	11,841,406,250

All this is, of course, pure speculation, for no one can know with any degree of certainty what the population of that world might have been, but I believe that these figures are not fantastic, but quite conservative. It is reasonable to assume that the population was at least equal to the population of the world today. There was sufficient time for such an increase in population, and the physical conditions conducive to population growth were most favorable. Dr. E. A. Ross of the University of Michigan,[2] an authority on population, estimates that if the population of the world increases at its present rate, it will treble in the next century, which would mean that by the year 2023 the world population would be about 5,000,000,000. Dr. Ross also makes the interesting observation that if the human race had started at about the time when Marcus Aurelius was emperor of Rome, and since then had multiplied at the present rate, the population today would be 1,700,000,000. Or in other words, according to this estimate, a period about equal in length to the antediluvian age would be sufficient to increase the human race to a number of 1,700,000,000 provided the race had increased as rapidly as it did during the last century. For reasons already stated it is reasonable to assume that the growth of population in the world of Adam and Noah was greater than that of the last century, and Drs. Guy Irving Burch and Elmer Pendell, both experts in the field of population, state in their recent book, *Human Breeding and Survival*, that between 1900 and 1940 the population of the earth increased by 563,000,000, and during the ten years immediately preceding World War II, by 200,000,000. They claim that if India's death rate could be lowered to the level of that of the United States, India with her present birth rate could fill five earths as full as ours, in a single century. China could do the same, and it would not take the U. S. S. R. much longer. The assumed estimate of the antediluvian population must therefore be regarded as extremely conservative.

But if the population had grown into numbers such as indicated, it would be reasonable to assume that man had scattered far beyond the immediate vicinity of the Garden of Eden and had taken possession of the greater part of the face of the earth as God had commanded him. That the latter actually was the case would seem to follow from the fact that God destroyed the whole earth and all the beasts and creeping things therein. God destroyed the earth because of the wickedness of man. He would hardly have destroyed the whole earth with all its creatures had this wickedness been confined to a small area, say, of the Euphrates and Tigris Valleys, as has been suggested. God punished the wickedness of Nineveh and destroyed that great city, but not all of Asia. He punished the apostasy of Israel, but because of their unbelief he did not destroy the whole Roman Empire. "The soul that sinneth, it shall die."

The question now arises: What do the rocks reveal concerning the possible spread of the human race? Have we the same evidence here as we have in the case of plants and animals? Strange to say, on this question the rocks are astonishingly silent. There is only very meager fossil evidence concerning the geographical distribution of the human race in the antediluvian world, and in many cases the interpretation of the available evidence is questioned by competent authorities. However, we are not left altogether in the dark. There is some fairly reliable evidence gathered in nearly every part of the earth, and as time goes on, further remains of antediluvian man and his civilization no doubt will be found.

Prof. Hugo Obermaier of the University of Madrid has accumulated a great deal of material on man's early existence in this world.[3] He found that of the European countries, France has the greatest number of human fossils. But fossil human remains are by no means limited to France or Europe alone. Of the material that he has gathered, I shall select only a few examples.

Obermaier reports the discovery of a cave in France where human remains were found together with the bones of the cave bear, the cave hyena, the cave lion, the leopard, the great deer, the mammoth, the wolf, the woolly rhinoceros, and the reindeer. That is, man is found with the remains of animals which are now either extinct or never had their habitat in those parts of the world during historic times.

According to the same author, a human skull was found in 1865 near Colmar in Alsace in a deposit of loess, 2½ meters below the surface and associated with the woolly mammoth, the bison, and other prehistoric animals.

In 1914 a complete human skeleton was found near Strassburg in a deposit intermixed with pebbles and also associated with the remains of a prehistoric mammoth.

In Belgium, near Namur, human remains were found associated with the remains of the mammoth, the woolly rhinoceros, the giant deer, the reindeer, and other animals.

In 1857 human remains were found in Devonshire, England, again with the same prehistoric animal remains already enumerated.

The Rock of Gibraltar has yielded up human remains together with the remains of a flora and fauna quite different from that found in that region today.

In 1914 human fossils were found in a quarry near Weimar, Germany, at a depth of 11.9 meters below the surface. Associated with these human remains were found wood ashes, flint implements, the remains of the rhinoceros and the cave bear. And two years later, in the same vicinity, the skeletal remains of a child were discovered together with the fossils of a rhinoceros, a cave bear, and other prehistoric animals.

In Honan, China, human remains were found in a deep loess deposit with the remains of the wild boar, the bison, and the mammoth.

A very important discovery was made in northern Rhodesia, Africa, in 1921, while men were working in the mine known as the "Bone Cave." Here were found a great number of fossilized and partly fossilized remains, including the elephant, lion, rhinoceros, antelope, and the bones of many smaller animals and birds. Amidst this strange accumulation of animal bones was also found an almost complete human skull with other human bones.

In the year 1700 Duke Erhardt Ludwig of Wuerttemberg caused some excavations to be made at Cannstadt, near Stuttgart, where a human skull was found with remains of animals, among which were the mammoth, the bear, and the hyena.[4]

In 1833 M. M. Schmerling published a treatise on the ossiferous fossils discovered in the province of Liege, Belgium. The author shows that human remains were found here together with those of the rhinoceros, the hyena, and the cave bear. In one cave the remains of three individuals were found, the skull of a young person being imbedded by the side of a mammoth tooth. Flint knives, polished, needle-shaped bones, with holes pierced through them, were found in the same deposit together with a rhinoceros. In 1860 Sir Charles Lyell revisited the caves near Liege and confirmed the previous reports.

Between 1840 and 1846 Boucher de Perthes discovered in the so-called quaternary gravels in the valley of the Somme at Abbeville a large number of flint implements whose origin was ascribed by the noted Professor Prestwich and Mr. John Evans as dating from a period when the mammoth and his companions were still living in that region.

While visiting America, Sir Charles Lyell examined the human remains found near Natchez on the Mississippi. Here human fossils were found on the base of the loess cliff with the remains of the mastodon, the bones of a horse, the remains of an elephant, a rhinoceros, and other animals now extinct or found only in a tropical climate.

In 1874 Professor Anghey found a large paleolithic arrow, or spearhead, below 20 feet of loess deposit a few miles southwest of Omaha, and associated with these man-made implements were found the vertebrae of an elephant. Other arrowheads were found fifteen feet below in a loess deposit in the valley of the Republican River in Nebraska.

Human remains and man-made implements were also found together with prehistoric animals in Pennsylvania and New Mexico and elsewhere. In South America similar remains were found in Brazil and other countries.

Dr. G. F. Wright writes that at Lansing, Kansas, near Leavenworth, a human skeleton was found buried at the foot of a deposit of loess, proving that man was in the valley of the Missouri River before this great loess deposit was laid down.[5]

The Angus, Nebraska, Mammoth. The remains of this mammoth were found near Angus, Nebraska, by A. M. Brooking of the Hastings, Nebraska, Museum

In 1931 A. M. Brooking of the Hastings (Nebraska) Museum excavated a large mammoth near Angus, Nebraska, and found under the left scapula a large fluted arrow, proving that man was a contemporary of the mammoth in the territory now a part of the State of Nebraska.

In 1932 another man-made projectile was found together with the fossil remains of a mammoth near Derit, a small town in Weld County, Colorado.

Still further proof of the contemporaneity of man and the mammoth in North America was furnished in 1938, when Dr. Cyrus N. Roy and Dr. Kirk Byron found man-made implements with the remains of mammoth bones about thirty miles southwest of Abilene, Texas. Other artifacts were found in a gravel pit between Clovis and Portales, New Mexico, together with the remains of a mammoth, a bison, and a horse. Similar evidence has been found in western Canada as far north as Ponoka, Alberta, and east as far as Regina, Saskatchewan.

In a bed of coarse gravel near Scottsbluff, Nebraska, known as the Scottsbluff Bison Quarry, arrowheads, knives, and scrapers were found, associated with the remains of an extinct bison and fossil skulls. Today this is a very dry country and not suitable for farming unless the land can be irrigated. These fossils were found at a great depth. Similar remains were found near Grand Island, Nebraska.

One of the most important discoveries of human remains of great antiquity was made in the Sandra Cave in the Las Huertas Canyon, New Mexico. In this cave were found a variety of man-made implements together with the fossil remains of such animals as the horse, the camel, the bison, the mammoth, the ground sloth, and the wolf.

It is interesting to note that the geological evidence found in the strata indicates that the layers underlying the fossiliferous deposits were laid down in water. This is all the more significant since the entire region is now extremely arid.

One of the most valuable discoveries of ancient human remains is the so-called Calaveras skull found in 1886 in Bald Hill, Calaveras County, California. This skull was found in a shaft of a mine one hundred and thirty feet below the surface in a layer of gravel overlaid by several beds of lava and gravel.

In 1915 Dr. E. H. Sellards found the remains of a man near Vero, Florida, in a stratum which had been laid down by water. In the same vicinity but somewhat removed were found specimens of an extinct fauna, including the mammoth. Similar remains were found near Melbourne, Florida.

In 1929 a human skull was found at Bishop's Cap Peak, New Mexico, by Roscoe Conkling. This skull was found twelve feet below the surface, and at a depth of twenty-one feet a second human skull was found, associated with the bones of the horse, the cave bear, the camel, and the sloth. The strata in which these remains were found show clear evidences of water action.

In 1926 a mammoth skull and below it some artifacts and the bones of a bison and a horse were found twelve miles northwest of Douglas in southwestern Arizona. A careful survey of the surrounding territory yielded further evidence of the existence of prehistoric man in these parts of North America. Among the remains found were grinding stones associated with the bones of the horse, the bison, the pronghorn antelope, an extinct species of the wolf, the coyote, and the mammoth.

In 1930 Dr. Mark Harrington found some human remains together with the fossils of a now extinct ground sloth and of an extinct camel in the gypsum cave sixteen miles east of Las Vegas, Nevada.

In 1935 J. C. McKinley discovered a human skull and other bones on the banks of the Cimarron River a little more than thirteen feet below the surface. In 1931 highway workers at Pelican Rapids, Minnesota, uncovered an almost complete human skeleton at a depth of ten feet in so-called glacial silt. The experts agreed that the geological evidence points to a great antiquity of these remains.

In 1933 William K. Jensen discovered a human skeleton in association with artifacts of recognized antiquity at Browns Valley, Traverse County, Minnesota. Again the geological evidence shows that the gravel ridge had been formed by the action of water.[6]

In 1929 the University of Pennsylvania conducted an extensive excavation at the ancient site of Ur in the lower Euphrates Valley, under the direction of Professor Woolley. After digging through the remains of several cities that had existed successively on the same site, Professor Woolley finally came to a thick deposit of blue clay, and digging through it, he discovered another city representing an older and more magnificent civilization than those above this level. Dr. Woolley classified this lower city as being antediluvian in origin. Other scholars have examined his findings and have confirmed his interpretation.[7]

Bassett Digby, F. R. G. S., has accumulated a great deal of material on this subject. He writes: "We have two kinds of convincing evidence of man's existence with the mammoths. The first is, numerous discoveries of intermingled bones of man and the mammoth in caves and subterranean deposits, sometimes with the implements, ornaments, and weapons, carved from mammoth ivory of fine quality. The second is the remarkable series of engravings on bones, ivory, and the roofs and walls of caves that have been found during the last sixty years in Spain, the south of France, and Belgium." [8]

This author enumerates a great number of such discoveries. In the cave of Spica on the Jurassic Mountains in northern Moravia, bones of the mammoth, the woolly rhinoceros, the charred remains of several campfires, flint implements, and parts of human jawbones, and human teeth were found. In Croatia, fragments of a dozen human skulls were found mixed up with the bones of the woolly rhi-

38

noceros and the mammoth. In another place in Moravia, near Prerov, mammoth bones were found not only below and on the same level as the bones of men, but also above them. More than 25,000 flint implements and hundreds of objects, many of them highly artistic, of reindeer horns, mammoth ivory and bone have been brought to light along with several human skulls and bones. Besides this, a sepulchral chamber containing fourteen complete human skeletons and parts of six others was discovered. Around the neck of one of these skeletons, that of a child, was a necklace of fourteen small mammoth ivory beads. Mammoth bones and flint implements were found near Villendorf, lower Austria. A human skeleton, over which lay a mammoth tusk and the shoulder blade of a mammoth, and near by some woolly rhinoceros ribs were found at Brunn, the chief town of Moravia. Similar discoveries were made in parts of Germany, France, Spain, Belgium, and elsewhere.

There is also a possibility that much of what historians have ascribed to Sumerian civilization in the Babylonian Valley and elsewhere really belongs to the antediluvian period.

Sir William Dawson in speaking about the early appearance of man on this earth has this to say: "In the meantime we may consider it as established beyond cavil that man was already in Europe immediately after the glacial period and was contemporary with the species of animals, many of them large and formidable, which at that time occupied the land. He must have entered upon the possession of a world more ample and richer in resources than that which remains to us." [9] Likewise F. A. Lucus of the American Museum of Natural History writes: "That man was a contemporary of the mammoth in southern Europe is fairly certain, and not only are the remains of the mammoth and man's flint weapons found together, but in a few instances some primeval lancer carved on slate, ivory, or reindeer antlers, sketchy outlines of the beast." [10]

This may suffice to show that there is some evidence in the form of human remains which seems to indicate a fairly wide distribution of the antediluvian race, and that it is not unreasonable to assume that man had taken possession of a very large part of the earth as it then existed. But it must also be admitted that the interpretation of some of this evidence is very uncertain and has been disputed by competent judges. Clear and unmistakable fossil remains preserved in the rocks, such as we have in such great abundance of plant and animal life, are still comparatively few. It may be said, however, that the earth has been barely scratched and that only at a few isolated places have careful excavations been undertaken, and future discoveries may bring further evidence to light. It is also quite possible that the areas which were most densely populated are now submerged below the sea or buried by thousands of feet of debris. Sodom and Gomorrah were not only destroyed by fire and brimstone, but the very sites on which they stood are buried below the briny water of the Salt Sea, so that no human eye shall ever again behold the cursed ground on which this wicked race once trod. And so it might be with many of the chief population centers of the world that perished in the Flood. For the present at least, it would seem that it was God's deliberate plan, not only to destroy, but utterly to wipe out the memory of that ungodly race of men on account of which this terrible destruction was brought upon this wonderful world which He had made.

CHAPTER III

The Civilization of the Antediluvian World

To complete our picture of the world before the Flood, we must add a word about the condition of man and the civilization as it existed in that world. By civilization we mean the general level of enlightenment and progress of the human race, including the social, moral, and religious conditions of that time.

In a textbook for ancient history which has been widely used in the high schools of the United States and Canada, the author introduces the subject of the first men on earth as follows: "The first men were more helpless than the lowest savages in the world today. They had neither fire nor light, no tools or weapons except their hands, and chance clubs or stones. We do not know a great deal about the earliest steps upward, towards civilization, but they must have been very slow. The first marked gain was the discovery by some savage that he could chip off flakes from a flint stone by striking it with other stones to give it a sharp edge, a keen point, and a convenient shape for the hand to grasp. This invention lifted man into the first stone age. In Europe the stone age began at least 100 thousand years ago." [1]

H. G. Wells in his *Outline of History*, a book which has had the tremendous distribution of nearly three million copies in English and other languages, describes the early history of man in similar words but with much greater detail. He writes of the savage ancestor of the human race with the vividness and the assurance of an American newspaper reporter. He speaks as though he had actually seen that race and had observed its gradual emergence from the state of savagery to its modern form of civilization.

The same views are found in other textbooks used in our American high schools, colleges, and universities. But willfully these textbook writers and their disciples remain ignorant, as Peter says. The Bible has proved itself to be a reliable and an accurate record of the most ancient historical events. In fact, for many large areas of ancient history the Bible is the only record we have. Archaeology, excavation, and honest historical research have proved the Bible to be an absolutely reliable source book. And yet, when writing these textbooks, modern historians disregard this source material entirely and treat it as though it were non-existent. But this is unscientific, unscholarly, and nothing less than intellectual dishonesty. That branches of the human race have lived in caves, no one will doubt; that large sections of the human family degenerated to the level of savagery cannot be questioned; but to conclude from this that the entire human race has sprung from a race of cave dwellers or has evolved from a race of savages or of beings even lower than a savage, is drawing an unwarranted conclusion.

The account which the Bible gives us of the early history of man is quite different from that of these "historical" and "scientific" textbooks. Man begins as a perfect being, created in the image of God and endowed with the most wonderful intellect and gift of human language. In Gen. 2:20 we read that Adam gave names to all the cattle, the fowl of the air, and to every beast of the field. This is mentioned only incidentally, as it were, but this brief incidental remark provides sufficient evidence to show that the first man was endowed with a keen intellect. It presupposes not only a remarkable insight into the nature of the creatures which were brought before him and which he saw for the first time, but also is proof for his outstanding vocabulary, which enabled him to describe or name with fitting designations the things which God had made. There are few, if any, scientists living today who could recognize and name with such supreme ease all living creatures now found in the world. If there be such, they have acquired this knowledge after years and years of intensive study.

To say, however, that man had his beginning as a being created in the image of God and endowed with a superior intellect does not mean that man was supplied with all the material equipment we commonly connect with the term of civilization. God gave him this earth as his abode and commanded him to occupy it and subdue it. This meant that he was to work out for himself a civilization in keeping with his position as lord and ruler of all that God had made. Hence Adam started his career by inventing the most rudimentary implements and tools. We may assume that he knew the use of fire from the beginning. With that and an untarnished intellect, he had all that was necessary to subdue the world and take possession of it.

When sin came into the world, the human intellect suffered as did the rest of his faculties. But even after sin had come into the world, men remained superior beings, and the first race was decidedly a superior one.

In Gen. 4:17 we read that Cain built a city after the name of his own son Enoch. Savages do not build cities. But the most interesting record of the civilization of this age we find in the verses that follow in the same chapter. We read: "And Adah bare Jabal; he was the father of such as dwell in tents and of such as have cattle. And his brother's name was Jubal; he was the father of all such as handle the harp and the organ. And Zillah, she also bare Tubalcain, an instructor of every artificer in brass and iron." And further on we read: "And Lamech said unto his wives, Adah and Zillah: Hear my voice, ye wives of Lamech. Hearken unto my speech; for I have slain a man to my wounding, and a young man to my hurt."

Here we have condensed in a few verses an interesting *Kulturbild*. We are told of those that dwelt in cities and those that followed the free and wild life of the nomad and the cattleman. We are informed that musical instruments of the string and the wind variety had been invented and that there were those who were able to play them. Tubalcain was an inventor and a master craftsman in brass and iron and a teacher of all such as work in these metals. This does not only presuppose the mining of these minerals, but a knowledge of smelting and purifying them and of molding and shaping them into all manner of useful tools, implements, and weapons. In the words which Lamech addresses to his wives we have the opening line of a poem or a song which he composed to glorify his own murderous deeds. Gen. 2:11-12 we find a reference to fine gold and precious stones in the Garden of Eden. Savages and cavemen have no use for, nor appreciation of, gold and precious stones. Somewhat later Noah is commanded to build an ark of dimensions which would be considered a large building or boat today. This again presupposes a considerable knowledge of mathematics, the possession and use of tools, and an advanced understanding of the art of building.

In other words, we have here at the very beginning of the human race various types of farming, industries, arts, and inventions, music and poetry, or those higher things of life which are only found in an advanced stage of civilization. The inventions of Jubal and Tubalcain were basic and must be counted among the greatest inventions of all time.

We must beware, however, not to assume that the civilization and culture of the antediluvian was on the same high level in every part of the inhabited earth. In that respect, conditions no doubt were then as they are now. Individuals or groups who separated themselves too far from the parent stock, or became completely isolated from the rest of the race over a long period of time, or for other reasons, declined and degenerated. There were savages and barbarous cave dwellers and nomads then as in the world of today. But the race also reached high peaks of civilization and accomplishments, comparable to that of the ancient Babylonians, Assyrians, and Egyptians. It is, of course, very difficult to say just what the world was like in Noah's lifetime. In addition to the very brief reference in the Bible, there are two other possible clues which may give us an answer to that question. The one must be sought in the stage which civilization had attained in the earliest dawn of its postdiluvian nations; the other in the results of modern excavations on the sites of ancient civilizations.

It is one of the most remarkable facts of history that the oldest civilizations of the present world known to us, such as the ones found in the valleys of the Nile and the Euphrates, in Crete, in Asia Minor and southern Greece, have peculiar similarities both as to the stages of their development and as to their colossal designs. And all of them are separated by only a comparatively short period of time from the age of Noah and the antediluvian world. Judging from the civilization we find there, Noah must have lived amidst a race enjoying many of the highest results of social and political maturity. In the remotest period of which records survive, we find Egypt exhibiting a degree of civilization that is inexplicable, except on the theory that she had received most of the secrets as a priceless heritage from the world that had perished in the Flood. The magnificent pyramids illustrate the triumphs of architectural science; for their masonry is still unrivaled, their finish still commands admiration, and their proportion and structure reveal an advanced knowledge of geometry and mathematics. Sculpture and statuary had reached a perfection, whether in wood, alabaster, or the hardest granite, which later ages never surpassed in Egypt. The art of picture writing had been perfected. The king's court exhibited all the state and circumstances of well-defined precedence and form. The army, the civil service, and the hierarchy were minutely organized, and society had already divided itself into separate classes, from the wealthy lord to the humble workman and slave. The glass blower, the gold worker, the potter, the tailor, the baker, the butler, the barber, the waiting maids, and the nurse were part of an establishment of the nobility and the priests. The acrobat, the dancer, the harpist, and the singer ministered to the public pleasure, and games of chance and skill were already common.

The records of Babylon and of the countries of the Aegean lead to the same conclusion. On Crete a palace dating back to the earliest postdiluvian period has been unearthed spreading over nearly four acres of ground with splendid halls, corridors, living rooms, throne rooms, and treasure rooms and with many frescoes depicting the brilliant life of the lords and ladies of the court. Especially amazing are the bathrooms with a drainage system superior to anything in Europe until the 19th century. The pipes could be flushed, and a mantrap permitted inspection and repair.

Clay tablets found with writing show that the art of writing was advanced even beyond that of Egypt. In the remains of Mycenae in southern Greece we find the colossal paired with artistic beauty, reminding one of the builders of the pyramids and the Tower of Babel.

The Code of Hammurabi, discovered by a French explorer in 1902 in Susa, dates back to the time of Abraham. This is the oldest known code of laws in the world, and it shows that the people for whom it was made were already far advanced in civilization. It guarded against bribery of judges and witnesses in court, against careless medical practice, and against ignorant or dishonest building contractors, as well as against the oppression of widows and orphans. Property rights, deeds, wills, marriage settlements, and legal contracts were carefully safeguarded. A similar advanced civilization is found in China and India dating back to about the same period when these early civilizations flourished.

There is but one explanation for this rapid progress among the nations following the Flood, and that is that they continued where the generation of Noah left off. They transplanted the civilization of the old world to the new, just as the early European immigrant brought with him the culture and civilization of his homeland to America to give it a fresh start in this new and virgin land.

These conclusions are confirmed by the recent excavation on the site of Biblical Ur in the lower Euphrates Valley, the ancient home of Abraham. In 1922 the University of Pennsylvania and the British Museum agreed to undertake a joint excavation expedition on the ancient site of Ur in Chaldea. Mr. Leonard Woolley was placed in charge of the undertaking. The results surpassed all expectations. As Schliemann found a series of cities, one superimposed upon the other, at the old site of Homer's Troy, so Woolley discovered at the ancient city of Ur the remains of several cities and civilizations, each built on the remains of the one preceding it. And one of the most surprising and by far the most magnificent discoveries was beneath the remains of what appeared to be the first, or foundation, city. Far down below its foundations he found that deep pits had been sunk and subsequently filled in with different materials, and at the bottom of these pits he found the tombs of great chiefs, kings, and queens, by the side of whose burial chambers lay the bones of maid servants, harpists, men at arms, and charioteers. He also found ornaments of gold and lapis lazuli and other remains of exquisite art. One of the skeletons, believed to be that of a queen, had on its head a beautiful helmet or headpiece made of gold.

Mr. Woolley, the director of the expedition, gives a very interesting account of these discoveries in his book, *Ur of the Chaldees*. A few selections from his description will help to make more real the picture of that interesting age.

He writes: "At the very end of the season, 1926–7, two important discoveries were made. At the bottom of an earth shaft, amongst masses of copper weapons, there was found the famous gold dagger of Ur, a wonderful weapon whose blade was of gold, its hilt of lapis lazuli decorated with gold studs, and its sheath of gold beautifully worked with an open-work pattern derived from platted grass; with it was another object scarcely less remarkable, a cone-shaped reticule of gold ornamented with a spiral pattern and containing a set of little toilet instruments, tweezers, lancet, and pencil, also of gold. Nothing like these things had ever before come from the soil of Mesopotamia; they revealed an art hitherto unsuspected, and they gave promise of future discoveries outstripping all our hopes. . . . At the end, on the remains of a wooden bier, lay the body of the queen, a gold cup near her hand; the upper part of the body was entirely hidden by a mass of beads of gold, silver, lapis lazuli, carnelian, agate, and chalcedony, long strings of which, hanging from a collar, had formed a cloak reaching to the waist and bordered below with a broad band of tubular beads of lapis, carnelian, and gold; against the right arm were three long gold pins with lapis heads and three amulets in the form of fish, two of gold and one of lapis, and a fourth in the form of two [sic] seated gazelles, also of gold."[2]

On another page Mr. Woolley gives a detailed description of the helmet worn by the king, whose remains they found in that grave. He writes: "It was a helmet of beaten gold made to fit low over the head with cheekpieces to protect the face, and it was in the form of a wig, the locks of hair hammered up in relief, the individual hairs shown by delicate, engraved lines. Parted down the middle, the hair covers the head in flat, wavy tresses and is bound with a twisted fillet; behind it is tied into a little chignon, and below the fillet hangs in rows of formal curls about the ears, which are rendered in high relief and are pierced so as not to interfere with the hearing; similar curls on the cheekpieces to represent whiskers; round the edge of the metal are small holes for the laces which secured inside it a padded cap, of which some traces yet remained.

"As an example of goldsmith's work this is the most beautiful thing we have found in the cemetery, finer than the gold daggers or the heads of bulls, and if there were nothing else by which the art of these ancient Sumerians could be judged, we should still, on the strength of it alone, accord them high rank in the roll of civilized races." On the basis of these discoveries Woolley evaluates the civilization of the age represented by these remains as follows: "The contents of the tombs illustrate a very highly developed state of society of an urban type, a society in which the architect was familiar with all the basic principles of construction known to us today. The artist, capable at times of a most vivid realism, followed for the most part standards and conventions whose excellence had been approved by many generations working before him; the craftsman in metal possessed a knowledge of metallurgy and a technical skill which few ancient peoples ever rivaled; the merchant carried on a far-flung trade and recorded his transactions in writing; the army was well organized and victorious; agriculture prospered, and great wealth gave scope to luxury." [8] Woolley himself interpreted his discoveries as representing a most ancient civilization.

It is not unreasonable to conclude, therefore, that man before the Flood had not only multiplied and become a great people, but had also taken possession of the earth and had reached a high stage of civilization and culture. He had achieved great things. It was the golden age in the history of man, of which the various mythologies of later ages are but a faint and indistinct echo.

Left — Woman's Headdress from the Great Death Pit at Ur

Right — The Gold Dagger of Ur

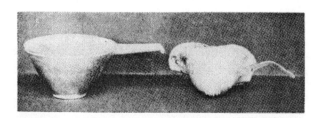

Gold Vessels of Queen Shubad of Ur

But there is another side to this picture. For parallel with these great material and cultural achievements, there runs a steady course of moral decay and spiritual degeneracy. Polygamy began early in the generation of Cain. Murder and violence increased. Lamech killed a young man and boasted of it in a song and poetry to his wives.

In the genealogies of Genesis 4 and 5 is traced the development of the human race through two fundamentally different lines, headed by Cain and Seth respectively. The one line is called the children of God and the other the children of men. The characteristic traits of these two brothers were passed on to their descendants. The Cainites were wicked and worldly like their father. The Sethites represented the Church of God on earth during this period, through whom the hope of the promised Savior was kept alive. But as time went on and men began to multiply, these two streams gradually approached each other, and lines of demarcation which had separated them were gradually wiped away. The children of God were influenced by their ungodly neighbors and became like them. This spiritual change first manifested itself when the sons of God saw the daughters of men that they were fair and took them wives of all which they chose. These words indicate that they were no longer being guided by the Spirit of God, but gave way to unrestrained freedom, or license. The result was that the children of God became like the children of men, carnal and worldly. They were no longer restrained by the will of God, but were governed by the lusts of the eyes, the lusts of the flesh, and the lusts of the world. This intermarriage with the ungodly, followed by a general moral decay and corruption, resulted in evil growing rampant and gradually destroying all that was good in the world. The line of Seth was completely merged with that of Cain, and with the exception of Noah and his family, and a few of the surviving patriarchs, there was now but one generation left on the face of the earth, namely, that of the ungodly. The moral and social conditions of this age are further described in these words: "There were giants in the earth in those days; and also after that when the sons of God came in unto the daughters of men and they bare children to them, the same became mighty men which were of old, men of renown. And God saw that the wickedness of man was great in the earth and that the imagination and the thoughts of his heart were only evil continually. . . . The earth also was corrupt before God, and the earth was filled with violence. And God looked upon the earth, and, behold, it was corrupt; for all flesh had corrupted his way upon the earth."

There were giants, says the sacred writer. Luther translates this word with tyrants. Giants is the translation of the Hebrew word *nephilim*, which means "those who fall upon others, brigands, thugs, tyrants." Luther says: "Sie werden recht genannt *nephilim*, darum dass sie ueberfallen und unterdruecken die unter sie getan sind." [4]

These *nephilim* were famous and renowned in the world. They were great in the affairs of the world, great chiefs who made themselves great names by deeds of war, filling the earth with violence. They were not only godless in their family relations and unrestrained in their carnal lusts, but also violent and lawless in their actions toward their fellow men. There was no fear of God and no respect for His Law. Note how the words *corrupt* or *corrupted, violence, wickedness,* and *flesh* are repeated over and over. Note also that God complains that every imagination of the thoughts of their hearts was only evil continually. Their thoughts were bent only upon doing evil, and as man thinketh, so he is. The generation before the Flood was not a pagan or idolatrous race. Mr. Woolley, in describing the prehistoric graves which he discovered at Ur, makes this interesting observation: "*In no single grave has there been any figure of a god, any symbol or ornament that strikes one as being of a religious nature.*" [5]

Idolatry apparently was a later development and is first mentioned after the Flood. The people were proud, lawless, and utterly unconcerned about God and His will. They were progressive and great in the things of this world, but materialistic and carnal in their philosophy of life. In short, man in that age resembled the civilized nations in the world today. Jesus, in describing the age of Noah, says of them: "They were eating and drinking, marrying and giving in marriage, until the day that Noah entered into the ark." In short, they were concerned only about the things of the world. Their philosophy of life was a "this world" philosophy.

The wickedness of the world was so great that God resolved to destroy the world which He had made. For He said: "My Spirit shall not always strive with man, for that he also is flesh; yet his days shall be an hundred and twenty years." Only Noah found grace in the eyes of the Lord, for he was a just man and perfect in his generation. And Noah walked with God.

This is a picture of the world before the Flood. The physical world was great and beautiful beyond our present conception. The race of man then living had increased to great numbers and had taken possession of the earth. It was a superior race in matters of this world, progressive, cultured, and enterprising; but arrogant, godless, and wicked. And because of their wickedness God wiped them away and blotted out their memory and with them even destroyed the earth and everything that was therein.

PART II

The Biblical Account of the Flood

CHAPTER IV

Warning of the Coming Flood

THE Biblical account of the Flood is found in the sixth, seventh, eighth, and ninth chapters of Genesis. The language of this extraordinary narrative is simple and direct. There is no appearance of legend or poetry, nothing fanciful or extravagant as in the case of the Flood traditions of other nations. It is a masterpiece in descriptive narrative, gripping and dramatic in style.

We are told that man had become altogether wicked and "that every imagination of the thoughts of his heart was only evil continually." Up to a certain period in that early history of the human race the children of God had kept themselves separate from the children of men; but, as men began to multiply, the line of demarcation gradually vanished. Cordial relations came to exist. The godly intermarried with the ungodly. The result was that the godly were absorbed by the ungodly. Only one class remained. God warned them. He gave them 120 years time for repentance, but to no avail. The downward course once entered upon was continued, and it "repented the Lord that He had made man." The language used here is an expression of the figure of speech called anthropomorphism, by which the thoughts and acts of God are described in language that would be appropriate to men in like circumstances. "And God said unto Noah,

The end of all flesh is come before Me, for the earth is filled with violence through them, and, behold, I will destroy them with the earth." Less severe measures would not meet the case. It was necessary to wipe out this wicked generation to save the human race from total annihilation and to make possible the fulfillment of the promise concerning the Seed of the woman. To perpetuate the race, Noah and his family were chosen. We are told that "Noah found grace in the eyes of the Lord." He is called a just man and perfect in his generation, and, like Enoch, he walked with God. Noah testified against the wickedness and corruption of his age, for Peter, in his Second Epistle, calls him a "preacher of righteousness" (2 Peter 2:5). But neither God's warning nor Noah's preaching was of any avail, and so God commanded Noah to build an ark for himself and his family and for a place of refuge for every species of animals. God had resolved to bring a flood upon the earth to destroy it. The Hebrew word "*mabbul*," translated "flood," is used only for the waters of Noah; and it is used only here and in Ps. 29:10. Noah was to build him an ark, or a vessel, to escape the Flood. The word "ark" seems to be derived from the Egyptian language and signifies "chest" or something to float. The word occurs only twice in the Bible, here for the ark of Noah and again in Ex. 2:3-5 for the ark of bulrushes in which the infant Moses was saved from the cruel decree of Pharaoh.

The ark was built of gopher wood and caulked with pitch within and without. The word "gopher" as used here is merely a transliteration of the Hebrew word. Its exact meaning is not known. Luther translates it with "*Tannenholz.*" Other scholars are of the opinion that the cypress is meant, because cypress wood was used very extensively for shipbuilding in ancient times and also because this species of wood is found in great abundance in the Two-River Valley, where the ark may have been built.

Other specifications for the ark were: "Rooms [cabins or cells] shalt thou make in the ark. The length of the ark shall be 300 cubits; the breadth of it 50 cubits; and the height of it 30 cubits; a window shalt thou make to the ark, and in a cubit shalt thou finish it above; and the door of the ark shalt thou set in the side thereof; with lower, second, and third stories shalt thou make it." (Gen. 6:14-16.)

The dimensions of the ark are given in cubits. The cubit was a common unit of measurement in ancient times among the Babylonians, Egyptians, and Hebrews. At least two kinds of cubits were known, the common cubit and a cubit which was a handbreadth longer than the common cubit. It is generally supposed that the cubit was the distance from the point of the elbow to the tip of the middle finger. Translated into our own standard of measurements, the common cubit is estimated at about 18 inches. But Petrie, a noted Egyptologist, is of the opinion that it measured 22½ inches. Whether or not Noah's cubit was comparable to any of the cubits now known to us, no one is able to determine. It is not unreasonable, however, to assume that, in keeping with nature about him, man before the Flood was more fully developed and was of a larger stature than now and the length from his elbow to the tip of his finger was even longer than the suggested 22½ inches. Two feet may be more nearly correct. However, it is obviously impossible to determine with any degree of certainty the exact size of Noah's ark. But accepting the lower figures and placing the cubit at eighteen inches and then again at twenty-four inches, we get the following results: According to the lower standard, the ark would have measured 450 feet in length, seventy-five feet in width, and forty-five feet in height. According to the higher figure, the length would have been six hundred feet; the width, one hundred feet; the height, sixty feet. For the sake of comparison, we may note that the well-known battleship *Oregon*, 348 feet long and sixty-nine feet wide, was built in the same proportions as to length and width as the ark. The famous *Titanic* was 825 feet long and ninety-three feet wide, with a displacement of 46,000 tons. The ships of the maritime nations of the world never approached the dimensions of the ark until about a half century ago. The ships of the ancient Phoenicians and Romans or the ships of the seafaring nations of the Middle Ages were mere toys when compared with the ark. Marine experts have estimated that since the ark was built with a flat bottom and there was no waste space on the bow or stern, it being square on both ends and straight up on its side, it would have had a displacement of about 43,000 tons, according to the lower figures, a displacement nearly equal to that of the ill-fated *Titanic.*

According to Leonard W. King, the ark had its antetype in a kind of boat still used on the Lower Tigris and Euphrates Rivers. Of this vessel, Mr. King writes as follows: "A Kuffah, the familiar pitched coracle of Bagdad, would provide an admirable model for the gigantic vessel in which Ut Napishtim rode out the Deluge. Without stem or stern, quite round like a shield — so Herodotus described the Kuffah of his day; so, too, is it represented on Assyrian slabs from Nineveh, where we see it employed for the transport of heavy building material; its form and structure, indeed, suggests a prehistoric origin. The Kuffah is one of those examples of perfect adjustment to conditions of use which cannot be improved. Anyone who has traveled in one of these crafts will agree that their storage capacity is immense, for their circular form and curved sides allow for every inch of space to be utilized. It is almost impossible to upset them, and their only disadvantage is lack of speed. For their guidance, all that is required is a steersman with a paddle, as is indicated in the Epic. It is true that the larger Kuffah of today tends to increase in diameter as compared to height, but this detail might well be ignored in picturing the vessel of Ut Napishtim. . . . The use of pitch and bitumen for smearing the vessel inside and out, though unusual even in Mesopotamian shipbuilding, is precisely the method employed in the Kuffah's construction." [1]

A further specification for the ark was: "A window shalt thou make unto the ark and in a cubit shalt thou finish it above" (Gen. 6:16). The question is: "What was meant by this window and where was it placed?" Luther says the Hebrew word translated *window* literally means "the light of noonday." The new American translation renders it: "You are to make a roof for the ark, finishing it off at the top to the width of a cubit." Delitzsch says the Hebrew word means "double light," or "midday." The passage can signify only that a hole or opening for light and air was to be constructed so as to reach within a cubit of the edge of the roof. A window only a cubit square could not possibly be intended, for the Hebrew word signifies generally a space for light, or a space by which light could be admitted into the ark and in which the window, or lattice for opening and shutting, could be fixed. Dr. Stoeckhardt took a similar view and understood it to mean an opening of some kind to be left all around the top of the ark, a cubit below the roof. The exact meaning is therefore not absolutely certain. So much, however, is clear that Noah was to provide some kind of an opening in the ark to admit the necessary light and make provision for ventilation.

Father Kircher, in his book *Arca Noe,* published in 1675, presents an interesting description of the ark. He divides it into small compartments for the various species, provides for a drinking place on each floor. The land animals he placed on the first floor, the food he stored on the second floor, and the birds and Noah's family were placed on the third floor. He greatly reduces the number of species of animals and maintains that besides the window mentioned in Genesis there were small openings all over the ark through which the air entered and that the ventilation system was similar to that of the large ocean liner of today with its windows and portholes. The book is in the New York Public Library.

61

The three stories of the ark were to be subdivided into cabins or cells. This would also imply that these cabins were arranged according to some definite plan, possibly in rows on each side of the ark, with a passageway through the middle, or vice versa. And also that these cabins were to be placed in tiers, one above the other, for we know that the ark was at least 45 feet high, taking the smaller standard for our measurement. This would leave approximately 15 feet for each story, subtracting from this only the amount of space needed for the floors. We can, therefore, safely assume that this space was used in the most profitable way and that the cabins took up the entire space between the floor and the ceiling to make possible the placing of the larger and the smaller animals in a manner that would ensure the most economical use of space within the ark.

"Thus did Noah," continues the sacred writer; "according to all that God had commanded him, so did he" (Gen. 6:22). Like Enoch, Abraham, and other great saints, he believed the impossible because God had spoken it. It was a fearful and unheard-of thing which God had threatened to bring upon this earth. No one believed it, and no one considered it possible. The great masses of people, that is, the majorities of his age, were against him. The "wisdom" of that world as represented by the great men of thought and of action did not believe it. The experience of the past was against him. It seemed so utterly unreasonable that God should destroy the earth upon which He had lavished such magnificent kindness and which He had so recently made. Nor were there any outward or visible indications that this overwhelming calamity was approaching. But "by faith Noah, being warned of God of things not seen as yet, moved with fear, prepared an ark to the saving of his house, by the which he condemned the world and became heir of the righteousness which is by faith" (Heb. 11:7). We can well imagine that Noah suffered insult and derision from the scoffing curiosity of those who watched him build his ark. On the other hand, we can well

62

imagine that Noah hired workmen, carpenters, and ship-builders from among his ungodly neighbors to assist him in the building of his ark. For the heavy timbers required in the construction of a ship of such formidable dimensions make it well-nigh impossible that the building was done by Noah and his sons alone. But just as these men assisted Noah and his sons in the building of the ark which was to save the human race from total destruction, yet themselves perished in the Flood, so there are today men and women assisting in the building of the Christian Church, either by their own labors or by their contribution of talents and gifts, and yet themselves are lost, because they do not accept with all their heart the Gospel of Jesus Christ, the Savior of the world. "The long-suffering of God waited in the days of Noah while the ark was a preparing" (1 Peter 3:20).

But His waiting was without avail. The generations of Noah went on "eating and drinking, marrying and giving in marriage, until the day that Noe entered into the ark, and knew not until the Flood came and took them all away" (Matt. 24:38-39; Luke 17:27).

When the ark had been completed and the period of grace had expired, Noah received instructions to enter the ark with his own household and with the animals which were to be kept alive. At the beginning of the 600th year of Noah's life the ark was finished, and on the tenth day of the second month of that year he entered the ark. This raises the question what was the first month? If, as some hold, the first month corresponded to the end of our month of September and the beginning of October, it would mean that the Flood began, according to our reckoning, about November of the 600th year of Noah, or the 1,656th year of the world. And with Noah went into the ark his three sons, Shem, Ham, and Japheth, and their wives, eight souls altogether. They took two of every kind of animal, but of the clean animals they took seven, which, according to Luther and other inter-preters, means three pairs to continue the species and one male for the purpose of sacrifice. The distinction between clean and unclean beasts evidently did not originate with Moses, but dates back to the very beginning of the practice of worshiping God through the sacrifice of animals. Whether God Himself made this distinction, or whether, as Delitzsch thinks, it arose from a certain innate feeling of the human mind which detects types of sin and corruption in many animals and instinctively recoils from them, cannot be known.

Noah also took with him the necessary food for his family and for all the animals that were with him in the ark, as God had commanded him.

The embarkation was completed within a week. What a grand and impressive sight it must have been to see this conglomeration of animals gathering about Noah! Here were the great and the small, the fierce and the timid, the lion and the lamb, obediently entering the ark and taking their places in the compartments prepared for them by Noah. The last to enter were Noah and his family; and God Himself, as we are told, shut and sealed the door behind them. By closing the door Himself, God indicated that the time of grace for the rest of the world had come to an end. There was a finality about this act of God. The door closed to save those that were within and to seal the doom of those that remained without. The end of the world was at hand.

CHAPTER V

Some Problems Concerning the Ark and Its Cargo

THE Biblical account of the Deluge is a sane and sober narrative having all the characteristics of an eye-witness report, but this does not mean that every detail of this great world catastrophe is described or explained to the complete satisfaction of the modern reader. It would be folly to make such a claim. It must be admitted that there are a great many difficulties in the Biblical account of the Flood for which we are able to find only a partial solution or no solution at all. But this does not in any way militate against the trustworthiness of this record or against the historicity of the Flood itself.

The Egyptian pyramids have survived these many thousands of years as a magnificent monument to the greatness of the race that built them. We know something about these builders and also something about the arts and skills they had developed. But there remain innumerable questions for which we have no satisfactory answer. How, for example, was it possible for a people at the very dawn of human history to erect monuments of such colossal dimensions and construct them with blocks of stone so huge that today we could move them only with the aid of steam and electrical power and the most gigantic machinery yet devised by man? How were these massive rocks transported to the place where these pyramids were built? How were the stones cut and polished with such precision? How was it possible for those ancient engineers to raise these enormous blocks of stone to heights which have not been reached by the building arts until very recent times? And so we could continue to raise questions and find no answer altogether adequate or satisfactory. Many arguments could be advanced to show that no race of men could have built these pyramids at a time when man is supposed to have been just emerging from savagery. And yet there they are, and there they have been these four thousand years, and all the arguments of the skeptics will not remove them.

Furthermore, we must remember that the Biblical account of the Flood is extremely brief, when considering the magnitude of the catastrophe it describes.

On February 10, 1942, the luxury liner *Normandie* in some mysterious way caught fire in New York harbor and was all but completely wrecked. The report of the *St. Louis Post-Dispatch*, describing the disaster, consisted of 141 lines of standard newspaper-column length. And though the report, written by an expert reporter, was graphic and quite complete in its description of what happened, it left many important questions unanswered. The Biblical account of the Flood, beginning with the covenant God made with Noah and ending with the sacrifice of thanksgiving at the end of the Flood, consists of 210 lines of about the same length as the standard newspaper-column lines. But the report on the Flood proper, that is, the section which deals with the actual event of the Flood, from the day that Noah entered the ark until his disembarking a little more than a year later, consists of 140 lines or is about of the same length as the *Post-Dispatch* report on the *Normandie* disaster. Here the report dealt with a disaster of only one ship, the loss of one human life, and a period of time dealing in hours only.

The Biblical report deals with a world disaster, the wiping out of the entire human race except Noah and his family, the destruction of animals and plants in every part of the earth and involving forces of nature on a scale unparalleled in all the history of the earth. If 140 lines of newspaper report were not sufficient to clear up all the problems arising out of the *Normandie* disaster, but required further extensive congressional investigation, how then can we expect that 140 lines or 210 lines, or 2,000 lines for that matter, would be sufficient to tell all that we should like to know about this world disaster. The sacred writer evidently had no intention of describing in detail all that happened when that first world came to an end. To do that would have required a book larger than the whole Bible itself. We must expect, therefore, to find many questions that we can answer only by guessing.

One of the questions which has given rise to doubt and serious skepticism in the minds of many is the question concerning the ark. Was the ark large enough to serve the purpose for which Noah was to build it; that is, would it serve as a shelter for Noah and his family and for representatives of all the animals not able to live in water and, in addition, have room for a sufficient quantity of food to keep them alive for the duration of the Flood? Without a doubt this is one of the greatest difficulties connected with the Flood, and one need not wonder that because of it skeptics have denied the possibility or at least have denied the universality, of the Flood.

According to the Brockhaus Encyclopedia, the number of living species of animals is estimated at 500,000. Other estimates range from one to three million. That all these were in the ark, not as single individuals, but in pairs, or even in groups of seven; that, in addition, a sufficient quantity of food was stored to keep this immense cargo of living creatures alive for more than one year, seems utterly incredible and a physical impossibility.

To find a solution for this problem, we must first answer two other questions. (1) What was the capacity of the ark? (2) How many species of animals are there, and how many of these had to be taken into the ark to preserve their kind?

Concerning the first question, Charles A. Totten, professor of Military Science and Tactics at Yale University, writes as follows: "The dimensions of the ark are given in the Bible as 300 cubits long, fifty cubits wide and thirty cubits high. It had three decks. Regarding the cubit as eighteen inches, the floor space on one deck would be 33,750 square feet. On the three decks of the ark there was then a total of 101,250 square feet of deck space. But since it was likely that the small and medium-sized animals were put in cages, in tiers, one above the other, not only the floor space, but the cubic space must be considered. The cubic capacity of the ark, at 18 inches as the measure of the cubit, was for each deck 500,000 cubic feet, or 1,500,000 cubic feet for the three decks.

"However, as we have seen, it is not at all certain that the cubit of the ark was eighteen inches. There was never any definite length of the cubit in ancient days. Different cubits existed. Most common was the cubit of the elbow, that is, the distance from the elbow to the finger tip. There was also the cubit of the arm pit or the distance of the whole arm. Naturally these lengths vary with the size of the person measured. The cubit also varied from country to country. Ancient Egypt had two lengths for it at different times. One was the length of a new-born child; the other was the length of the king at a certain age. We may say that a cubit of 20.7 inches was about the standard measure of the Egyptian and also of the Assyrian, Chaldean, and Babylonian Empires. Moses was directed to work according to a pattern shown him. The so-called 'great cubit' of Ezekiel revealed to him by God was an ordinary cubit plus a hand's breadth, or about two feet.

"Supposing this to have been the length of the cubit, the ark was then 600 feet long and 100 feet wide and sixty feet high, having a capacity of 3,600,000 cubic feet. An ordinary cattle car on the railroad carries of cattle, from eighteen to twenty head; or of hogs, from sixty to eighty head; or of sheep, from eighty to one hundred head. One thousand of such cars, duly proportioned, could be stored away in Noah's ark. Such was the capacity of Noah's ark, a ship whose dimensions have, from general misunderstanding of their true significance, been persistently ridiculed as unequal for their task. Certainly there was room in such a craft for one hundred menageries larger than Barnum, the great American showman, ever saw in his wildest reveries, and room to spare for food." [1]

It must also be remembered that the large species of animals are comparatively few, even including those that are now extinct. It has been estimated that land mammalia above the size of sheep at the present time number about 290; those from the sheep to the rats, 757; and those smaller than the rats, 1,359. The average size is about that of a cat, a pair of which would require less than two square feet of space.

The second question concerns the problem of species. How many species were in the ark? The answer to that question depends upon how one regards the term *species*. Dr. Price writes: "And with the new light which we have received regarding the subject of species partly through experiments with changes in environments during the embryonic stage, and partly through crossing under the methods taught by Mendel, we now know that the old specific and generic distinctions were marked off on altogether too narrow lines. It is perfectly evident that both animals and plants have varied much more in a natural way than used to be thought possible, and hence two or more comparatively different forms may very well be supposed to be of common descent. From this, it further follows that the problem of accounting for the modern diversity of animals as the survivors of the universal deluge has been greatly simplified, for the more variation we admit as possible, the easier it is to account for the present fauna and flora since fewer original forms would be required to begin the present stock." [2]

And Mr. M. C. Edwards says: "Of course, all the once created species were not there (in the ark), but certain representative species found in that part of the globe were there with potentialities that were almost infinite. Take the classic case that Darwin quotes — the pigeon. He found that if the almost endless varieties of pigeons were allowed to breed together, they went back to the rock pigeon; therefore, if there were seven rock pigeons in the ark, there were thousands of varieties potentially preserved. The same may be said about others, e. g., the dog." [3]

The term *species* may be defined as a group of individuals of animals or plants which breed together freely and reproduce fertile offspring. It is known that species of the same genus are occasionally interfertile and, therefore, might have required only one pair to represent them in the ark. The same applies, for instance, to the cat genus with its many species (lions, tigers, panthers, leopards, etc.), to the numerous varieties and breeds of the dog family, etc. All horses, whether Shetland ponies, racers, or heavy draft horses, form one species and may have descended from a common ancestor. Likewise, a single pair of cattle may have represented the entire bovine family. Not every variety of this large group need to have been in the ark. A representative was sufficient to supply the great number of varieties of forms found on the earth today.

That this kind of argumentation is not unreasonable nor impossible can also be shown from the example of the human race. The entire human race as now existing in the world has descended from Noah and his three sons. Yet we know that mankind is now divided into a great variety of distinct colors and races. We speak of the Caucasian race, the Mongolian race, the Ethiopian race, the red and the brown race. All have come from the same stock, Noah, and yet what a

70

difference in size, color, build, and general appearance. When this change came or what caused the change has remained an anthropological mystery.

Concerning the difficult question of species Dr. Milton A. Petty of the Department of Plant Pathology, University of Maryland, writes: "The base unit in this natural system of classifying plants and animals is the species. Now this species is not a fixed and invariable group as mortal man knows them, but a species is a group of living, or once living, beings delineated by scientific description. They are therefore subject to more or less delineation by man if its *status quo* is not suitable. A species to a biologist is just a pigeon-hole for a group of beings that may still be a heterogeneous mixture of types. *A species is then a concept in the eye of the scientist.* Just what a species is in the eyes of the Creator we do not know. We do not know the division lines of 'after their kind.' "

"Grasses bring forth grass seed, and when we hear that some plant-breeder has successfully crossed two different species or even two different genera, do not fret . . . remember that these so described species and genera were delineated by man, not by God. These grasses still bring forth seed after their kind. The species of beings that we know are not altogether first. Environment may play a role so great as to make a single type in fifteen different habitats appear to be as many different types. Infinite variations may be obtained by the hybridization of two types. I have seen several thousands of types that originated from two beginning types. The ability of protoplasm to mold itself to difficult surroundings is absolutely essential to its continued existence." [4]

We must also note that after the Flood, God again repeated the blessing which He had pronounced upon Adam and the first world. Concerning the animals He said: "Bring forth with thee every living thing that is with thee, of all flesh, both of fowl and of cattle and of every creeping thing that creepeth upon the earth; that they may breed abundantly in the earth and be fruitful and multiply upon the earth" (Gen. 8:17). God's blessings are always effective. It was a creative blessing and implied that the world should again be filled with a great variety of each species able to survive and live in the new world emerging from the universal Flood.

The other problem to be noted here is the gathering of the animals by Noah and their entrance and sojourn in the ark. With regard to the entrance of the animals into the ark, it should be noticed that our text definitely states that they came two and two and that they came male and female of all flesh. In the expression "They came" it is clearly indicated that the animals collected about Noah and entered the ark of their own accord, that is, without any special effort on the part of Noah. The animals came by instinct, but God had planted in them this special instinct for this occasion. Just as, in the beginning, God had brought the animals to Adam that he should name them, so he now brought them to Noah that he might keep them in the ark for a replenishing of the earth after the Flood.

It has been objected that it would be impossible to conceive of an assemblage of all the living creatures of the different regions of the earth in any one spot. The unique fauna of Australia certainly could have neither reached the ark, nor regained their home after leaving it; for they are separated from the nearest continuous land by vast breadths of ocean. The polar bear surely could not survive a journey from his native icebergs to the sultry plains of Mesopotamia; nor could the animals of South America have reached these except by traveling the whole length of North America and after miraculously crossing the Bering Strait, having pressed westward across the whole breadth of Asia. That even a deer should accomplish such a pedestrian feat is inconceivable, but how could a sloth accomplish it, a creature which lives in trees, never, if possible, descending to the ground,

72

Animals Assembling at the Ark

and able to advance on it only by the slowest and most painful motions? Or how could tropical creatures find supplies of food in passing through such a variety of climates and over vast spaces of hideous deserts? [5]

Here is another problem which cannot be solved to the entire satisfaction of human reason and experience, but it must be remembered what was stated at the beginning, namely, that since Creation the Deluge is the most stupendous miracle in the history of our planet and that the miraculous element appears in all the phases of its history. And yet some of these difficulties will vanish when we bear in mind that the climatic conditions of the world before the Flood were quite different than now. There were no arctics and no deserts in that world, no high mountain barriers to separate one region from another, and this uniform climate also made possible a more uniform distribution of animals over the entire face of the earth. It is therefore not at all necessary to assume that the lumbering polar bear was called from his arctic habitat to the sultry plains of Mesopotamia to keep him and his generation from total annihilation, nor was it necessary to transport the animal denizens from Australia or South America to the valley of the Two Rivers to keep alive seed of their kind. There is every reason to believe that all of these animals were distributed over the face of the earth and therefore were found in the regions near or adjacent to the place where the ark was built.

Then, again, there is the question of species, to which reference was made before. The animals of the postdiluvian world found a changed world with respect to both climate and food supplies; but as these animals multiplied and spread to reoccupy the earth, they adapted themselves to the changed conditions, and differences developed which did not exist before. The animals which could not make this adaptation perished and disappeared entirely, as, for example, the many varieties of prehistoric reptiles and many others.

74

But even granting that the distribution of animals of the first world might have been according to biological zones, similar to what it is now, even then it would not necessarily follow that these animals could not have found their way into the ark. It must be recalled that God gave the world 120 years time for repentance, which means that the Flood was a long time in preparation, and the instinct which God implanted in the animals by which they were brought to Noah might have been operative for many generations. That is to say, the migration of those animals which God had intended to save might have extended over several generations of animals. Large migrations of certain species of animals over great distances have occurred since. Why could it not have taken place then? And, again, the distribution of land masses and their relation to one another was not necessarily the same as it is now, as was pointed out before. There is good evidence to show that large bodies of land which once existed have disappeared in the ocean and that other bodies of land were separated from the parent body by the inroads of the sea.

There still remain other problems concerning the ark and the animals in the ark, such as the food supply necessary to feed for a whole year all that were in the ark; the care of the animals. How was it possible for eight people to feed and to provide drink and other care for all the different animals that were with them in the ark; the cleaning of the ark; the natural increase of the animals in the ark; and other similar questions. Various suggestions have been offered as a possible solution. An English writer advances the theory that Noah was in possession of some mysterious oil of which a drop was sufficient to satisfy the hunger and the thirst of man and animals for a whole day at a time,[6] that is, a sort of antediluvian vitamin tablet. But this seems rather fantastic. Others have suggested that the animals hibernated during the greater part of the time while they were in the ark. This would solve many or all the problems mentioned, but it, too, implies a miraculous interference with the mode of life of most of the animals. But if we are willing to accept the possibility of the miraculous, some such solution is at least conceivable. The Flood as a whole was a stupendous, miraculous interference with the laws governing the entire universe; a temporary suspension of the laws governing the routine and habits of a select group of animals for one year is but an insignificant detail in comparison. The Biblical account of the Flood is so brief, and our knowledge of the world before the Flood, and particularly of the ark, is so limited that here, as elsewhere, many questions must remain unanswered.

Another problem that might be mentioned is the preservation of plant life during this great world catastrophe.

The question may well be raised, If the Flood was of such long duration and caused such tremendous changes on the face of the earth, how was it possible for plant life to survive? No positive or completely satisfactory answer can be given to that question. We know that Noah took all kinds of foods into the ark for his own family and for the animals that were with him, and this would imply seeds of the various plants known to him. But it is not likely that the plant life of the earth was preserved in that manner. It is true that the Flood was a world revolution which caused tremendous changes on the surface of the earth, but it is not unreasonable to assume that in God's providence some areas of the earth remained relatively undisturbed and there plant life in some form or another survived, and from there it gradually spread over the rest of the earth in the decades and centuries that followed, adapting itself to the changed conditions of the new world. It was not God's purpose to annihilate His creation completely but to punish the first world because of its godlessness. In His wisdom He found ways and means to preserve the animals in the ark and the plant life in some other miraculous manner, about which no further details are revealed in the Bible.

CHAPTER VI

Was the Ark Discovered?

URING the year 1942, readers of church papers, magazines, and the public press were aroused by a detailed report of an alleged discovery of the remains of Noah's ark on Mount Ararat. This most remarkable discovery was said to have been made by Mr. Vladimar Roskivitsky, a converted Russian aviator, who since then severed his connection with the godless Bolsheviks, came to America, and was selling Bibles when these articles first appeared. Because of the great interest these articles aroused and the wide discussion they caused, it is thought well to include here in this discussion of Noah's ark an account of this supposed discovery. The following is a verbatim account of this event as told by Mr. Roskivitsky and as reprinted in the *Banner* of the Reformed Church, dated November 27, 1942:

"It was in the days just before the Russian revolution that this story really begins. A group of us Russian aviators were stationed at a lonely temporary outpost about twenty-five miles northwest of Mount Ararat. The day was dry and terribly hot, as August days so often are in this semi-desert land.

"Even the lizards were flattened out under the shady sides of rocks or twigs, their mouths open and tongues lashing out as if each panting breath would be their last. Only occasionally would a tiny wisp of air rattle the parched vegetation and stir up a choking cloudlet of dust.

"Far up on the side of the mountain we could see a thundershower, while still farther up we could see the white snowcap of Mount Ararat, which has snow all the year around because of its great height. How we longed for some of that snow!

"Then the miracle happened. The captain walked in and announced that plane number seven had its new supercharger installed and was ready for high altitude tests, and ordered my buddy and me to make the test. At last we could escape the heat!

"Needless to say, we wasted no time getting on our parachutes, strapping on our oxygen cans, and doing all the half dozen other things that have to be done before 'going up.'

"Then a climb into the cockpits, safety belts fastened, a machinist gives the prop a flip and yells, 'Contact,' and in less time than it takes to tell it we were in the air. No use wasting time warming up the engine when the sun already had it nearly red hot.

"We circled the field several times until we hit the fourteen-thousand-foot mark and then stopped climbing for a few minutes to get used to the altitude.

"I looked over to the right at the beautiful snow-capped peak, now just a little above us, and, for some reason I can't explain, turned and headed the plane straight toward it.

"My buddy turned around and looked at me with question marks in his eyes, but there was too much noise for him to ask questions. After all, twenty-five miles doesn't mean much at a hundred miles an hour.

"As I looked down at the great stone battlements surrounding the lower part of the mountain, I remembered having heard it had never been climbed since the year seven hundred before Christ, when some pilgrims were supposed

78

to have gone up there to scrape tar off an old shipwreck to make good luck emblems to wear around their necks to prevent their crops being destroyed by excessive rainfall. The legend said they had left in haste after a bolt of lightning struck near them and had never returned. Silly ancients! Who ever heard of looking for a shipwreck on a mountaintop?

"A couple of circles around the snow-capped dome, and then a long swift glide down the south side, and then we suddenly came upon a perfect little gem of a lake, blue as an emerald, but still frozen over on the shady side. We circled around and returned for another look at it. Suddenly my companion whirled around and yelled something and excitedly pointed down at the overflow end of the lake. I looked and nearly fainted.

"A submarine? No, it wasn't, for it had stubby masts, but the top was rounded over with only a flat cat walk about five feet across down the length of it. What a strange craft, built as though the designer had expected the waves to roll over the top most of the time and had engineered it to wallow in the sea like a log, with those stubby masts carrying only enough sail to keep it facing the waves! (Years later, in the Great Lakes, I saw the famous 'whaleback' ore carriers with this same kind of rounded deck.)

"We flew down as close as safety permitted and took several circles around it. We were surprised when we got close to it at the immense size of the thing, for it was as long as a city block and would compare very favorably with the modern battleships of today. It was grounded on the shore of the lake with about one fourth of the rear end still running out into the water, and its extreme rear was three fourths under water. It had been partly dismantled on one side near the front, and on the other side there was a great door nearly twenty feet square but with the door gone. This seemed quite out of proportion as even today ships seldom have doors even half that large.

"After seeing all we could from the air, we broke all speed records back to the airport.

"When we related our find, the laughter was loud and long. Some accused us of getting drunk on too much oxygen, and there were many other remarks too numerous to relate.

"The captain, however, was serious. He asked several questions and ended by saying, 'Take me up there, I want to look at it.'

"We made the trip without incident and returned to the airport.

" 'What do you make of it?' I asked, as we climbed out of the plane.

" 'Astounding,' he replied. 'Do you know what ship that is?'

" 'Of course not, sir.'

" 'Ever hear of Noah's ark?'

" 'Yes sir. But I don't understand what the legend of Noah's ark has to do with us finding this strange thing fourteen thousand feet up on a mountaintop.'

" 'This strange craft,' explained the captain, 'is Noah's ark. It has been sitting up there for nearly five thousand years. Being frozen up for nine or ten months of the year, it couldn't rot and has been on cold storage, as it were, all this time. You have made the most amazing discovery of the age.'

"When the captain sent his report to the Russian government, it aroused considerable interest, and the Czar sent two special companies of soldiers to climb the mountain. One group of fifty men attacked on one side, and the other group of one hundred men attacked the mountain from the other side.

"Two weeks of hard work were required to chop out a trail along the cliffs of the lower part of the mountain, and it was nearly a month before the ark was reached.

"Complete measurements were taken and plans drawn of it as well as many photographs, all of which were sent to the Czar of Russia.

"The ark was found to contain hundreds of small rooms and some very large with high ceilings. The large rooms usually had a fence of great timbers across them, some of which were two feet thick, as though designed to hold beasts ten times as large as elephants, somewhat like one sees today at a poultry show; only instead of chicken wire, they had rows of thinly wrought iron bars along the fronts.

"Everything was heavily painted with a waxlike paint resembling shellac, and the workmanship of the craft showed all the signs of a high type of civilization.

"The wood used throughout was oleander, which belongs to the cypress family and never rots, which, of course, coupled with the facts of it being painted and it being frozen most of the time, accounted for its perfect preservation.

"The expedition found on the peak of the mountain above the ship the burned remains of the timbers which were missing out of the one side of the ship. It seems that these timbers had been hauled up to the top of the peak and used to build a tiny one-room shrine, inside of which was a rough stone hearth like the altars the Hebrews use for sacrifices, and it had either caught fire from the altar or been struck by lightning, as the timbers were considerably burned and charred over and the roof was completely burned off.

"A few days after this expedition sent its report to the Czar, the government was overthrown and godless Bolshevism took over, so that the records were never made public and probably were destroyed in the zeal of the Bolsheviks to discredit all religion and belief in the truth of the Bible.

"We Russians of the air fleet escaped through Armenia, and four of us came to America where we could be free to live according to the 'good old Book,' which we had seen for ourselves to be absolutely true, even to as fantastic sounding a thing as a world flood."

That is the story as allegedly told by Mr. Roskivitsky. The question arises whether we are to accept this story or not. If it is true, we certainly would have a most remarkable testimony for the truth of the Biblical account of the Flood. However, I should like to call attention to the following facts:

1. The story is well told, and the subject is such as appeals to the imagination. Every Bible student would like just such evidence to annihilate forever all skepticism and cheap ridicule that has been leveled at Noah's ark and the story of the Biblical Flood. But for that very reason the reader must not be carried away with unreasonable enthusiasm, for it is very easy in a case like this for the wish to become the father of the belief.

2. The report claims that a great number of men, numbering more than 150, actually saw the ark on Mount Ararat, but, strangely enough, of this great number there is only one known eyewitness to tell the story of this most remarkable discovery. The official report prepared for the Czar was lost or willfully destroyed by the Bolsheviks because of their hostility to the Bible. It is possible, of course, but we must consider it strange indeed that this most important document, dealing with one of the greatest archaeological discoveries ever made, would reach its destination just in time to meet with such a disastrous fate. One would also expect that a copy of such an important report would have been retained and signed by all the witnesses because of its significance to science and Bible knowledge and that, of the 150 odd men that are supposed to have visited the scene and carefully investigated the ark, at least one or a few men would have reported this strange discovery.

3. It is claimed that the ark was discovered at an elevation of fourteen thousand feet and that it required about a

month for the searching expedition of 150 men to reach the place where it was held in eternal ice. This raises several important questions. If the ark actually came to rest at that elevation, how could the animals in the ark have descended from so high a mountain down its steep, icy, and impassable slopes? It is conceivable that some of the animals could have descended without receiving harm, but many would have perished.

The Bible says that the ark rested on Mount Ararat, but this does not mean that it necessarily rested on one of the very highest peaks of this rugged mountain chain. Mountain peaks of fourteen thousand feet elevation are covered with ice and snow the year round. It is admitted that the wood of the ark may have been preserved during these millennia, being kept in a constant frozen condition, but what about snow slides, rock movements, or the fearful storms that occur in mountain regions? It seems incredible that a structure so large as the ark could have escaped uninjured or complete destruction during the 4,500 years of action by snow, rocks, and mountain storms.

4. It is extremely difficult to verify or disprove the report. Just which of the many mountain peaks in the Armenian Highlands was Mount Ararat? On which of these did the ark come to rest? If the exact peak or even in a general way the location of this discovery had been given, the story could be verified. But to send an expedition to the Armenian Mountain Range for the search of Mount Ararat and the ark with so little direction is like looking for the proverbial needle in a haystack. It would be an extremely costly expedition and, therefore, very difficult to find an archaeologically minded millionaire to finance such an undertaking. In short, the story has all the characteristics of the Old Testament Apocrypha. It is good to read, it appeals to the imagination, but lacks positive proof.

CHAPTER VII

The Beginning and the
Duration of the Flood

A FTER all preparations had been completed and Noah and his family had entered the ark, the storm broke, and there followed the most destructive catastrophe this world has ever experienced or will experience until heaven and earth will pass away on the day of final Judgment. The record of this event is given in simple language, terse and majestic. The account reads like the logbook of a sea captain, and it is quite possible that Noah actually did record from day to day the events here related. The account reads as follows: "In the 600th year of Noah's life, on the 17th day of the second month, on that very day the fountains of the great abyss were all broken open, and the windows of the heavens were opened. (The rain fell on the earth for forty days and nights.) That same day Noah with Shem, Ham, and Japheth, Noah's sons, and Noah's wife, and the three wives of his sons accompanying them, went into the ark, together with all the various kinds of wild beasts, all the various kinds of domestic animals, all the various kinds of land reptiles, and all the various kinds of birds, everything with feathers and wings; of all creatures in which there was the breath of life, a pair of each, joined Noah in the ark.

Those that entered were a male and a female of every kind of animal, as God had commanded him. Then the Lord shut him in. The flood continued for forty days upon the earth. The waters mounted and lifted the ark so that it rose above the earth. The waters rose and increased greatly on the earth, so that the ark floated on the surface of the waters. The waters rose higher and higher on the earth, until the highest mountains everywhere under the heavens were all covered. Fifteen cubits above them the waters rose, so that the mountains were covered. Every creature that moved on the earth perished, including birds, domestic animals, wild beasts, all the land reptiles, and all mankind. Of all that was on the land, everything in whose nostrils was the breath of life died; every living thing was blotted off the face of the earth, both men and animals and reptiles and birds; they were blotted off the earth, so that Noah alone was left, and those that were with him in the ark. The waters rose on the earth for 150 days." (Gen. 7:11-24. Smith and Goodspeed Version.)

There is a majestic awfulness and awe-inspiring solemnity about this picture. There is nothing here of the trivial or the spectacular, nothing to arouse the carnal sympathies for those men and women and children that perished in this fearful destruction. We see nothing of the death struggle; we hear not the cry of despair; we are not called upon to witness the frantic agonies of husband and wife, of parent and child, as they flee in terror before the rising waters, climbing from hilltop and to ever greater heights, only to be pursued even there by a remorseless foe until they all perished. Nor is a word said of the sadness of those who were safe within the ark, looking out upon the destruction that was wrought all about them. The Babylonian tradition of the Flood, which in many respects is similar to the Biblical, differs widely at this point. Tears are shed in heaven over this catastrophe, and even consternation seizes upon the heavenly inhabitants, while within the ark itself the

And the Rain Was Upon the Earth Forty Days and Forty Nights

Chaldean Noah is represented as saying: "When the storm came to an end and the terrible water spouts ceased, I opened the window and the light smote upon my face; I looked at the sea, tentatively observing, and the whole humanity had returned to mud. Like seaweed the corpses floated. I was seized with sadness; I sat down and wept, and my tears fell upon my face."

There is one profound impression left upon the reader of the Biblical account of the Flood, and that is that of utter desolation. There is a scene of indescribable sadness all about Noah, and there prevails an awful silence, the silence of universal death. We hear nothing but the moaning of the surging waters that bear up the ark. We see not an object to break the monotony of the dull and shoreless expanse of this universal ocean. "All flesh died that moved upon the earth, both of fowl and of cattle and of beast and of every creeping thing that creepeth upon the earth and every man. . . . They were destroyed from the earth, and Noah only remained alive and they that were with him in the ark."

Macaulay has pictured the appalling ruin of the Deluge in the following lines:

From the heaven streams down amain
For forty days the sheeted rain;
And from her ancient barriers free,
With a deafening roar, the sea
Comes foaming up the land.

Mother, cast thy babe aside;
Bridegroom, quit thy virgin bride;
Brother, pass thy brother by;
'Tis for life, for life ye fly!

Along the drear horizon raves
The swift advancing line of waves.
On, on; their frothy crests appear
Each moment nearer, and more near.

Urge the dromedaries speed,
Spur to death the reeling steed,
If, perchance, ye yet may gain
The mountains that o'erhang the plain.

On that proud mountain's crown
The few surviving sons and daughters
Shall see their latest sun go down
Upon a boundless waste of waters.
None salutes, and none replies;
None heaves a groan or breathes a prayer;
They crouch on earth with tearless eyes
And clenched hands and bristling hair.

The rain pours on, no star illumes
The blackness of the roaring sky;
And each successive billow booms
Higher still and still more high.

And now upon the howling blast
The wreaths of spray come thick and fast;
And a great billow, by the tempest curled,
Falls with a thundering crash, and all is o'er:

And what is left of all this glorious world?
A sky without a beam, a sea without a shore.[1]

With the words "Then God remembered Noah and all
them within the ark," the narrative turns to the description
of the gradual decrease of the water until dry land again
appeared. The falling of the waters is described with the
same pictorial language as its rapid rise. God remembered
Noah. This was a dynamic remembering and produced
definite results. For forty days the Flood had increased so
that the waters covered the highest mountains to the depth
of fifteen cubits of water, and it remained at that level for
150 days.

The statement that the waters covered all the highest
hills under the whole heaven clearly indicates that the
Deluge was a universal flood. In fact, the universality of the
Flood is everywhere implied in the entire Biblical account, as
passages such as the following clearly show: "And the Lord
said: I will destroy man, whom I have created, from the *face*
of the earth, both man and beast and the creeping thing and
the fowls of the air, for it repenteth Me that I have made
them." Or, "And God said unto Noah, The end of all flesh
has come before Me . . . and, behold, I will destroy them

The Rising of the Water (Gen. 7:19), by Doré

with the earth." Or, "Behold, I, even I, do bring a flood of waters upon the earth to destroy all flesh wherein is the breath of life from under heaven, and everything that is in the earth shall die. . . . For yet seven days, and I will cause it to rain upon the earth forty days and forty nights, and every living substance that I have made will I destroy from off the face of the earth." These and other statements similar to them cannot be interpreted to mean anything else but that the entire earth, even the highest elevation on the face of the earth, was completely submerged by the floods of the Deluge.

Some have argued that a universal Flood cannot be meant because of the difficulties involved, but that the words of the Jewish writer must be interpreted in the sense of what he meant by the whole world. To the Jew, when Genesis was written, the world was very small, comprising in general the territory bounded in the north by the Black Sea and the Armenian Highlands; in the east, by the territory immediately beyond the Tigris; in the south, by the Persian Gulf and Abyssinia in Africa; and in the west, by the eastern islands of the Mediterranean Sea.[2] But in reply to this and similar views it must be said that it is not a question of what the Jews knew about the world and the extent of man's habitation when Genesis was written, but that the sacred writer clearly states that the whole earth, be it large or small, was destroyed by the Flood and that the entire human race was wiped off the face of the earth, except the eight souls of the family of Noah. And when Jesus and the Apostles in the New Testament refer to the Flood, their statements imply that they understood it to have been a universal flood, just as Moses describes it. We accept Genesis and the rest of the Bible as more than a mere human document. It is God's own infallible record, and therefore no other interpretation is possible.

After the end of the 150 days, the waters were abated. On the seventeenth day of the seventh month the ark rested upon Mount Ararat. The Ararat Mountains are located in Armenia between the Black and Caspian Seas. The tallest peak is said to be 17,750 feet high and is still called by the natives the Kuhi Nuch, that is, the Mountain of Noah. Ararat is also the name of the country. That the ark settled on Ararat does not mean that it settled on that tall peak towering 17,000 feet into the air. All this statement implies is that the ark came to rest somewhere in the highland of Ararat. The waters continued to subside, and so by the first of the tenth month the tops of the mountains had become visible. Noah waited patiently forty days longer, which brings us to the eleventh day of the eleventh month, when he sent forth a raven to find out to what extent the surface of the earth had dried up. The raven flew to and fro, that is, from the mountaintop to the ark and back, or from mountain peak to mountain peak, but he was not taken back into the ark, because he found sufficient food to satisfy his needs. After that, Noah sent out a dove. Three times in succession he sent out doves at regular intervals of seven days. The first dove returned shortly because it found no place to alight and rest. The dove is a bird which will settle only upon such places or objects as are dry and clean. The second dove, a week later, returned in the evening of that day; that is, it had tarried longer than the first dove, and it brought with it a fresh olive leaf. This was the first sign of new life re-appearing on the desolated earth. The third dove did not return. Noah now perceived that the earth was dry. This, however, does not necessarily imply that the whole earth had completely dried off in all places. There is good evidence to show that this was not the case, but that in large inland basins great bodies of water remained for a long period of time after Noah left the ark, possibly for centuries or more. In Asia, in western North America, in northern Africa, and in Australia there are found large areas which are called interior basins, without exterior drainage to the sea, but with interior drainage to some lake or fossil lake. The phys-

The Sending Forth of the Dove (Gen. 8:8),
by Doré

ical evidence points with convincing proof to the fact that these basins were at one time full of water. The Great Salt Lake in Utah is but a remnant of a much larger lake that once occupied this region. Another similar body of water was west of this lake and occupied the greater part of the present States of Nevada, Utah, Idaho, Oregon, and California. Another so-called fossil lake was Lake Agassiz, named for the great scientist and father of American glacial geology. This ancient lake covered an area of land in the present territory of Saskatchewan, Manitoba, North Dakota, Ontario, and Minnesota. 650 miles long and more than 200 miles wide, it covered an area of about 110,000 square miles and had a depth of 500 feet. The present Lake Winnipegosis and Lake Winnipeg are remnants of this lake.

Even the present arid steppes of Mongolia and Turkestan in Central Asia were not always arid, for concerning this region, Upton Close writes: "Now semi-arid waste stretches of sand and gravel very like the American State of Wyoming, it was once a lush lake country." (See Ch. XIV, Glacial and Fossil Lakes.)

Similar bodies of water existed in other places on this and other continents. Their disappearance greatly affected the climate and also plant and animal life in these regions.

On the first day of Noah's 601st year, Noah removed the covering of the ark and saw that the earth was dry, and on the 27th day of the second month the earth was dried, and God commanded him to leave the ark. The Flood had begun on the 17th day of the 600th year of Noah, and Noah left the ark on the 27th day of the 601st year of his life, which makes the duration of the Flood one year and ten days.

It is difficult to realize what must have been the feeling of Noah and his family when they came forth from the ark and set their feet for the first time on the new earth, the only living human beings in all the world. What a change had been wrought all about them! Everywhere the remains of a dead world — dead people, dead animals, dead cities,

93

and a dead civilization. How indescribably lonely they must have felt and what a dread and fear must have come upon them!

The first act of Noah was to bring unto God a sacrifice of thanksgiving for having so graciously protected him and all that were with him in the ark. And God was pleased with this act of Noah. "He smelled a sweet savor," the text says. That is, He graciously accepted the sacrifice of Noah; and He made a covenant with Noah that He would never again curse the ground for man's sake. He gave him a visible token of this covenant and said: "While the earth remaineth, seedtime and harvest, and cold and heat, and summer and winter, and day and night, shall not cease." "And God said: This is the token of the covenant which I make between Me and you and every living creature that is with you for perpetual generations. I do set my bow in the cloud, and it shall be for a token of a covenant between Me and the earth. And it shall come to pass, when I bring a cloud over the earth, that the bow shall be seen in the cloud, and I will remember My covenant which is between Me and you and every living creature of all flesh, and the waters shall no more become a flood to destroy all flesh." And God blessed Noah and his sons with the blessing of Adam and Eve and said unto them: "Be fruitful and multiply and replenish the earth," and He again gave them dominion over all the beasts of the field (Gen. 9:1-7).

This is the history of the Flood as recorded by Moses in the first book of the Bible. To countless millions of all ages this book has been and still is the inspired Word of God, and therefore correct in every detail, also when dealing with natural phenomena and scientific facts. The Bible is not a textbook on geology or any other science, but whenever it touches fields of knowledge belonging to these categories, it is reliable and not merely representing in poetical or allegorical language the erroneous, naive, or limited views current at the time when it was written. But the historicity of the

Deluge does not depend upon Genesis alone. It is confirmed by other sacred writers of the Bible in both the Old and New Testaments and by Christ Himself. Thus Job refers to the Flood in Chapter 22:15-16: "Hast thou marked the old way which wicked men have trodden, which were cut down out of time, whose foundation was overflown with a flood?" Or Is. 54:9: "For this is as the waters of Noah unto Me. For as I have sworn that the waters of Noah should no more go over the earth, so have I sworn that I would not be wroth with thee nor rebuke thee." And in Luke 3:36 Noah and his son Shem are mentioned in the genealogy of Christ. In Matt. 24:37-38 our Savior refers to the Flood in the following words: "But as the days of Noah were, so shall also the coming of the Son of Man be; for as in the days that were before the Flood they were eating and drinking, marrying and given in marriage until the day that Noe entered into the ark." And in Heb. 11:7 Noah is numbered among the heroes of faith. And Peter refers to Noah and the Flood (1 Peter 3:20) as follows: "Which sometime were disobedient, when once the long-suffering of God waited in the days of Noah, while the ark was a preparing, wherein few, that is, eight souls, were saved by water." And 2 Peter 2:5: "And spared not the old world, but saved Noah, the eighth person . . . bringing in the flood upon the world of the ungodly." The Apocryphal book "The Wisdom of Solomon," written between 150 B. C. and 50 B. C., has a reference to the Flood (chap. 10:4), indicating that the Jews of that time considered the Flood of Noah an historical fact.

For the unbiased reader there cannot be any doubt that Moses and other inspired writers mentioned above, including our Lord Himself, regarded the Deluge as a universal flood and a great historical fact. To deny this means to question the infallibility of the Bible and that of Christ Himself.

CHAPTER VIII

Further Problems Connected with the Flood

THE ark with its animal cargo was the first serious stumbling block we encountered in the Mosaic record of the Flood, but we face another and possibly even a more formidable one when we proceed to consider the magnitude of the Deluge and the cosmic revolution required to bring it about. It is evident beyond a doubt that Moses intended to convey the idea that the Deluge was a universal flood, that every continent, every island, and every place inhabited by man or beast was covered with water, and that the flood rose to a height sufficient to cover the loftiest mountains with fifteen cubits of water. As we contemplate these facts with all their implications, the problems involved grow to such proportions as to make it well-nigh impossible to believe that the literal meaning of the words was intended, and hence that some other interpretation must be sought.

The very first questions which stare us in the face in this picture are: Whence came the water sufficient to submerge the entire earth? And what became of the water when the Flood subsided?

The answer found in Genesis is: "The same day were all the fountains of the great deep broken up, and the windows of heaven were opened," and there came pouring rain upon the earth forty days and forty nights. The waters came from heaven above and from the earth below. But that raises two further questions: What was the source of the water that poured forth from the windows of heaven? And what was the source of the water that came from the great deep? Some Bible students have held that this universe is surrounded by a vast sea of water. They base this view on Gen. 1:6-7, where we are told that God placed a firmament over the earth and divided the waters which were under the firmament from those over the firmament. And the same interpreters hold that the waters of the Flood which poured forth "from the windows of heaven" came from this vast supply of water surrounding the universe. There are very serious objections to this view which need not be discussed here.

The Hebrew word translated with "firmament" in the English and "*Feste*" in the German Bible has caused great difficulties to the translator because it is hard to know the real meaning. The literal meaning is "a spreading out," then "dome of heaven." The purpose of the firmament was, according to Genesis, to divide the waters which still constituted a part of the chaos on the emerging earth from the waters which were above. The meaning of this statement can only be a separation between the solid and gaseous matter, between the water in liquid form on earth and the water in gaseous form in the atmosphere. The work of the second day of creation therefore consisted in the creation of the atmosphere surrounding the earth, with the laws governing the atmosphere. The source of the water that came from above must therefore be sought here. Either it came from the atmosphere directly, that is, it was, as it were, wrung out of the atmosphere itself by reducing its water content, or it came from the clouds in the atmosphere or from both sources. And who is able to estimate the amount of water contained in the atmosphere surrounding our globe today? There are good reasons to believe that the atmosphere of the first world contained a greater amount of humidity than it does today. The climate and the vegetation which existed in the world seem to demand this. Who is able to calculate the vast seas of water contained in the atmosphere surrounding our globe at that time, and who is able to measure the water which floats over our heads in the form of clouds? It has been estimated that a single cloud supplying four inches of rainfall over a territory with a radius of one hundred miles contains approximately nine billion tons of water. It is quite possible that the water contained in the prediluvian atmosphere and that which floated over the earth in clouds was equal to the total amount of water on the face of the earth.

The Biblical expression "the windows [or the sluices] of heaven were opened" is the Hebrew way of describing an incessant torrential rain pouring down upon the face of the earth. But we need not even assume that such great changes affected the atmosphere. It is quite possible that the rains of the Deluge came from the same source which supplies the water for the rains today, that is, through the process of evaporation and cloud formation.

Now, it is true that the water cycle on our planet operates in a closed system. That is to say, evaporation increases the rainfall in a given area but does not thereby increase the total quantity of water on the face of our earth, but merely distributes it. However, it must be remembered that the Flood changed the original balance between land and water segments, and a rain of 40 days and 40 nights would contribute very materially to such a change. But that immediately raises another question: How could the clouds form fast enough and continue to form and to produce those quantities of water required for a rain as described in Gen. 7:12? What produced the necessary evaporation? This is another of those questions for which we have no completely satisfactory answer, simply because we have no way of knowing the exact conditions of the atmosphere in the antediluvian world or the changes that were brought about by the world catastrophe. The best we can do is to guess at a possible or probable answer. Even in normal times nature is full of difficult questions and unsolved mysteries; the great Flood was something extremely abnormal and a violent interference with the regular laws of nature; hence it need not disturb us unduly if unsolved difficulties remain. However, in answer to that question, it might, first of all, be said that there are areas in the tropics of the world today where there is but one season, namely, the rainy season, where rains continue to fall without interruption day after day, year in and year out. An unbelievable quantity of water circulates there between the earth and the sky through the normal process of evaporation and rainfall, and all that under perfectly normal conditions.

In the second place, there is indisputable evidence, to which further reference will be made later, that the Flood was accompanied by an abrupt change in climate resulting ultimately in the rigors of the arctic and antarctic regions of our present world. The impact of this sudden change must have been terrific as the cold air and the cold water currents met and mingled with the warm. Mountains of fog and clouds would rise into the air only to discharge their load again in the form of torrential rains, such as are described in the account of the Flood.

And, finally, there is also the possibility that extensive volcanic activities in every part of the earth contributed toward the formation of clouds and the fall of rain on a scale postulated in the Biblical Flood account. That the Flood was accompanied by volcanic activities on an unprecedented scale will be shown later. Here it will be sufficient to call attention to this fact and to point out that the action of volcanoes may well have had something to do with producing clouds and a rainfall unequaled in all the history of our earth. That active volcanoes give off vapor in quantities almost beyond comprehension is a fact established by observation. Steam equivalent to 460 million gallons of water has been observed to issue from one of the subsidiary cones of Mount Etna within one hundred days, which would mean 4,600,000 gallons of water a day, and that only from one secondary cone of one volcano. And then imagine hundreds and thousands of volcanoes in furious activity all over the earth and in the seas, and the cloud-forming possibilities at once appear as beyond calculation. We must always bear in mind that the Deluge was an act of God's judgment upon the wickedness of man. It was therefore a divine interference with the regular and established laws of nature, and yet the forces by which this judgment was carried out and the destruction of the world was wrought were latent in nature. Even in the Deluge the laws of nature were operating, but on a scale unprecedented in the entire history of the universe.

The other sources of the Deluge waters mentioned are the fountains of the deep. The question here is: "What is meant by the fountains of the great deep?" The Hebrew word *t'hom* is translated by Gesenius as *"Urwasser, Ozean, das grosze Weltmeer."* Delitzsch translates it with "unfathomable ocean." By the great deep evidently, then, is meant the water of àll the oceans of the world; the breaking forth of the fountains of the great deep would, then, mean that the ocean broke out and poured over the land. But what caused the waters to break forth? We are told that all the fountains of the great deep broke open. When we hear such words as fountains, wells, or springs, the average person thinks of water welling forth from some orifice in the earth, in more or less quiet and orderly fashion. Springs and fountains always call up pleasant pictures in the mind, and we think of meadows, pasture land, and mountainsides with water bubbling or gushing forth to water the thirsty land or to bring cool refreshment to man and beast. Many of our adult mental images are the unaltered remnants of childhood experiences. This is true especially of such images as were based on verbal description or on pure imagination. Our first impressions of the Deluge were received in early childhood, and the picture drawn for us then was interpreted in the light of our childhood experiences. This picture was carried into adult life with but few modifications. Hence, when the Bible tells us that the fountains of the great deep broke open, we are apt to think of springs and fountains such as were known to us in our meadows or on the mountainsides quietly welling forth their water in refreshing streams or babbling brooks. But the statement that the fountains of the great deep were broken open implies a great deal more. It means that the earth was rent, that great fissures and chasms appeared on the surface of the earth. But that happens only in violent cataclysms, such as are caused by earthquakes or volcanic activities. The Deluge was a terrible judgment of God which He brought upon the world because of the wickedness of men and which is comparable only with the final Judgment, awaiting the world at the end of time. When God came down on Mount Sinai to proclaim His Law, He descended in a dark and threatening cloud. Lightning and thunder accompanied Him, and the whole mountain and the earth round about trembled. When God had finally determined the complete destruction of Pharaoh, he first struck terror into the hearts of the Egyptian hosts, causing them to flee even before the water had come upon them. And the last Judgment of the world is described in the New Testament as a day of fearful wrath and consternation for the wicked. They are described as crying out to the mountains, "Fall upon us," and to the hills, "Cover us." And the Apostle, referring to this day, writes that it is a fearful thing to fall into the hand of the living God.

The Deluge was a day of judgment for the first world. Hence it is certain that God manifested His anger before the Flood destroyed man. That wicked and godless genera-

101

tion was to realize before death overtook them that they had fallen into the hands of the living God, whom they would not acknowledge. Heaven and earth were thrown into a furious and terrible revolution. The lightning flashed without ceasing, and the thunders rolled from pole to pole throughout the heavens. These were the trumpets and bugle calls of God announcing that the day of judgment had come. The earth heaved and trembled in its very foundations. Its writhing convulsions encircled the earth. Volcanoes belched forth fire, water, steam, and brimstone, to add more horrors to this terrifying spectacle of divine judgment. This is not a mere fancy of the imagination. If all the foundations of the great deep broke open, as Moses says, this certainly implies such violent and cosmic disturbances as just described. And that something like this did occur somewhere in the remote past of our earth's history is verified by the condition of the rocks in the earth's crust. Geologists are acquainted with these conditions and describe them accurately, attributing them to violent upheavals and continental revolutions, but because it is regarded as unscientific to accept the Biblical account of a world-wide catastrophe, they find other explanations and place these events in the nebulous past of millions and billions of years ago.

Until about 125 years ago geologists accepted one kind of a flood theory or another. Cuvier, for example, believed in a series of catastrophic floods, with a new creation of life after each. But since then it is no longer regarded as orthodox geology. Hence the modern men of science refuse to accept it. Today it is difficult to find a textbook on geology with even so much as a reference to the Biblical Flood. This would be heretical science, and such books are therefore promptly placed on the *Index Librorum Prohibitorum*. But there are still a few lone voices crying in the wilderness of modern geology who accept Genesis as a trustworthy record of the early history of our earth, and foremost among these is George McCready Price, an able geologist and a brilliant

102

writer. Others are the late Sir J. William Dawson of Canada and a few geology teachers in some church colleges. Concerning such a world-wide revolution and the traces it left on the rocks of the earth, Dr. Price writes: "In the rocks of all parts of the world, ancient displacements have been detected, with throws of vertical range measuring from 200 to 2,000 feet; and if these were suddenly brought about, as all analysis seems to indicate, there must have, at some time in the past, been earthquakes of indescribable violence." [1]

And Edward Suess, the noted Austrian geologist, says: "The earthquakes of the present day are certainly but a faint reminiscence of those telluric movements to which the structure of almost every mountain range bears witness. Numerous examples of great mountain chains suggest by their structure the possibility, and in certain cases the probability, of occasional intervention in the course of great geological processes of episodal disturbances of such indescribable and overpowering violence that the imagination refuses to follow the understanding and to complete the picture of which the outlines are furnished by observation of facts. Such catastrophes have not occurred since the existence of man, at least not since the time of written records." [2]

Earthquakes as described are capable of doing just what the words of Moses imply, viz., to tear the earth into great fissures and cause the fountains of the deep to open, to pour forth water, steam, and molten rock. In the year 1783 a great earthquake occurred in Calabria which caused fissures to be opened 500 feet wide and a thousand feet long, and down them were precipitated men, women, and children, houses, churches, public buildings, and whole farms. Some of the gaping chasms closed again. Others remained open until nature slowly healed its scars.

Simultaneously with the terrible earthquake in Lisbon in 1755, a wide fissure was torn open in Morocco across the straits from the Spanish Peninsula, and an entire village with a population of 8,000 people was literally swallowed up.

In the earthquake which shook the South Island of New Zealand in 1848, a fissure was formed averaging eighteen inches in width and traceable for a distance of sixty miles. The subsequent earthquake seven years later in the same region gave rise to a fissure traceable for ninety miles.

The earthquake of Owens Valley, California, in 1872 was accompanied by the formation of a fault forty miles in length and with a vertical displacement of five to twenty feet. In an earthquake in 1887 in Arizona and Mexico, a zigzag fault thirty-five miles long, with a maximum throw of twenty feet, was produced.

The great Japanese earthquake of 1891 was accompanied by a fault forty miles in length, with throws exceeding thirty-three feet in height, in one of which one side was placed permanently at a different level from the other.

From 1811 to 1812 occurred one of the greatest earthquakes in the history of our country. The loss of life was comparatively small because the country was still very sparsely settled and there were no populous cities in the stricken area. This may account for the fact that this catastrophe is not so well known as other historic earthquakes which resulted in the destruction of great cities and caused the death of thousands of people.

This earthquake is known as "the great earthquake in the West." It occurred in the Mississippi Valley, affecting a region along the Mississippi and some of its tributaries about 300 miles long between the mouth of the Ohio and that of the St. Francis. But serious shocks were also felt far beyond in the mountain region of Tennessee and as far east as Pittsburgh and the Atlantic Ocean.

The greatest intensity of the quake was experienced at New Madrid, a small town about one hundred miles south of St. Louis. Shock followed shock at varying intervals between December, 1811, and February, 1812. The water of the river was changed to a reddish hue and became thick with mud thrown up from the bottom of its bed. The earth on the shores opened in gaping fissures and, closing again, threw the water, sand, and mud in huge jets higher than the tops of the trees. The atmosphere was filled with a thick vapor or gas, to which the light imparted an eerie purple tinge. The current of the Mississippi was driven back in its course with appalling velocity for several hours in consequence of an elevation of its bed, but before long the accumulated waters came booming back with a tremendous roar, carrying everything ruthlessly before them.

The change wrought in the topography in the stricken area was staggering. Thousands of acres of fine forest land were completely swallowed up. Hills had disappeared, and new lakes were found in their place. The earth was rent into innumerable fissures which swallowed up whatever happened to be in their course. In many places the gaping earth revealed unsuspected secrets. Human graves were torn open and their contents scattered over the surface. Bones of the extinct mastodon and the ichthyosaurus were brought to light to the astonishment of the natives. Numerous lakes became elevated ground over the surface of which vast heaps of sand and other debris were scattered. In other places upland forest regions dropped fifty to one hundred feet, forming awesome chasms or new lakes. One of the lakes thus formed was about seventy miles long and from three to twenty miles wide. Similar topographical changes were caused in Tennessee and at other places along the river which had been affected by the earthquake.

The country around New Madrid, Missouri, is since then known as "the sunk country."

Multiply these events and the scenes of New Madrid by ten thousand times ten thousand, and try to visualize that similar scenes occurred simultaneously in every part of the earth, and then we shall be able to construct for ourselves an approximate picture of what is implied in the few but pregnant words of Genesis "and the fountains of the great deep broke open."

But even that is not all. These violent earthquakes not only caused the earth to be rent, forcing it to yield up whatever streams or reservoirs of water were contained in its bowels, but earthquakes, especially when occurring near the sea or on the floor of the ocean, cause gigantic tidal waves known to have risen to heights of ten, twenty, thirty, even fifty and sixty feet or more, above the normal tide level. Large areas of land have thus been inundated, and the force with which these tidal waves strike has irresistibly swept away everything before them. Forests have been uprooted; the works of man wiped out as so much dust; large blocks of rock lifted and moved to higher levels, and over great distances; deposits of sand and gravel and other superficial accumulations have been torn up and swept away, while ruin, destruction, desolation, debris, in short, a completely altered topography were left in the wake.

One of the most lucid descriptions of such a wave is given by Darwin in *The Voyage of the Beagle*, chapter 14.[3] Darwin writes: "The disturbances seem generally, as in the case of Concepcion, to have been of two kinds: first, at the instant of the shock, the water swells high up on the beach with a gentle motion, and then as quietly retreats; secondly, some time afterwards, the whole body of the sea retires from the coast, and then returns in waves of overwhelming force. . . .

"Shortly after the shock a great wave was seen from the distance of three or four miles, approaching in the middle of the bay with a smooth outline; but along the shore it tore up cottages and trees as it swept onwards with irresistible force. At the head of the bay it broke in a fearful line of white breakers, which rushed up to a height of twenty-three vertical feet above the highest spring tides.

"Their force must have been prodigious; for at the fort a cannon with its carriage, estimated at four tons in weight, was moved fifteen feet inwards. A schooner was left in the midst of the ruins two hundred yards from the beach.

"The first wave was followed by two others, which in their retreat carried away a vast wreck of floating objects. In one part of the bay a ship was pitched high and dry on shore, and then was carried off, again driven on shore, and again carried off. In another part two large vessels anchored near together were whirled about and their cables were thrice wound around each other; though anchored at a depth of thirty-six feet, they were for some minutes aground."

An earthquake which occurred on the Island of Sicily and in southern Italy in 1908 practically wiped out the two cities of Messina and Reggio with an approximate loss of human life of 200,000. It has been called "the world's most cruel earthquake." These two cities are located nearly opposite each other on the strait of Messina. At first the sea retired, as a result of the earthquake, and then rolled back, with furious destruction, followed by others and ever rising higher. At Messina the height of the waves was nearly twenty-six or twenty-seven feet, and at San Allessio as high as forty feet, sweeping everything before them. What had not been destroyed by the earthquake was wiped out by the water.

An earthquake at Concepcion, Chile, set in motion a wave that traversed the ocean to the Society and Navigator Islands, three and four thousand miles away, causing incalculable damage.

Concerning the devastating power of an earthquake, d'Orbigny, a noted French geologist of the last century, has the following to say: "After having seen at Callao in Peru the ravages which a sweeping earthquake may make, I am justified in believing that the upheaval of the Andes would suffice to destroy at one stroke by a movement of water all the terrestrial fauna of the globe. At Callao, during the earthquake which occurred at the end of the last century, the waters carried over the land ships there at anchor and changed the whole aspect of the country."[4]

The devastating earthquakes accompanying the Flood

were supplemented, or rather were produced either in part or entirely, by volcanic activities simultaneously occurring in every part of the earth. This, too, is not mere speculation, but is borne out by the physical evidence found in the crust of the earth, particularly in the mountain areas, but by no means confined to those sections. In speaking of this evidence, Dr. Price writes: "Extinct volcanoes are found in all parts of the world. Great numbers of badly eroded volcanic necks or plugs, often with radiating dikes, like the spokes of a cart wheel, showing where they once were. The Rocky Mountains contain many such wrecks of former volcanoes; but almost every corner of the globe, including many regions where no volcanic activities have been seen within historic times, shows signs of former action. Many such relics of old volcanoes are to be seen in the New England States and in Eastern Canada, in the British Isles, in France and Germany, and, indeed, in many regions where the thought of volcanic activity seems almost as strange as that of snow in the tropics." [5]

Other evidence for universal volcanic activity at the time of the Flood is found in the presence of loess in every part of the world and in the conditions under which it was deposited. The soil called "loess" is believed by diluvial geologists to be of volcanic origin, while the manner in which, and the places where, it has been deposited, its ubiquity, the lateness of its deposition, its disregard for watersheds, seems to postulate the action of water on a scale equal only to the great Flood described in Genesis; however, other geologists regard loess as a wind deposit.

An interesting paper on the subject "Scientific Proof of a Universal Flood" was read before the Philosophical Society of Great Britain in February, 1929, by Dr. Philip J. Le Riche, M. R. C. S., L. R. C. P. In this paper, Dr. Le Riche builds up a formidable argument to show that loess is of volcanic origin and that its ubiquity and the character of its deposition argues in favor of a universal flood. While some of the other arguments advanced by the speaker were questioned by members of that learned society, no one seems to have challenged this argument. Concerning these loess deposits, Dr. Le Riche said: "One of the most interesting and the most superficial of all deposits is called 'loess.' It is a yellow homogeneous clay or loam, unstratified, and when crushed in the fingers forms an impalpable dust. It is found as the topmost of all deposits, and its distribution is extensive. It covers a wide area in Central Europe, in Northern France and Belgium, up the valleys of the Rhine and its tributaries. It spreads across Silesia, over the plains of Poland and Southern Russia. It extends into Bohemia, Moravia, Galicia, Hungary, Transylvania and Roumania, sweeping far up into the Carpathians, where it reaches a height of two thousand feet. In the United States it is widely distributed in the great basin of the Mississippi.

"The loess is found extensively in China. In Shansi it reaches a height of nine thousand feet. In hilly regions it fills up valleys and traverses mountain chains. It spreads over the ground so completely as to conceal inequalities. In the Mississippi Valley of the United States, and in Europe in the Rhine Valley, the loess rests in places upon elevations of eight hundred feet above the river, but does not occur at higher levels. This would clearly indicate that it is a water deposit.

"What is the origin of the loess? Sir Henry Howorth compares the loess to the 'Moya,' or volcanic mud, that is thrown out in certain districts, and its calcareous ingredients seem to point to a subterranean origin; and he shows that it consists of comminuted angular particles, free from structure and from the presence of foraminifera, and that it is charged with carbonates. The loess is apparently a substance of volcanic origin deposited slowly in water and then acted upon by the wind in many places after its deposition. That it is not of marine origin, the microscopical evidence clearly shows.

Eruption of Etna, 1771. The Cascade of Fire

The Earthquake of Lisbon, 1755

The Sea Wave on the Coast of Ceylon

The Birth of a New Volcano in Mexico. In a few months the homestead of a humble Mexican farmer grew from a flat surface to a 1,500-foot volcanic mountain

The Eruption Cloud of Mount Pelée,
December 16, 1902

Gigantic Lava Flow Craters of the Moon, Idaho. View looking southeastward from Big Cinder Butte, showing a double line of cinder cones, many of them grass-covered and all of them vents of numerous flows which unite southward into one great field of lava, lonely and uninhabited. The symmetrical crater bowl on the south-east side of Big Cinder Butte lies in the foreground

"Those who assert that the loess is the product of glacial action, in fact, is 'glacial milk,' cannot maintain that glacial products are fertilizing agents, whereas it is well known that volcanic products are fertilizing agents. My belief is that the loess is the product of subterranean volcanic eruptions ... and that it is volcanic dust. It fulfills the conditions necessary for a volcanic product, viz.: that it is extremely light in the air or in water, and it is one of the most fertile of soils, its fertility being in the loess itself. . . . Silica is known to be a product of volcanic action, and this would explain its occurrence with loess. . . .

"The distribution of the loess in positions so far apart as China, the Danube and the Rhine, and in North America, lying everywhere in the same stratigraphical position — and the surmise that it was deposited in water — leads one to suppose that it was the very latest of all the sedimentary deposits."

In the *Voyage of the Challenger*, Sir C. Wyville Thompson states that over a large part of the bed of the Atlantic Ocean, pumice occurs in quantity in different stages of decay, and that this is more especially evident in the "red clay" area; and he traces a great part of the material of the red clay to this source. Nodules containing a large proportion of manganese peroxide, he says, are usually more or less abundant in the "red clay," and are believed to be derived from the decomposition of volcanic products.

Here again we have evidence of volcanic products being found as a superficial deposit, as ocean deposits.

Dr. G. Frederick Wright, in his *Man and the Glacial Period*, states: "The connection of lava-flows on the Pacific Coast with the Glacial Period is unquestionably close. For some reason which we do not understand, the vast accumulation of ice in North America is correlated with enormous eruptions of lava west of the Rockies. The extent of outflow of lava west of the Rockies is almost beyond comprehension. Literally hundreds of thousands of square miles have been covered by them to a depth — in many places — of thousands of feet.

"Here again we find volcanoes exerting their influence at the higher levels in the strata; but in the Rockies it is more as if the tired earth, in its last throes, had belched forth these enormous emanations of lava, as it were, in its dying effort. So from the lowest to the highest layers of the earth's crust we find that volcanoes and volcanic products have been in the main causes (if not the entire cause) of stratification. The volcanic mud of the Old Red Sandstone, the Argillaceous material of the oil-shales of the carboniferous, the lavas of the Tertiary, the pumice of the Atlantic Ocean, the loess — ubiquitous and most superficial — all these are of undoubted volcanic origin." [6]

So much for the evidence of volcanic activity on a worldwide scale somewhere in the past history of our earth. And now a word about the potential effects these may have had in changing the face of the earth.

We have already pointed out that volcanic activity may greatly increase the normal process of evaporation and thus seriously affect the climate in a given region. But that is not all. For just as the destructive forces of earthquakes are not limited to the tremors of the earth itself, but are seriously aggravated by the tidal waves which they produce, so the destructive potentialities of a volcano are not limited to the eruption itself, to the lava flows or the falling of cinders and volcanic ash, but are enormously augmented by the disturbance they cause in the sea. To realize what unbelievable devastation the sea may cause on land and to the works of man in a moment of time, when disturbed by volcanic activities, one need but read the descriptions of the historic eruptions of the world's great volcanoes, such as Vesuvius, Krakatoa, Mount Pelée, and others.[7] One example will suffice here, and I shall choose the eruption of Krakatoa which occurred in the latter part of August, 1883.[8]

Krakatoa is located on an island of the Dutch East Indies of the same name, about one hundred miles from Batavia, Java. Until the year 1883 few had ever heard of Krakatoa, but in that year there were symptoms that the volcanic powers in this defunct volcano were about to awake from the slumber that had endured for many generations. Notable warnings were given. Earthquakes were felt, and deep rumblings proceeded from the earth, showing that some disturbance was in preparation. At first the eruption did not threaten to be of any serious type. In fact, the people of Batavia arranged a picnic expedition to the island to observe at close range the strange actions of this mountain.

As the summer of this dread year advanced, the vigor of Krakatoa steadily increased. The noises became more and more vehement and more audible on shores ten miles distant, then twenty miles, and still these noises waxed louder and louder until they could be heard over an area equal to about two Midwestern States. With each successive convulsion, quantities of fine dust were projected aloft into the clouds. The wind could not carry this dust away as rapidly as it was hurled upward by Krakatoa, and accordingly the atmosphere became heavily charged with suspended particles, a pall of darkness thus spreading over the adjoining seas and islands. Such was the thickness and the density of this atmospheric dust that for a hundred miles around, the darkness of midnight prevailed at midday. Then the awful tragedy of Krakatoa took place. Many thousands of the unfortunate inhabitants of the adjacent shores of Sumatra and Java were destined never to behold the sun again. They were swept away to destruction in an invasion of tremendous waves with which the seas surrounding Krakatoa were agitated. Gradually the development of the volcanic energy proceeded, and gradually the terror of the inhabitants of the surrounding coast rose to a climax. July had ended before the manifestation of Krakatoa had attained even full violence. As the days of August passed by, the spasms of Krakatoa waxed more and more vehement. By the middle of that month the panic was widespread, for the supreme catastrophe was at hand.

On the night of Sunday, August 26, 1883, the blackness of the dust clouds, now much thicker than ever in the straits of Sunda and adjacent parts of Sumatra and Java, was only occasionally illuminated by lurid flames from the volcano. The Krakatoa thunders were on the point of their complete development.

At the town of Batavia, a hundred miles distant, there was no quiet that night. The houses trembled with the subterranean violence, and the windows rattled as if heavy artillery were being discharged in the streets, and still these efforts seemed to be only rehearsing for the supreme display. By ten o'clock on Monday morning, August 27, 1883, the rehearsals were over, and the performance began. An overture consisting of two or three introductory explosions was succeeded by a frightful convulsion which tore away a large part of the island of Krakatoa and scattered it to the winds of heaven. In that final effort all records of previous explosions on this earth were completely broken.

Never before was a noise of such intensity heard on this globe. It must, indeed, have been a loud noise which could travel from Krakatoa to Batavia and preserve its vehemence over so great a distance; but we should form a very inadequate conception of the energy of the eruption of Krakatoa if we thought that its sounds were heard by those merely a hundred miles off. This would be little indeed compared with what is recorded in testimony which it is impossible to doubt. The explosion was heard 3,000 miles away, just four hours after the explosion had occurred. It is estimated that the explosion blew about a cubic mile of solid material into ashes which rose in the form of a dark cloud seventeen miles into the atmosphere, completely hiding the sun by its denseness over the vast area and finally encircling the earth. The disturbance in the atmosphere was registered by thermometers over the whole world. Huge waves, up to one hundred feet above high tide, were generated in the sea and rushed along the low-lying coast of Java and Sumatra, sweeping far inland and destroying 1,295 towns, villages, and lives of nearly 40,000 people. By the force of the tidal waves a large ship was carried inland for a mile and a half and left stranded thirty feet above the sea level. Great blocks of stone weighing from thirty to fifty tons were also carried inland for two or three miles.

During the days, weeks, and months of the Flood when judgment was being executed on the first world, there were probably ten thousand and more Krakatoas, Mount Pelées, and Vesuviuses shaking and tearing at the foundation of the earth, roaring their incessant thunders as a terrible funeral dirge, belching forth dust and steam and lava and boulders, and illuminating the death struggles of a perishing world with their terrifying and lurid volcanic fires.

This is not a fantastic assumption or a mere figment of the imagination. The very foundation rocks of our earth bear evidence that these things happened. And as one contemplates this world judgment and the cosmic forces latent in the universe, in the atmosphere, in the earth, and in the sea released and becoming operative simultaneously in every part of the world for the duration of the Flood and extending even beyond, then there are no longer any serious difficulties in solving the problems of the Flood waters. In addition, we also find in this event or series of events a key to many of the vexing problems of geology, such as the enormous foldings and faults, found in the rocks, lava flows and lava intrusions in unexpected places, the problem of erratics and drifts, and a thousand other unexplainable features found on the surface or in the crust of our earth.

These planetary seismic and volcanic revolutions no doubt were accompanied by the larger movements of land and sea segments both up and downward, thus forcing the water of the sea over the entire land areas. Such movements of land and water segments have been observed repeatedly since geologic or historic time. A well-known example, and one that is generally found in standard textbooks of geology, is the Temple of Jupiter Serapis in the Bay of Naples. This temple was built in Roman times and probably began to sink while still in use, as appears from the two ancient pavements, one above the other. There is evidence that the building was submerged to the depth of nearly twenty feet. Since then the land has again risen, but just when the re-elevation began is not definitely known. There is some documentary evidence, however, to show that it was in progress during the early years of the sixteenth century and was probably completed in 1538, when a volcanic eruption in the neighborhood resulted in the formation of Monte Nuovo.

On the coast of Egypt ancient rock-cut tombs are now visible beneath the waters of the Mediterranean, showing both down and upward movements. The testimony of old buildings shows that the eastern end of the Island of Crete is sinking while the west and south are rising. South of Stockholm in Sweden the remains of an ancient hut were found sixty-five feet below the surface, buried in marine deposits which contained shells of the same species now living in the Baltic. The west coast of Greenland is sinking. Buried forests have been found on the delta of the Mississippi and on the shore of the Chesapeake Bay, also in Holland and northern Germany.[9]

Geikie states that raised coral reefs, formed by living species of coral, are a conspicuous feature of the geology of the West Indies region. The terraces of Barbados are particularly striking. In Cuba a raised coral reef occurs at a height of one thousand or eleven hundred feet above the sea. In Peru modern coral limestone has been found 2,900 or 3,000 feet above sea level. Again, in the Solomon Islands, evidence of a recent uprise is furnished by coral reefs lying at a height of eleven hundred feet. Similar evidence occurs among the New Hebrides at fifteen hundred feet. Raised beaches are found in the higher altitudes of the northern and southern hemispheres. They occur in many parts of the coast line of Britain. The coast line on both sides of Scotland is likewise fringed with raised beaches, sometimes several occurring one after the other. And the list of examples could be multiplied to show that ever since historic times up- and downward movements of land masses have been observed. It is not claiming the impossible therefore or even the unusual to assume that the complete submergence of the face of the earth was due at least in part to the subsidence of large masses of land below sea level and a corresponding raising of the bottom of the sea to higher levels, thus bringing about a more equal distribution of the existing quantity of water over the earth's entire surface.[10]

The "great deep" of Genesis is the ancient universal ocean, from which the dry land emerged when God commanded these two elements to separate on the third day of Creation. According to the Bible, it is the dry land that is the uncertain element on the surface of this earth and liable to submergence at any time when "the bounds placed on the sea by its Maker shall be loosened." For it is God "who gave the sea His decree that it should not pass His limits," who "shut up the sea with doors," who "appointed to the waters bounds that they may not pass, that they return not to cover the earth." The element of mutability is therefore in the solid earth rather than in the sea; and when God for a season removed the bounds of the sea which He had first given by decree, and raised the bars which had been closed against the "proud waves," the sea again engulfed the whole earth and returned to a condition prevailing before the third day of creation. (Prov. 8:29; Job 38:8-11; Ps. 104:9.)

But there is still another question which needs to be considered in this connection, and that is the question concerning the altitude of the antediluvian mountains. The Mosaic account states that the water of the Flood rose to a height of fifteen cubits over the highest mountains. Does this mean that the water rose to an elevation to cover such heights as Pikes Peak, Mount Everest, Mount McKinley, and all the other highest peaks in the world's mountain ranges? This does not necessarily follow. On the contrary, we may well assume that the mountains of the world before the Flood were not of the same altitude as the mountains of our world today. The uniform springlike climate which prevailed over the entire earth before the Flood and the complete absence of desert or arctic regions would seem to preclude the existence of such lofty mountain barriers as we know them today. Besides, it is a well-known fact that the tops of our mountains are overlaid with strata of fossiliferous rocks, which show that these rocks were laid down in water and that they were formed after life had appeared on the earth. This evidence is found not only throughout the length and breadth of the mountain ranges on this continent, but also in the Himalayas, the Alps of Europe, and in other great mountain ranges of the earth.

And, finally, the question must be answered: "Is there enough water on our planet to cover the entire earth?" Apelles, an heretical teacher, raised this question as early as the second century of our era. The Gnostics and Manichaeans in the same age likewise questioned the universality of the Flood, for similar reasons, and since then this question has been raised again and again. The answer must be a very emphatic yes! Geographers estimate the total land surface of our globe at approximately 58,000,000 square miles. The proportion of land to water area on our earth is about three tenths to seven tenths. That is, there is more than twice as much water as land. The area of the Pacific Ocean alone is nearly ten million square miles greater than all the continents and the islands of the sea added together. If the water now stored in the form of glacial ice on Greenland and Antarctica alone were released, the volume of the sea would be raised by one hundred and fifty feet.[11]

The average depth of the ocean is twelve thousand feet.

That is equal to twelve times the average height of the land surface. The volume of all the ocean water is therefore greater than the mass of land protruding above sea level. If all the deeper parts of the ocean were filled up by materials to a mean depth, and all of the highest elevations on land would be planed down to an average level, a universal ocean covering the entire earth to the depth of one and a half miles would result. Surely the objection that there was not enough water on the earth to produce the Flood, therefore, cannot stand, nor would anyone seriously contend that the omnipotent God and Creator of the universe lacked the physical means by which such a deluge could have been brought upon the earth.

This chapter might therefore quite fittingly be concluded with a quotation from an article by Lt. Col. Davies which appeared in the *Journal of Transactions of the Victoria Institute* of London in 1930: "The question as to where the water came from and where it went to will only trouble those who hold extreme views as to the fixidity of oceanic and continental levels. If the sea beds can rise and the continents sink, there is no difficulty whatever in finding enough water, even for a universal flood." (P. 95.)

The Deluge, we must remember, was both a miracle and a natural event. It was a miracle because it was an intervention of divine power and justice in the laws of nature, which God Himself had fixed; and it was a natural event because it was carried out by forces already latent in nature. In this it resembles the destruction of Sodom and Gomorrah, the plagues of Egypt, the destruction of Pharaoh's host in the Red Sea. The omnipotent God, who created heaven and earth, has placed infinite forces in the universe itself. He released these forces for a season, and the destruction of the world was the result. The Flood is a miracle and therefore beyond the comprehension of finite man. It is a mystery which can be understood only through faith in the omnipotent Creator and Ruler of the universe.

PART III

Extra-Biblical Evidence for the Flood

CHAPTER IX

Flood Traditions Among the Nations of the World

Until about one hundred years ago the historical fact of the Flood was almost universally accepted, not only by members of the Church, both Catholic and Protestant, but also by the men of science. Then arose the so-called doctrine of uniformitarianism, and, with that, Darwinism; the catastrophe of the Flood did not fit into this system. It was rejected for geological, biological, and historical reasons. The textbooks of these sciences continue to ignore the Flood altogether, and anyone who still seriously contends for a belief in the universal Flood meets with opposition, scorn, and ridicule even in many quarters of the Church. For this reason we shall next turn to evidence for a universal flood found outside the Bible.

The first evidence to be noted is that of the Flood traditions. The account of the Flood in Genesis does not stand alone. Traditions similar to this record are found among nearly all the nations and tribes of the human race. And this is as one would expect it to be. If that awful world catastrophe, as described in the Bible, actually happened, the existence of the Flood traditions among the widely separated and primitive people is just what is to be expected. It is only natural that the memory of such an event was rehearsed in the ears of the children of the survivors again and again and possibly made the basis of some religious observances. The religious ceremonies connected with these traditions, as found, e. g., in Egypt, Mexico, and among some tribes of the American Indians, can be satisfactorily explained only in this light. This awful disaster left an indelible impression upon the minds of men before they were scattered abroad; and whether we go to ancient Babylon, to the Sumerians or to the Chaldeans, to the Chinese or to the American Indians, to the natives of the Pacific Islands or to the ancient inhabitants of India, everywhere is found some trace of a Flood tradition and a memory of a fearful catastrophe which destroyed mankind and left but one or a few survivors.

But, as might be expected, these traditions have been modified through the ages and have been influenced by the customs of the various peoples and by the environment in which they are found and thus have taken on local color and sometimes extravagant and fantastic proportions, so that the kernel of truth in many cases is seriously obscured. And yet, when stripped of the accretions which have accumulated as they were handed down from father to son through the generations, the essential facts of this great catastrophe are easily discernible. There is almost complete agreement among them all on the three main features: 1. There is a universal destruction of the human race and all other living things by water. 2. An ark, or boat, is provided as the means of escape. 3. A seed of mankind is preserved to perpetuate the human race. To these might be added a fourth, which, though not occurring in all the traditions, occurs very frequently, namely, that the wickedness of man is given as the cause of the Flood.

Naturally, these Flood traditions have aroused the curiosity of scholars. They have been collected and studied, but the men who collected them were not necessarily interested in establishing the truth of the Biblical account of the Flood.

128

Some of them at least had other interests and treated these as other traditions and mythologies found among the nations of the world. Among the noted scholars of the last generation who worked in the field of traditions and myths, including the Flood traditions, were men like Frazer [1] and the German scholar Wundt.[2] In recent years a collection of mythologies of all races has been published by the Archaeological Institute of America. This collection includes the Flood traditions of many peoples. In Germany Dr. Johannes Riem has made an extensive study of this subject and has embodied the results of his findings in his book *Die Sintflut in Sage und Wissenschaft*.[3] In the introduction to this book the author makes the following significant statement: "Among all traditions there is none so general, so widespread on earth, and so apt to show what may develop from the same material according to the varying spiritual character of a people as the Flood tradition. Lengthy and thorough discussions with Dr. Kunike have convinced me of the evident correctness of his position that the fact of the Deluge is granted because at the basis of all myths, particularly nature myths, there is a real fact, but that during a subsequent period the material was given its present mythical character and form." [4]

Dr. Riem furnishes a map of the world indicating where Flood and rainbow traditions are found. According to this map, Flood traditions are most common in Asia and on the islands immediately south of Asia and on the North American continent. Though found in Africa, they are not nearly as common as on other continents. Studies dealing with the Babylonian, Assyrian, or Sumerian Flood traditions are very numerous. Dr. Richard Andree, another German scholar, has compiled another collection of Flood traditions. He has collected eighty-eight different Flood traditions. Twenty of these have an Asiatic origin; five come from Europe; seven were found in Africa; ten in Australia and the South Sea Islands; and forty-six were found among the aborigines of the Americas.[5] Hugh Miller, the famous Scottish geologist of the last century, also enumerates a great number of Flood traditions and expresses the following opinion concerning them: "There is, however, one special tradition which seems to be more deeply impressed and more widely spread than any of the others. The destruction of well-nigh the whole human race, in an early age of the world's history, by a great deluge, appears to have so impressed the minds of the few survivors, and seems to have been handed down to their children, in consequence, with such terror-struck impressiveness that their remote descendants of the present day have not even yet forgotten it. It appears in almost every mythology, and lives in the most distant countries, and among the most barbarous tribes. It was the laudable ambition of Humboldt, first entertained at a very early period of life, — to penetrate into distant regions, unknown to the natives of Europe at the time, that he might acquaint himself in fields of research altogether fresh and new, with men and with nature in their most primitive conditions. In carrying out his design, he journeyed far into the woody wilderness that surrounds the Orinoco and found himself among tribes of wild Indians whose very names were unknown to the civilized world. And yet among even these forgotten races of the human family he found the tradition of the deluge still fresh and distinct; not confined to single tribes, but general among the scattered nations of that great region, and intertwined with curious additions, suggestive of the inventions of classic mythology of the Old World. 'The belief in the great deluge,' we find him saying, 'is not confined to one nation singly, the Tamanacs, it makes part of a system of historical tradition, of which we find scattered notions among the Maypures of the great cataracts; among the Indians of the Rio Erevato, which runs into the Caura; and among almost all the tribes of the upper Orinoco. When the Tamanacs are asked how the human race survived this great deluge — the age of water — of the Mexicans, they say,

130

a man and a woman saved themselves on a high mountain called Tamanacu, situated on the banks of the Asiveru, and casting behind them over their heads the fruits of the mauritia palm tree, they saw the seeds contained in these fruits produce men and women, who re-peopled the earth.' " [6]

For very obvious reasons it will be impossible to deal with all or even many of these traditions. A few must suffice to give examples of their content and character and to show that they are found in all ages among people of various cultural levels and in all lands and countries of the earth.

Our first selection will be taken from those found among the American Indians, and the first of these is one found among the Athapascan Tribe on the West Coast of our country. The story begins with the making of a new sky to replace the old one, which is threatening to fall. After describing in some detail the rebuilding of a new heaven, the story continues:

"Then upon the earth that was they caused rain to fall. Every day it rained, every night it rained. All the people slept. The sky fell, the land was not. For a very great distance there was no land. The waters of the oceans came together. Animals of all kinds drowned. Where the waters went, there were no trees. There was no land. Water came, they say. The waters completely joined everywhere. Trees and grass were not. There were no fish or land animals or birds. Human beings and animals alike had been washed away. The wind did not blow through the portals of the world, nor was there snow, nor frost, nor rain. It did not thunder, nor did it lighten. Since there were no trees to be struck, it did not thunder. There were neither clouds nor fog, nor was there sun. It was very dark. Then it was that this earth with its great, long horns got up and walked away down this way from the north. As it walked along through the deep places, the water rose to its shoulders. When it came up into shallower places, it looked up. There is a ridge in the north upon which the waves break. When it came to the middle of the world in the east under the rising of the sun, it looked up again. There where it looked up will be a large land near to the coast. Far away to the south it continued, looking up. It walked under the ground. Having come from the north, it traveled far south and laid down. Nagaitche, standing on earth's head, had been carried to the south. Where earth laid down, Nagaitche placed its head as it should be and spread gray clay between its eyes on each horn. Upon the clay he placed a layer of reeds and then another layer of clay. In this he placed upright blue grass, brush and trees. 'I have finished,' he said. 'Let there be mountain peaks here on its head. Let the waves of the sea break against them.' " [7]

According to the historian Bancroft, the Papago Indians of Arizona have the following Flood tradition: "The Great Spirit first made the earth and its creatures. Then he came down to look at his handiwork. Digging in the ground he had made, he found some clay. He took this back into the sky with him and let it fall back into the hole he had excavated.

"Immediately there came out man, in the form of Montezuma, the hero of this legend. With his help there also came forth all the Indian tribes in order. The last to come were the Apaches, wildest of all tribes, who scattered to the four winds as soon as they issued forth. Peace and happiness was in the world those first days. The sun being nearer to the earth than it is now, all the seasons were warm, and no one wore clothing. Men and animals shared a common tongue, and all were brothers.

"Then a fearful catastrophe shattered the golden days. A great flood destroyed all flesh wherein was the breath of life, except Montezuma and a coyote who was his friend. The coyote had prophesied the flood's coming, and Montezuma, his friend, had believed him. He hollowed out a boat for himself and kept it waiting on a mountaintop. The coyote was pretty wise, too. He gnawed out a great cane

132

by the river bank, calked it with gum, and with the coming of the waters clambered into it.

"The great waters rose, but Montezuma and the coyote floated upon them and were saved. When the waters receded, the man Montezuma and the wolf who had warned him met on dry land. Anxious to discover how much dry land was left, the man sent out the coyote to explore, and the animal reported that to the west, the south, and the east there was sea, but to the north he could find no sea, though he had journeyed until he was weary. Meanwhile the Great Spirit, with the help of good old Montezuma, had restocked the earth with men and animals.

"Another legend of the great flood is similar, with an eagle substituting for the wolf." [8]

The Arapaho Flood tradition as recorded by Sherman Coolidge, an educated member of that tribe, reads as follows: "Long ago before there was any animal life on earth, the entire surface of the planet was covered with water, except the top of one high mountain. Upon this mountain sat a lone Arapaho, poor, weeping, and in great distress. The Great Spirit saw him and felt sorry for him, and in his pity sent three ducks down to the poor Indian. The Arapaho ordered the ducks to dive down into the waters and bring up some dirt. The first and second tried, but after remaining under water for a long time, each returned without any dirt. Then the third went down and was gone so long that the surface of the water where he disappeared had become still and quiet. The Arapaho believed this duck to be dead, when she returned to the surface with some dirt in her bill. As soon as the Arapaho received this bit of dirt, the waters began to subside.

"In a short time the waters had receded so far that they could not be seen from the top of the highest mountains, but this Arapaho, who was endowed with supernatural wisdom and power, knew that they surrounded the earth, even as they do to this day. The Arapaho, who had been saved by the ducks, then became the sole possessor of the land. He made the rivers and made the trees to grow and then the buffaloes, elks, deer, and other animals, all the birds of the air and the fishes in the water and all the trees and bushes and all other things that can be grown by planting seed in the ground." [9]

Another interesting Indian Flood tradition is that of the Algonquins from the northeastern part of our continent. The story of this tradition runs as follows: Long ago there came a powerful snake when man had become evil. The strong snake was the enemy of living beings, and they became confused and hated one another. Then both fought and annihilated one another, not keeping their peace. The small man fought with the keeper of the dead. Then the powerful snake made a great resolve to destroy all men and living beings. She brought the black snake, the monster, the rushing waters. The rushing waters spread out over the mountains and destroyed all living things. On Turtle Island was Manabozho, the grandfather of the human race and of living beings. Being born creeping on Turtle Island, he is ready to move and to dwell. Men and living beings floated on the water, seeking the back of the turtle. The sea monsters were many, and they destroyed many (men). Then the daughter of one of the spirits helped them into a boat, and all together they cried out: "Come help, Manabozho, the grandfather of living beings, of men, and of turtles." Altogether on the back of the turtle the men were. Greatly frightened, Manabozho prayed the turtle to restore everything. Then the waters subsided, the mountains and plants became dry, and the evil one went elsewhere. [10]

"There are other portions of America in which the tradition of the flood is still more distinct than among the forests of the Orinoco. It is related by Herrera, one of the Spanish historians of America, that even the most barbarous of the Brazilians had some knowledge of the general deluge; that in Peru the ancient Indians reported that many years before there were any Incas all the people were drowned by a great flood, save six persons, the progenitors of the existing races, who were saved on a float; that among the Mechoachens it was believed that a single family was preserved, during the outburst of the waters, in an ark, with a sufficient number of animals to replenish the new world; and, more curious still, that it used to be told by the original inhabitants of Cuba that 'an old man, knowing the deluge was to come, built a great ship and went into it with his family and abundance of animals; and that, wearying during the continuance of the flood, he sent out a crow, which at first did not return, staying to feed on the dead bodies, but afterwards returned bearing with it a green branch.' The resemblance borne by this last tradition to the Mosaic narrative is so close as to awaken a doubt whether it may not have been but a mere recollection of the teaching of some early missionary. Nor can its genuineness now be tested, seeing that the race which cherished it has been long since extinct. It may be stated, however, that a similar suspicion crossed the mind of Humboldt when he was engaged in collecting the traditions of the Indians of the Orinoco; but that on further reflection and inquiry he dismissed the doubt as groundless. He even set himself to examine whether the district was not a fossiliferous one, and whether beds of sea shells, or deposits charged with the petrified remains of corals or of fishes, might not have originated among the aborigines some mere myth of a great inundation sufficient to account for the appearances in the rocks. But he found that the region was mainly a primary one, in which he could detect only a single patch of sedimentary rock, existing as an unfossiliferous sandstone. And so, though little prejudiced in favor of the Mosaic record, he could not avoid arriving at the conclusion, simply in his character as a philosophic inquirer who had no other object than to attain to the real and the true, that the legend of the wild Maypures and Tamanacs regarding a great destructive deluge was simply one of the many forms of that oldest of traditions which appears to be well-nigh coextensive with the human family, and which, in all its varied editions, seems to point at one and the same signal event." . . . "The admirable reflection of Humboldt suggested by the South American traditions seems, incidentally at least, to bear out this view. 'Those ancient traditions of the human race,' he says, 'which we find dispersed over the whole surface of the globe, like the relics of a vast shipwreck, are highly interesting in the philosophical study of our own species. How many different tongues belonging to branches that appear totally distinct transmit to us the same facts! The traditions concerning races that have been destroyed and the renewal of nature, scarcely vary in reality, though every nation gives them a local coloring. In the great continents, as in the smallest islands of the Pacific Ocean, it is always on the loftiest and nearest mountain that the remains of the human race have been saved; and this event appears the more recent in proportion as the nations are uncultivated, and as the knowledge they have of their own existence has no very remote date.' " [11]

According to a Mexican Flood tradition, Coxcox, also called Tezpi by other tribes, saved himself, his wife, his children, some animals, and some grain, from a great flood by embarking in a boat or raft. When the Great Spirit ordered the water to withdraw, Tezpi sent out from his ship a vulture. This bird feeds on carrion and hence did not return because of the great number of carcasses strewn all over the earth. Tezpi sent out other birds, of which the hummingbird alone returned, bringing with it a branch covered with leaves.

According to the *Buffalo Courier Express*, the recent Dana and Ginger expedition into an unexplored region of Mexico found remnants of an ancient Maya Flood tradition.[12]

Comment on these Indian Flood traditions is unnecessary. Some of the details are fantastic and have been influenced by the environment and mode of living of the primitive aborigines of this continent, but the basic elements of the Biblical Flood are easily discernible. There is a universal Flood covering the whole earth, destroying all men and every living thing. There is a Noah, who is saved with his family. There is also a boat or a raft by which the human race, animal, and plant life are saved from total annihilation. There are the birds, which were sent out to explore the surface of the earth after the Flood, and even the olive leaf has not been omitted. There are elements which may even be an echo of the confusion of the tongues at Babel.

The natives of Alaska have the following Flood traditions: Formerly the father of the Indian tribe lived toward the rising sun. Having been warned in a dream that a deluge would desolate the earth, he built a raft, on which he saved himself and his family and all the animals. He floated for several months on the water. The animals, who could then talk, complained and murmured against him. A new earth at length appeared. He thereafter alighted with all the animals, which then lost the gift of speech as a punishment for their complaining.[13]

The natives of Sudan call Lake Chad in Bornu Bahar el Nuh, i. e., the lake of Noah, and they believe that a flood submerging the whole earth had its origin in this lake. The Hottentots call the progenitors of their race Noh and Hingnoh, and the natives of Greenland have a tradition according to which ten generations of men had lived upon the earth when a universal flood came and the earth capsized like a boat and the whole human race was destroyed. Only one man saved himself. When he struck the earth with his rod, a woman was created for him. From this pair the present human race has descended.[14]

The Hawaiians say that long after the time of Kumuhonua, the first man, the earth became wicked and careless of worship of the gods. One man was righteous, Nu-u. He made a great canoe with a house on it and stored it with food, taking plants and animals into it. Then the waters came up over all the earth and destroyed all of mankind except Nu-u and his family. When he came out upon the land after the water had subsided, he looked up and saw the moon and thought that it was Cane, the great god; so he worshiped it. This displeased Cane, and he came down on a rainbow to reprove Nu-u, but he did not punish him, for Nu-u did this by mistake. When he returned to the sky, he left the rainbow behind him as a token of his forgiveness.

"In eastern Tartary the Mongols will tell you that it has been said from time immemorial that in remote antiquity the waters of the deluge flooded the district, and when they had receded, the places where they had been were covered with sand.

"The Battaks of Sumatra say that when the earth grew old and dirty, the Creator — whom they call Debata — sent a flood to destroy every living thing. Debata was angry. The last human pair had taken refuge, not in an ark, but on the top of the highest mountain, and the waters of the deluge had already reached their knees when Debata, the Lord of all, repented of his resolution to make an end to all mankind.

"Magnificently picturesque legends have grown up among the natives of Engano — an island to the west of Sumatra — and among the Sea Dyaks of Sarawak in Borneo. The Bugi-speaking Toradjas of the Central Celebes tell of a flood which covered the highest mountain, leaving bare only the tip of Mount Wawom Pebato. This time no lucky pair escaped. Instead, the only living creatures to survive the flood were a pregnant woman and a pregnant mouse.

"According to the legend of the primitive inhabitants of the Andaman Islands in the Bay of Bengal, some time after they had been created, men grew careless. They disobeyed the rules of the Creator, disregarded the commands he had given them. So, like Jehovah in Genesis, he sent a flood, and it covered all the land except one mountain, Saddle Peak, where the Creator himself lived.

138

"The Kurnai, an aboriginal Australian tribe of Gippsland in Victoria, tell that long ago a great flood came to their land, and all were drowned except a black man and two or three women. The Fijians, too, had a great flood, but they are uncertain in their memory whether it was partial or universal.

"Polynesia, Micronesia, Tahiti, New Zealand, Hawaii, New Guinea, and Melanesia, all have their flood tales, handed down from generation to generation over countless years.

"The Melanesians of the New Hebrides will tell how their legendary hero, Quat, disappeared from this world in a deluge." [15]

"An early Welsh legend states that once the lake of Llion burst, flooding all the lands so that everyone was drowned except Dwyfan and Dwyfach, who escaped with a pair of every kind of living thing, so that the descendants of this couple restocked with animals derived from those they had saved." [16]

A Lithuanian story is very similar. According to this, Pramzimas, the supreme deity, looked out of the window of heaven and observed the wickedness of mankind; so he determined to destroy them. He sent two great giants, Wandu and Wegas, that is to say, water and wind, to execute his orders, and after twenty days only a remnant of mankind was left upon the top of a high mountain. Pramzimas looked out again and noticed this. He was eating nuts at the time, and by an accident he let fall a nut shell which dropped upon the mountain. Into this everyone climbed and thus was saved. Only a single old couple remained on the spot, and they were naturally disturbed by the catastrophe. So the god sent them the rainbow to comfort them and told them to jump nine times over the bones of the earth. This they did, and nine fresh couples sprang up to become the ancestors of the nine tribes of the Lithuanians.[17]

According to a legend of the gypsies of Transylvania, there was a time when man lived forever and when neither worry nor sickness troubled them. Meat and fruits existed in abundance, and the rivers flowed with milk and wine. Men and animals lived happy lives and were without fear of death. Then it happened one day that a strange old man arrived at the house of an old couple and asked to lodge for the night. He slept in the cabin, and the man's wife took good care of him. As the man departed on the following day, he gave to his host a vessel in which there was a small fish and said: "Keep this fish, and do not eat it. When I come back in nine days and you return the fish to me, I will reward you." After that he departed. The woman desired the fish for supper, but her husband answered: "I have promised the old man to return the fish to him. You will have to promise me that you will spare the fish and keep it until our guest returns." The woman swore and said: "I will not kill that little fish, I will keep it, so help me God." In the absence of her husband, however, her desire to eat the fish grew stronger and stronger, and finally she took it out of the vessel and placed it on some hot coals. But barely had she done so, when there flashed the first lightning on earth, which struck and killed the woman. Thereupon it began to rain, and the river rose and overflowed its banks. On the ninth day the old man returned and said to his host: "You have kept your oath, and you did not kill the fish. Take another wife, gather your kinsfolk, and build a boat in which you shall save yourselves. All creatures and all men shall perish in the water, but you shall remain alone. Take also animals and seed of trees and herbs with which to replenish the earth. The old man departed, and the rain came and continued for a whole year, and nothing but water and sky could be seen. After a year the water subsided, and the man disembarked with his second wife, his relatives, and the animals. But now they had to labor, cultivate, and sow to live. Labor and sorrow was from now on in their life; to

140

this were added sickness and death. As a result, man multiplied very slowly, and it took many thousands of years
before mankind was again as numerous as they had been
before.

In this legend the basic elements of the Noachian Flood
are clearly discernible, but intermingled with it are faint
echoes of other historic facts, which have been distorted into
fantastic myths. The story of the fish seems to point to India
for its background, for the fish also plays an important role
in the Hindu flood saga. The reference to a time when
neither man nor animals feared death, and when labor and
sorrow had not yet entered the human life, evidently refers
to the state of man's original innocence in Paradise. The
woman's desire to eat the fish is clearly a variation of Eve's
temptation in the Garden of Eden, but this need not surprise us. Both traditions have survived in one form or another and frequently are found confused, as in this gypsy
flood tradition.

The traditions in India and China tell, with varying details, the same story of the carrying away of the old world
by a flood and the re-peopling of the earth by some who had
been miraculously preserved. Manu, whom the Hindus regard as the great progenitor of the race, was warned, so
their tradition goes, by a great fish that the earth was about
to be engulfed by water. He was told to build a ship and
to put into it all kinds of seeds, together with the seven
Rishis, or holy beings. The flood came as announced and
covered the whole earth. The ship was made fast to the
horns of the fish, which drew it on in safety and finally
landed it on the loftiest summit of the Himalayas. Manu
was permitted by God to create the new race of mankind.

It will be noticed here that there are seven companions
of Manu; hence eight were saved. This is the very number
mentioned in Genesis. Another fact is that Manu is called
Satya, that is, the righteous. It was said of Noah that he

141

was righteous among his generation. And then, to make this flood tradition still more remarkable, there is added this story as reported by Hugh Miller: "The holy Satyavrata, having on one occasion drunk mead, became senseless and lay asleep, naked, and Charma, one of three sons who had been born to him, finding him in that sad state, called on his two brothers to witness the shame of their father, and said to them, What has now befallen? In what state is our sire? But the two brothers were more dutiful than Charma and hid him with clothes; and recalled to his senses, and having recovered his intellect, and perfectly knowing what had passed, he cursed Charma saying, Thou shalt be a servant of servants." [18]

This certainly is a most remarkable and startling echo of the incident recorded in Gen. 9:20 ff. One would be inclined to doubt its authenticity if it were not reported by so eminent a scholar and careful scientist as Hugh Miller.

According to the Chinese traditions, Fah-he escaped from a deluge which destroyed the human race with the exception of himself, his wife, his three sons, and three daughters, and from these, the whole earth was peopled.

The Persians had a tradition that the world had been corrupted by Ahriman, the Prince of Darkness. It was necessary to cover it with a flood so as to sweep away its impurities. The rain fell in drops as large as a bull's head, and the flood rose to man's height above the earth, so that all the creatures of Ahriman were destroyed. [19]

Berosus, a Chaldean priest, a contemporary of Alexander the Great, compiled a history of the Chaldeans based on ancient Chaldean records and traditions for Seleucus Nicator, his king. In this account he reports the following legend as he found it: "In the reign of Xisuthros, the tenth king of Babylon, there was a great flood. Before this occurred, the god Kronos appeared to the king in a dream and warned him that on the 15th day of the month Daisios all

142

men would perish by a flood. He told him to write a history of the world from the beginning and to bury it in the city of the Sun at Sippara and then to build a ship and to enter it with his family and his dearest friends, to deposit in the ship provisions for food and drink and to cause wild animals and birds and quadrupeds to enter it, so as to prepare everything for the voyage. And when Xisuthros asked in which direction he ought to navigate the ship, he was told, Toward the gods, and he was bidden to pray that good might come to man. Xisuthros obeyed and built a ship five stadia in length and two in breadth, about three thousand feet long and twelve hundred feet wide. He collected together all that he had been ordered to do and embarked with his wife and his children and his intimate friends. The deluge having come and being on the wane, Xisuthros sent out some of the birds. These, finding no food nor resting place, returned to the ship. Some days after, Xisuthros sent them out again, but they returned again to the ship, with their feet full of clay. When they were released a third time, they returned no more. Thereupon Xisuthros learned that the earth was again bare. He made an opening in the roof of the ship and saw that it had rested upon a mountain. He thereupon disembarked with his wife and daughter and pilot, raised an altar and sacrificed to the gods, and at the same time disappeared with those who accompanied him. Meanwhile those who had remained in the ship, not seeing Xisuthros return, disembarked and proceeded to look for him, calling him by his name. They did not see Xisuthros again, but heard a voice from heaven bidding them be pious toward the gods, as he had, in fact, received the reward of his piety and had been taken away to live henceforth among the gods and that his wife, his daughter, and the pilot of the ship had shared his fortunes. The voice also told them to return to Babylon and, when there, following the decrees of destiny, to dig up the writings buried at Sippara and make them known among men. The voice added that this country where they were was Armenia. Having heard the voice, they sacrificed to the gods and returned on foot to Babylon. Of the ship of Xisuthros, which rested in Armenia, portions still remain in the mountains of Armenia, and pilgrims bring back the asphalt which they have scraped from the ruins, and it is used as a preservative against magic. The companions of Xisuthros went to Babylon, dug up the writings deposited at Sippara, founded numerous towns, built temples, and restored Babylon." [20]

Manetho, who lived about 250 B. C. and wrote the ancient history of the Egyptians, relates that there was a worldwide catastrophe in which one, called Toth, was saved. Before this cataclysm, Toth inscribed on a slab of stone in sacred language the principles of all knowledge and after the catastrophe translated the writing into common language. With the Deluge tradition the Egyptians connected the commemoration of the dead, which was done by symbolical ceremony, in which the priest placed the image of Osiris in a sacred ark and launched it out into the sea and there watched it disappear from sight. This ceremony was observed on the 17th day of Athyr, which corresponds to the date given in the Mosaic account of the Flood. [21]

In the ancient town of Apamea in Phrygia, there was a pillar on which was carved an ark, which, according to tradition, had come to rest on that very spot. A coin was also found on one side of which was represented an ark with the door wide open and a patriarchal figure receiving a returning bird into the ark. On the other side of the coin is shown a man and his wife leaving the ark. On the ark itself appears the name "Noe."

The Greeks had the following tradition: Prometheus had a son who reigned in Phthia and married Pyrrha, daughter of Epimetheus and Pandora. Because Zeus wished to destroy mankind, Deucalion, by the advice of Prometheus, made a coffer, or box, into which he put all the necessities of life

144

and into which he withdrew with Pyrrha. Zeus having caused a great rain to fall, the greater part of Greece was inundated. Deucalion, having been tossed about by the sea for nine days and nights, at length came to the shore at Parnassus. The rain having ceased, he came out of his coffer and offered a sacrifice to Zeus, who sent Hermes to ask him what he wanted. He replied that he wished to people the earth. By order of Zeus he and his wife then threw stones behind them. Those thrown by Deucalion became men, while those thrown by Pyrrha became women.[22]

The Greeks had another very interesting legend, with elements of Flood traditions, concerning the Island of Atlantis. According to this legend, there was a large island in the sea beyond the Pillars of Hercules. This was larger than Libya and Asia put together and was the way to other islands. From this island one could pass to the whole of the opposite continent, which surrounded the true ocean; for their sea, which is within the straits of Hercules, is only a harbor, having a narrow entrance, but that other is a real sea, and the surrounding land may be most truly called a continent. Now, in this Island of Atlantis, there was a great and wonderful empire which had control over other islands and parts of the continent. But in the course of history there occurred a violent earthquake and floods, and in a single day and night of misfortune all the warlike men in a body sank into the earth, and the Island of Atlantis in like manner disappeared and was sunk beneath the sea. Because of this, those parts of the sea are impenetrable because there is such a quantity of shallow mud in the way.

Plato treats the material of this tradition in his unfinished dialog *Critias*. After describing the division of the earth among the gods and the races of men, and after telling in some detail about the people, the government, and the ideal conditions prevailing upon the mythical Island of Atlantis, Plato continues: "For many generations, as long as the divine nature lasted in them, they were obedient to the laws and well affectioned toward the gods, who were their kinsmen; for they possessed true and in every way great spirits, practicing gentleness and wisdom in the various chances of life and in their intercourse with one another. They despised everything but virtue, not caring for their present state of life and thinking lightly of the possession of gold and other property, which seemed only a burden to them; neither were they intoxicated by luxury; nor did wealth deprive them of their self-control; but they were sober and saw clearly that all these goods were increased by virtuous friendship with one another and that by excessive zeal for them, and honor of them, the good of them is lost and friendship perishes with them. By such reflections and by the continuance in them of a divine nature, all that which we have described waxed and increased in them; but when this divine portion began to fade away in them, and became diluted too often and with too much of the mortal admixture, and the human nature got the upper hand, then they, being unable to bear their fortune, became unseemly, and to him who had an eye to see, they became base and had lost the fairest of their precious gifts; but to those who had no eye to see the true happiness they still appeared glorious and blessed at the very time when they were filled with unrighteous avarice and power. Zeus, the god of gods, who rules with law, and is able to see into such things, perceiving that an honorable race was in a most wretched state, and wanting to inflict punishment on them that they might be chastened and improve, collected all the gods into his most holy habitation, which, being placed in the center of the world, sees all things that partake of generation. And when he had called them together, he spake as follows: [23]

Here the dialog breaks off abruptly. No one knows why. It is evident, however, from the context that Plato was about to announce the displeasure of the gods and their judgment to an apostate people. The dialog, so far as we have it, is extremely interesting. It contains elements which betray faint memories of people, of a world, and of conditions in a world as existed before the Flood. There seem to be even some very faint echoes from Paradise and some indistinct relics of the confusion of tongues and definite memories of a great flood.

The Roman Flood tradition has been preserved by the well-known Latin poet Ovid in his work called *Metamorphoses*. Ovid lived and wrote at the time of Caesar Augustus, and for reasons unknown was banished from Rome, in the later part of his life, to the regions of the Black Sea, where he wrote the *Metamorphoses*. Roman and Greek mythologies formed the subject of a number of his poetic works. In this particular poem the Creation and Flood traditions formed the basis. Though highly poetic in language and treatment, the poem presents these legends as they were current among the Greeks and Romans from ancient times.

The poem begins with the story of creation. Man is described as "one of heavenly seed engendered, made in the likeness to the gods that govern everything." Man lived originally in a state of happiness, innocence, and blessedness.

Then sprang up first the golden age, which of itself maintained
The truth and right of everything, unforced and unconstrained.
There was no fear of punishment, there was no threatening law
In brazen tables nailed up, to keep the folk in awe.

There was no town enclosed yet with walls and ditches deep.
No horn nor trumpet was in use, no sword nor helmet worn.
The world was such that soldiers' help might easily be forborne.
The fertile earth as yet was free, untouched of spade or plough,
And yet it yielded of itself of everything enough.
And men themselves contented well with plain and simple food
That on the earth by Nature's gift without their travail stood.
The springtime lasted all the year, and Zephyr with his mild
And gentle blast did cherish things that grew of own accord.
The ground, untilled, all kind of fruits did plenteously afford.
No muck nor tillage was bestowed on lean and barren land
To make the corn of better head and ranker for to stand.
Then streams ran milk, then streams ran wine, and yellow honey
flowed
From each green tree whereon the rays of fiery Phoebus glowed.

Then came a change. Man was less carefree and was now forced to labor in the sweat of his brow —

And ancient springtime Jove abridged and made thereof anon
Four seasons: winter, summer, spring, and harvest off and on.
Then first of all began the air with fervent heat to swelt;
Then icicles hung roping down; then, for the cold was felt,
Men 'gan to shroud themselves in house; their houses were the
  thicks,
And bushy queaches, hollow caves, or hurdles made of sticks.
Then first of all were furrows drawn, and corn was cast in ground;
The simple ox with sorry sighs to heavy yoke was bound.
Next after this succeeded straight the third and brazen age;
More hard of nature, somewhat bent to cruel wars and rage,
But yet not wholly past all grace. Of iron is the last
In no part good and tractable as former ages past;
For when that of this wicked age once opened was the vein,
Therein all mischief rushed forth, the faith and truth were fain
And honest shame to hide their heads; for whom stepped stoutly in,
Craft, treason, violence, envy, pride, and wicked lust to win.

Conditions grew from bad to worse. Man became more wicked and lawless still —

All godliness lies under foot. . . . Men say that giants went about
  the realm of heaven to win,
To place themselves to reign as gods and lawless lords therein.

Jupiter, enraged by the arrogance and lawlessness of men, finally resolves to destroy the human race. He called a council of the gods to make known to them his decision.

Now when the gods assembled were, and each had ta'en his place,
Jove, standing up aloft and leaning on his ivory mace,
Right dreadfully his bushy locks did thrice or four times shake,
Wherewith he made both sea and land and heaven itself to quake,
And afterward in wrathful words his angry mind thus brake:
"I never was in greater care nor more perplexity
How to maintain my sovereign state and princely royalty,
When with their hundred hands apiece the adder-footed rout
Did practice for to conquer heaven and for to cast us out;
For though it were a cruel foe, yet did that war depend
Upon one ground, and in one stock it had his final end;
But now, as far as any sea about the world doth wind,
I must destroy both man and beast and all the mortal kind.
I swear by Styx's hideous streams that run within the ground,
All other means must first be sought; but when there can be found
No help to heal a festered sore, it must away be cut
Lest that the parts that yet are sound in danger should be put.

148

And therefore as they all offend, so am I fully bent
That all forthwith, as they deserve, shall have due punishment."
These words of Jove some of the gods did openly approve,
And with their sayings more to wrath his angry courage move.
And some did give assent by signs; yet did it grieve them all
That such destruction utterly on all mankind should fall:
Demanding what he purposed with all the earth to do
When that he had all mortal men so clean destroyed, and who
On holy altars afterwards should offer frankincense,
And whether that he were in mind to leave the earth from thence
To savage beasts to waste and spoil because of man's offense.
The King of Gods bade cease their thought and questions in that
    case
And cast the care thereof on him: within a little space
He promised for to frame a new, another kind of men
By wondrous means, unlike the first, to fill the world again.
And now his lightning he had thought on all the earth to throw,
But that he feared lest the flames perhaps so high should grow
As for to set the heaven on fire and burn up all the sky.
He did remember furthermore how that by destiny
A certain time should one day come wherein both sea and land
And heaven itself should feel the force of Vulcan's scorching brand,
So that the huge and goodly work of all the world so wide
Should go to wreck; for doubt whereof forthwith he laid aside
His weapons that the Cyclops made, intending to correct
Man's trespass by a punishment contrary in effect;
And, namely, with incessant showers, from heaven poured down,
He full determined with himself the mortal kind to drown.

As soon as he between his hands the hanging clouds had crushed,
With rattling noise adown from heaven the rain full sadly gushed.
The rainbow, Juno's messenger, bedecked in sundry hue,
To maintain moisture in the clouds great waters thither drew:
The corn was beaten to the ground, the tillman's hope of gain,
For which he toiled all the year, lay drowned in the rain.
Jove's indignation and his wrath began to grow so hot
That for to quench the rage thereof his heaven sufficed not;
His brother Neptune with his waves was fain to do him ease,
Who straight assembling all the streams that fall into the seas,
Said to them standing in his house: "Sirs, get you home apace —
You must not look to have me use long preaching in this case.
Pour out your force (for so is need), your heads each one
    unpenned,
And from your open springs your streams with flowing waters
    send."
He had no sooner said the word but that returning back
Each one of them unloosed his spring and let his waters slack;

And to the sea with flowing streams swollen above their banks,
One rolling in another's neck, they rushed forth by ranks.
Himself with his three-tined mace did lend the earth a blow
That made it shake and open ways for waters forth to flow.
The floods at random where they list through all the fields did
    stray;
Men, beasts, trees, corn, and with their gods were churches
    washed away.
If any house were built so strong against their force to stand,
Yet did water hide the top, and turrets in that pond
Were overwhelmed: no difference was between the sea and ground,
For all was sea; there was no shore nor landing to be found.
Some climbed up to tops of hills, and some rowed to and fro
In boats, where they not long before to plough and cart did go.
One over corn and tops of towns whom waves did overwhelm
Doth sail in ship, another sits a-fishing in an elm.
In meadows green were anchors cast (so fortune did provide),
And crooked ships did shadow vines, the which the flood did hide.
And where but th' other day before did feed the hungry goat,
The ugly seals and porpoises now to and fro did float.
The sea-nymphs wondered under waves the towns and groves
    to see,
And dolphins played among the tops and boughs of every tree.
The grim and greedy wolf did swim among the silly sheep,
The lion and the tiger fierce were borne upon the deep.
It booted not the foaming boar his crooked tusks to whet,
The running hart could in the stream by swiftness nothing get.
The fleeting fowls long having sought for land to rest upon,
Into the sea with weary wings were driven to fall anon.
The outrageous swelling of the sea the lesser hillocks drowned;
Unwonted waves on highest tops of mountains did rebound.
The greatest part of men were drowned, and such as 'scaped the
    flood,
Forlorn with fasting overlong, did die for want of food.
Against the fields of Aonia and Attic lies a land
That Phocis hight, a fertile ground while that it was a land:
But at that time a part of sea, and even a champion field
Of sudden waters which the flood by forced rage did yield,
Whereas a hill with forked top the which Parnassus hight
Doth pierce the clouds and to the stars doth raise his head upright.
When at this hill (for yet the sea had whelmed all beside)
Deucalion and his bedfellow without all other guide
Arrived in a little barque, immediately they went
And to the nymphs of Corycus with full devout intent
Did honour due and to the gods to whom that famous hill
Was sacred, and to Themis, in whose most holy will

Consisted then the oracles. In all the world so round
A better nor more righteous man could never yet be found
Than was Deucalion, nor again a woman, maid nor wife,
That feared God so much as she, nor led so good a life.
When Jove beheld how all the world stood like a splash of rain
And of so many thousand men and women did remain
But one of each, howbeit those both just and both devout,
He broke the clouds and did command that Boreas with his stout
And sturdy blasts should chase the flood that earth might see
    the sky
And heaven the earth; the seas also began immediately
Their raging fury for to cease. Their ruler laid away
His dreadful mace, and with his words their woodness did allay.

Then 'gan the sea to have a shore and brooks to find a bank,
And swelling streams of flowing floods within their channels sank.
Then hills did rise above the waves that had them overflow,
And as the waters did decrease, the ground did seem to grow.
And after long and tedious time the trees did show their tops,
All bare save that upon the boughs the mud did hang in knops.
The world restored was again, which though Deucalion joyed
Then to behold, yet for because he saw the earth was void
And silent like a wilderness, with sad and weeping eyes
And ruthful voice he then did speak to Pyrrha in this wise:
"O sister, O my loving spouse, O silly woman, left
As only remnant of thy sex that water hath bereft,
Whom Nature first by right of birth hath linked to me fast
In that we brother's children been, and, secondly, the chaste
And steadfast bond of lawful bed, and, lastly now of all,
The present perils of the time that lately did befall;
On all the earth, from east to west, where Phoebus shows his face,
There is no more but thou and I of all the mortal race.
The sea hath swallowed all the rest, and scarcely are we sure
That our two lives from dreadful death in safety shall endure,
For even as yet the dusky clouds do make my heart adrad.

Would God I could my father's art of clay to fashion men
And give them life that people might frequent the earth again.
Mankind, alas! doth only now within us two consist
As moulds whereby to fashion men, for so the gods do list."
And with these words the bitter tears did trickle down their cheek
Until at length between themselves they did agree to seek
To God by prayer for his grace, and to demand his aid
By answer of his oracle. . . .[24]

Their prayers were answered. The goddess bade them
pick up stones and throw them over their backs behind them.

At first they hesitated because they did not understand, but then they did as they were told, and the stones thrown by Deucalion turned into men, while those thrown by Pyrrha were formed into women, and thus came into being a new race of men to reoccupy the earth.

One cannot read the amazing Flood tradition of the ancient Romans presented here in highly poetic form by the great poet Ovid without being deeply impressed. It is not difficult to recognize in this poetic account elements of the primeval history of the human race, such as the creation of man, the state of innocence of original man, the perfection and happiness of Paradise, the fall of man, the curse of sin, and the Flood, all skillfully woven together in this beautiful poem. Time could not erase these profound memories of the race, and hence we find them recurring in varying forms and shades with different people. The Roman story of the Flood as presented by Ovid is, next to the Babylonian, the most interesting of the many Flood traditions found among the nations of the world.

CHAPTER X

The Babylonian Flood Account

THE most remarkable of all Flood stories outside the Bible is the Babylonian account of the Flood, which was brought with thousands of other clay tablets from the ancient library of Assurbanipal in Nineveh to the British Museum, where it was accidentally discovered by George Smith, a British orientalist, in 1872. As early as 1845 Layard had begun to dig in a mound which proved to be the site of Nineveh, the ancient capital of Assyria. In this mound he found the ruins of two palaces that had been destroyed by fire. One turned out to be that of Sennacherib, known to us from the Second Book of Kings. The other was the ruined palace of Assurbanipal, who reigned from 668 to 626 B. C. From these palatial ruins, especially those of Assurbanipal's palace, he brought back a number of treasures, including about 20,000 clay tablets and fragments of clay tablets covered with cuneiform inscriptions. The work of sorting and deciphering these tablets was a difficult one. Mr. Smith was engaged to make copies of the inscriptions of the more important tablets for foreign scholars, and in doing so he acquired a thorough knowledge of the cuneiform script, which was at that time still little understood. While engaged at this task, he accidentally came across a small fragment of a tablet on which he read these words: "The mountain of Nisir stopped the ship. I sent forth a dove, and it left. The dove went and turned, and a resting place it did not find, and it returned."

Smith perceived at once that these lines resembled an incident in the account of the Flood of Noah as recorded in Genesis, and he began an untiring search for the missing fragment. His labors were rewarded beyond expectation. He found not only many fragments of this account of the Flood but parts of two other copies. When he had assembled all the fragments that he could find, he made a careful translation of the whole text, in which there were, of course, still many gaps. He published the result of this most remarkable discovery before a meeting of the Society of Biblical Archaeology on December 30, 1872.

Naturally, this discovery created a great stir not only among scholars, but among the public in general. Until then it had been generally believed that the Babylonian version of the Flood tradition as related by Berosus had been borrowed from the Book of Genesis during the Babylonian Captivity. But here was a Flood tradition almost identical in many of the smallest details, yet dating from a period long before the Babylonian Captivity and forming a part of a larger epic, evidently of considerable antiquity.

Immediately after this discovery became known, the owners of the *London Daily Telegraph* invited Mr. Smith to go out to Assyria at their expense to search for further Flood tablets. He had not labored very long on the site of Assurbanipal's palace when something next to the miraculous happened, for he actually found further fragments of the tablets which he had first discovered in the British Museum. He returned three times to ancient Nineveh, but while there during his third expedition, he succumbed to an illness brought on very largely by overwork and his zeal for research.

The following is a translation prepared by Dr. Alexander Heidel (died in 1955) brilliant Assyriologist at the Oriental Institute of the University of Chicago. This is a part of *The Gilgamesh Epic,* published by the University of Chicago Press.

TABLET XI

1. Gilgamesh said to him, to Utnapishtim the Distant:
2. "I look upon thee, Utnapishtim,
3. Thine appearance is not different; thou art like unto me.
4. Yea, thou art not different; thou art like unto me.
5. My heart had pictured thee as one perfect for the doing of battle;
6. (But) thou liest (idly) on (thy) side, (or), on thy back.
7. (Tell me), how didst thou enter into the company of the gods and obtain life (everlasting)?"
8. Utnapishtim said to him, to Gilgamesh:
9. "Gilgamesh, I will reveal unto thee a hidden thing,
10. Namely, a secret of the gods will I tell thee.
11. Shurippak [1] — a city which thou knowest,
12. (And which) is situated (on the bank of) the river Euphrates —
13. That city was (already) old, and the gods were in its midst.
14. (Now) their heart prompted the great gods (to) bring a deluge.
15. (There was [?]) Anu, their father;
16. Warlike Enlil, their counselor.
17. Ninurta, their representative;
18. Ennugi, their vizier;
19. Ninigiku (that is) Ea, also sat with them.
20. Their speech he repeated to a reed hut: [2]
21. 'Reed hut, reed hut! Wall, wall!
22. Reed hut, hearken! Wall, consider!
23. Man of Shurippak, [3] son of Ubara-Tutu!
24. Tear down (thy) house, build a ship!
25. Abandon (thy) possessions, seek (to save) life!
26. Disregard (thy) goods, and save (thy) life;
27. (Cause to) go up into the ship the seed of all living creatures.
28. The ship which thou shalt build,

---

[1] Usually called Shuruppak.

[2] Probably the dwelling of Utnapishtim. Some good photographs of reed houses have recently been published by John van Ess in *The National Geographic Magazine* LXXXII (1942) 410 f.

[3] This expression, as shown by the following lines, refers to Utnapishtim.

29. Its measurements shall be (accurately) measured;
30. Its width and its length shall be equal.
31. Cover it (li)ke the subterranean waters.'
32. When I understood this, I said to Ea, my lord:
33. '(Behold), my lord, what thou hast thus commanded
34. (I) will honor (and) carry out.
35. (But what) shall I answer the city, the people, and the elders?'
36. Ea opened his mouth and said,
37. Speaking to me, his servant:
38. 'Thus shalt thou say to them:
39. (I have le)arned that Enlil hates me,
40. That I may no (longer) dwell in yo(ur) city,
41. Nor turn my face to the land of Enlil.
42. (I will therefore g)o down to the *apsû* and dwell with Ea, my (lor)d.[4]
43. (On) you he will (then) rain down plenty;
44. (. . . of b)irds(?) . . . of fishes.
45. (. . .) harvest wealth.
46. (In the evening the sender) of the storm (?)
47. Will cause a wheat rain to rain down upon you.'[5]
48. As soon as (the first shimmer of mor)ning beamed forth,
49. The land was gathered (about me).
50–53. (Too fragmentary for translation.)
54. The child (brou)ght pitch,
55. (While) the strong brought (whatever else) was needful.
56. On the fifth day (I) laid its framework.
57. One *ikû*[6] was its floor space, one hundred twenty cubits each was the height of its walls;
58. One hundred twenty cubits measured each side of its deck[7]

---

[4] The apsû, the place where Ea had his dwelling, was the subterranean sweet-water ocean, from which, e. g., the water of the river was thought to spring forth. But in this line it probably refers to the Persian Gulf.

[5] Here the original obviously has a play on words, the purpose of which is to deceive the inhabitants of Shurippak to the last moment (cf. Carl Frank in *Zeitschrift fuer Assyriologie* XXXVI (1925) 218. This line can also be translated "He will cause a destructive rain (lit. a rain of misfortune) to rain down upon you." This evidently is the intended meaning of the passage. But Ea knew that the people of Shurippak would interpret these words differently.

[6] About 3,600 square meters or approximately an acre (see A. J. Sachs in the *Bulletin of the American Schools of Oriental Research,* No. 96 (December, 1944), pp. 29–39.

[7] Placing the Babylonian cubit at about half a meter (see the article by Sachs referred to above), the deck had a surface of approximately 3,600 square mëters, or one *ikû.* Utnapishtim's boat was an exact cube.

59. I 'laid the shape' of the outside (and) fashioned it.[8]
60. Six (lower) decks I built into it.
61. (Thus) dividing (it) into seven (stories).
62. Its ground plan I divided into nine (sections).[9]
63. I drove water-stoppers into it.[10]
64. I provided punting poles and stored up a supply.[11]
65. Six *shar* [12] of pitch I poured into the furnace,
66. (And) three *shar* of asphalt (I poured) into it.
67. Three *shar* of oil the basket carriers brought: [13]
68. Besides a *shar* of oil which the saturation ([?] of the water stoppers) consumed.
69. Two *shar* of oil (which) the boatman stowed away.
70. Bullocks I slaughtered for (the people).
71. Sheep I killed every day.
72. Must, red wine, oil, and white wine,
73. (I gave) the workmen (to drink) as if it were river water,
74. (So that) they made a feast as on New Year's Day.
75. I (. . .) ointment I put my hands.
76. (. . .) the ship was completed.
77. Difficult was (the . . .).
78. . . . above and below.

---

[8] The ship. Utnapishtim now attached the planking to the framework.

[9] Each of the seven stories was divided into nine sections, or compartments.

[10] This line probably means that he drove pointed pieces of wood between the seams to help make the boat watertight. Thus Paul Haupt in *Beiträge zur Assyriologie* X, Heft 2 (1927), 6, and Armas Salonen, *Die Wasserfahrzeuge in Babylonien* (Helsinki, 1939) p. 100 f.

[11] Or: what was needful (cf. line 55).

[12] Var.: three *shar*. One *shar* is 3,600. The measure is not given in these lines. Perhaps we have to supply *sutû*; one *sutû* was equal to a little over two gallons. Three *shar* would then correspond to about 24,000 gallons (cf. Schott, *op. cit.*, p. 67, n. 11.)

[13] If the translation "basket carriers" is correct, we may perhaps assume that the baskets were coated with asphalt, or some such substance (so Haupt in *Beitrage zur Assyriologie*, X, Heft 2, 18). But I am rather inclined to believe that the oil was contained in vessels carried in some kind of sling. Thus in Egypt large pottery amphorae filled with wine were transported in netted pot slings carried on a pole (for a beautiful and easily accessible illustration see *The National Geographic Magazine*, LXXX [1941] 495.) The same mode of transportation is depicted on a plaque discovered by the Oriental Institute among the ruins of Opis, in Babylonia (a good picture of this plaque is found in J. H. Breasted, *Ancient Times*, Boston, etc., 1935), p. 155. Attention may be drawn also to the manner in which a demijohn is enclosed and carried. Salonen's view (*op. cit.*, p. 15. N. 2) that *sussullu* denotes a kind of ladle has been refuted by Meier in *Orientalistische Literaturzeitung*, XLIII, col. 306.

79. (. . .) its two thirds.
80. (Whatever I had I) loaded aboard her;
81. Whatever I had of silver I loaded aboard her;
82. Whatever I (had) of gold I loaded aboard her;
83. Whatever I had of the seed of all living creatures (I loaded) aboard her.
84. After I had caused all my family and relations to go up into the ship,
85. I caused the game of the field, the beasts of the field, (and) all the craftsmen to go (into it.)
86. Shamash [14] set for me a definite time:
87. 'When the sender of the sto(rm [?]) causes a destructive rain to rain down in the evening,
88. Enter the ship, and close thy door.' [15]
89. That definite time arrived:
90. In the evening the sender of the sto(rm [?]) caused a destructive rain to rain down.
91. I viewed the appearance of the weather;
92. The weather was frightful to behold.
93. I entered the ship and closed my door.
94. For the navigation (?) of the ship to the boatman Pazur-Amurri
95. I entrusted the mighty structure with its goods.
96. As soon as the first shimmer of morning beamed forth,
97. A black cloud came up from out the horizon.
98. And thundered [16] within it,
99. While Shullat and Hanish went before,
100. Coming as heralds over hill and plain;
101. Irragal [17] pulls out the masts;
102. Ninurta [18] comes along (and) causes the dykes to give way;
103. The Anunnaki [19] raised (their) torches,
104. Lighting up the land with their brightness; [20]
105. The raging of Adad reaches unto heaven
106. (And) turns into darkness all that was light.

---

[14] The sun god.

[15] Var., the ship.

[16] The god of storm and rain.

[17] Another name of Nergal, the god of the underworld.

[18] God of war and lord of the wells and irrigation works (Knut Tallqvist, *Akkadische Goetterepitheta*, Helsinki, 1938, pp. 424–26.

[19] The judges in the underworld.

[20] These two lines perhaps refer to sheet lightning on the horizon; forked lightning, which is accompanied by thunder peals, is attributed to Adad (Jensen, *op. cit.*, p. 496, and Ebeling in *Reallexikon der Assyriologie*, Vol. I, (Berlin and Leipzig, 1932), p. 24.

107. (. . .) the land he broke (?) like a po(t [?])
108. (For) one day the tem([pest] blew).
109. Fast it blew and (. . .)
110. Like a battle (it ca)me over the p(eople).
111. No man could see his fellow.
112. The people could not be recognized from heaven.
113. (Even) the gods were terror-stricken at the deluge.
114. They fled (and) ascended to the heaven of Anu; [21]
115. The gods cowered like dogs (and) crouched in distress (?)
116. Ishtar cried out like a woman in travail;
117. The lovely voiced lady of the g(ods) lamented:
118. 'In truth, the olden time has turned to clay,
119. Because I commanded evil in the assembly of the gods!
120. How could I command (such) evil in the assembly of the gods!
121. (How)could I command war to destroy my people,
122. (For) it is I who bring forth [22] (these) my people!
123. Like the spawn of fish they (now) fill the sea.'
124. The Anunnaki-gods wept with her;
125. The gods sat bowed (and) weeping.
126. Covered were their lips . . .
127. Six days and (six) nights
128. The wind blew, the downpour, the tempest, (and) the fl(ood) overwhelmed the land.
129. When the seventh day arrived, the tempest, the flood,
130. Which had fought like an army, subsided in (its) onslaught.
131. The sea grew quiet, the storm abated, the flood ceased.
132. I looked upon the sea, (all) was silence.
133. And all mankind had turned to clay;
134. The . . . was as level as a (flat) roof.
135. I opened a window, and light fell upon my face.[23]
136. I bowed, sat down, and wept.
137. My tears running down over my face.
138. I looked in (all) directions for the boundaries of the sea.
139. At (a distance of) twelve [24] (double hours) there emerged a stretch of land.
140. On Mount Nisir [25] the ship landed.
141. Mount Nisir held the ship fast and did not let (it) move.
142. One day, a second day, Mount Nisir held the ship fast and did not let (it) move.

---

[21] The sky god.
[22] Lit., gives birth to.
[23] On the transposition of this line see Schott in *Zeitschrift fuer Assyriologie*, XLII, p. 139 ff.
[24] Var.: fourteen.
[25] This name could also be read Nimush.

143. A third day, a fourth day, Mount Nisir held the ship fast and did not let (it) move.

144. A fifth day, a sixth day, Mount Nisir held the ship fast and did not let (it) move.[26]

145. When the seventh day arrived,

146. I sent forth a dove and let (her) go.

147. The dove went away and came back to me;

148. There was no resting place, and so she returned.

149. (Then) I sent forth a swallow and let (her) go.

150. The swallow went away and came back to me;

151. There was no resting place, and so she returned.

152. (Then) I sent forth a raven and let (her) go.

153. The raven went away, and when she saw that the waters had abated,

154. She ate, she flew about, she cawed, (and) did not return.

155. (Then) I sent forth (everything) to the four winds and offered a sacrifice.

156. I poured out a libation on the peak of the mountain.

157. Seven and (yet) seven kettles I set up.

158. Under them I heaped up (sweet) cane, cedar, and myrtle.

159. The gods smelled the savor,

160. The gods smelled the sweet savor.

161. The gods gathered like flies over the sacrificer.

162. As soon as the great goddess [27] arrived,

163. She lifted up the great jewels which Anu had made according to her wish:

164. 'O ye gods here present, as surely as I shall not forget the lapis lazuli on my neck,

165. I shall remember these days and shall not forget (them) ever!

166. Let the gods come near to the offering;

167. (But) Enlil shall not come near to the offering,

168. Because without reflection he brought on the deluge

169. And consigned my people to destruction!'

170. As soon as Enlil arrived

171. And saw the ship, Enlil was wroth;

172. He was filled with anger against the gods, the Igigi: [28]

---

[26] In place of the words "held the ship fast and did not let (it) move," in lines 142–144, the original has the sign of reduplication or repetition, which means that the statement is to be completed on the basis of the preceding line. In this instance, the sign of reduplication could be rendered with "etc."

[27] That is, Ishtar.

[28] The gods of heaven.

173. 'Has any of the mortals escaped? No man was to live through the destruction!'

174. Ninurta opened his mouth and said, speaking to warrior Enl(il):

175. 'Who can do things without Ea?

176. For Ea alone understands every matter.'

177. Ea opened his mouth and said, speaking to warrior Enlil:

178. 'O warrior, thou wisest among the gods!

179. How, O how couldst thou without reflection bring on (this) deluge?

180. On the sinner lay his sin; on the transgressor lay his transgression!

181. Let loose, that he shall not be cut off; pull tight, that he may not ge(t) (too loose).²⁹

182. Instead of sending a deluge, would that a lion had come and diminished mankind!

183. (Or) instead of thy sending a deluge, would that a wolf had come and dim(inished) mankind!

184. (Or) instead of thy sending a deluge, would that a famine had occurred and (destroyed) the land!

185. (Or) instead of thy sending a deluge, would that Irra ³⁰ had come and smitten mankind!

186. (Moreover) it was not I who revealed the secret of the great gods;

187. (But) to Atrahasis ³⁰ I showed a dream, and so he learned the secret of the gods.

188. And now take counsel concerning him.'

189. Then Enlil went up into the ship.

190. He took my hand and caused me to go aboard.

191. He caused my wife to go aboard (and) to kneel down at my side.

192. Standing between us, he touched our foreheads and blessed us:

193. 'Hitherto Utnapishtim has been but a man;

194. But now Utnapishtim and his wife shall be like unto us gods.

195. In the distance, at the mouth of the rivers, Utnapishtim shall dwell!'

196. So they took me and caused me to dwell in the distance, at the mouth of rivers."

---

²⁹ *I. e.*, punish man, lest he get too wild; but do not be too severe lest he perish (cf. Ebeling, in *Archiv fuer Orientforschung*, 231).

³⁰ Irra is the god of pestilence; Atrahasis is a descriptive epithet meaning "the exceedingly wise" — is another designation for Utnapishtim.

The remarkable similarity between this and the Biblical Flood is truly amazing. According to both accounts, the Flood is brought on because the earth was full of violence. In both cases the dimensions of the ship are given though differing in details. In both cases representatives of all animals are taken into the ark. In the Babylonian account the Flood lasts seven days. In the Bible narrative the embarkation takes seven days. In both cases a raven and a dove are sent forth from the ark. The Babylonian accounts add a swallow. In both accounts, a thanksgiving offering is made after the Flood and in both cases is favorably received by God or the gods respectively. The rainbow of Genesis is represented by the great jewels of Ishtar. In both there is a covenant guaranteeing that no world Flood is ever to come upon the earth again to destroy it. And both accounts end with a blessing being pronounced upon the hero and his wife.

This remarkable Flood story is part of the great Gilgamesh Epic. It was found in the ruins of the Assurbanipal library in Nineveh. The original was written centuries before Moses wrote Genesis. Though there is a striking similarity between the two narratives, one is not based upon the other, but both describe independently an actual historical event.

It had become fashionable with scholars like Delitzsch, King, Skinner, Driver, Wundt, Jastrow, and others who followed them to ascribe the Hebrew Flood account to Babylonian sources. Some held that this story was brought from Babylon to Canaan by Abraham; others said that they were transmitted to the West in the so-called Amarna period, but the great majority of scholars hold that knowledge of it was obtained in Babylon at the time of the Exile. Two arguments are generally advanced for this position: the one argument is the great age of Babylonian civilization, which involved the idea that civilization in the West had only developed a little before 2000 B. C. by Arabs from Arabia; the other argument is based on the frequency of inundations in Babylonia, which gave rise to these so-called nature myths. In 1909, Albert Clay opposed these theories and held that the Babylonian origin of the Biblical Deluge story was without foundation. He argued that the Biblical Deluge story was indigenous to the West and that, on the other hand, the Babylonian Deluge story as preserved in the Gilgamesh Epic had West-Semitic elements and that therefore the influence was rather from the West.

Dr. Alexander Heidel is of the opinion that both the Biblical and the Babylonian Flood accounts revert to a common source of some kind. This source need not at all have sprung from Palestine soil, but may have originated in the land of Babylonia, where the Book of Genesis (11:1-9) localizes the home of postdiluvian mankind and from where Abraham emigrated to Palestine. Since we know that several different Deluge versions were current in the Tigris-Euphrates area, this explanation is a very distinct possibility.

No fair- and open-minded person can, in the face of this accumulation of Flood traditions, which are found with so many people, persist in relegating the Biblical story of the world-wide Flood to the realm of meaningless fable, as Huxley does. Even the great Wundt, whom no one will accuse of being unduly influenced by Biblical evidence, and who does his utmost to find a reasonable case for an independent origin of the various flood sagas, is forced to admit: "Of the combination of all these elements into a whole (the destruction of the earth by water, the rescue of a single man and seed of animals by means of a boat, etc.), however, we may say without hesitation, it could not have arisen twice independently." [1]

And Sir J. William Dawson, LL. D., the famous Canadian geologist, writes: "Further, we know now that the Deluge of Noah is not a mere myth or fancy of primitive man or solely a doctrine of the Hebrew Scriptures. The record of the catastrophe is preserved in some of the oldest historical documents of several distinct races of men, and is indirectly corroborated by the whole tenor of the early history of most of the civilized races.

"As to the actual occurrence of the Deluge as a widespread catastrophe affecting, with a few stated exceptions, the whole human race, we have thus a concurrence of the testimony of ancient history and tradition, and of geological and archaeological evidence, as well as of the inspired records of the Hebrew and Christian revelation. Thus no historical event, ancient or modern, can be more firmly established as matter of fact than this." [2]

To deny that, is to cast away not only the Word of God, but to reject also the most ancient and most sacred traditions of universal humanity.

And Hugh Miller concludes his observations on the Flood traditions with the following remarks: "Such are some of the traditions of the great catastrophe which overtook the human family in its infancy and made so deep an impression on the memories of the few awe-struck survivors that the race never forgot it. Ere the dispersal of the family it would have of course existed as but one unique recollection — a single reflection on the face of an unbroken mirror. But the mirror has since been shattered into a thousand pieces, and now we find the object, originally but one, pictured in each broken fragment, with various degrees of distinctness, according to the various degrees of injury received by the reflecting medium." [3]

In conclusion we may therefore say: "If there was not such a world catastrophe of which all the Flood traditions bear witness, how can they be accounted for?" Nature myths have their origin in a great historical fact. We cannot escape the conclusion that these Flood traditions are an indisputable proof that the world catastrophe as described in Genesis is one of the greatest facts of all history. It has left an indelible impression on the memory of the entire human race.

CHAPTER XI

Other Historical Evidence for the Flood

O NE of the most remarkable chapters in the first section of Genesis is the chapter dealing with the genealogical tables of the antediluvian patriarchs. This chapter is remarkable not only because of its accurate enumeration of the chief representatives of the ten generations preceding the Flood, including the exact age of each of the patriarchs at the birth of his first son and his full age at the time of his death, but also because of the enormous ages to which these antediluvian fathers lived before death overtook them. According to this genealogy, Adam lived 930 years, Methuselah, the oldest man of the human race, 969 years, while the shortest life reported is that of Enoch, who was 365 years old when he was translated into heaven without seeing death. The full meaning of these ages can only be appreciated by comparison. If we translate these ages into our own time, it would mean that the fathers of the present generation would have lived and associated with the men and women who were born at the time of St. Paul or St. John. No wonder, therefore, that this chapter, above others, has been subjected to much criticism, skepticism, and

ridicule. But it is a most significant fact that these ten antediluvian generations reappear with a most stubborn per-
sistency in the ancient traditions of the various races and
that they end, as the Bible says, with a great flood.

In the following table the reader will find in parallel
columns the names of the antediluvian Biblical patriarchs
and the ten antediluvian kings of Egypt and Babylon as
found in the respective traditions of these countries.

Patriarchs	Egypt	Chaldean Kings
Adam	Ptah	Alorus
Seth	Ra	Alaparus
Enos	Su	Almelon
Cainan	Seb	Ammenon
Mahalaleel	Hosiri	Amegalarus
Jared	Set	Daonus
Enoch	Hor	Aedorachus
Methuselah	Tut	Amempsin
Lamech	Ma	Otiartes
Noah	Hor	Xisuthros [1]

The long lives of the Biblical patriarchs have been length-
ened by grotesque exaggerations in both the Egyptian and
Chaldean traditions. The first king of the Babylonian chronology ruled 36,000 years. Their oldest king ruled 64,800
years. The Babylonian genealogies and chronologies are reported by Berosus, whose unit of chronology is the *sarus*.
There is some reasonable doubt as to the exact meaning of
this word. Suidas informs us that it had at least two values
among the Babylonians, the one astronomical, corresponding
to 3,600 years; the other civil, corresponding to eighteen and
a half years. If we take the latter meaning, these exaggerated
ages are reduced considerably and become almost identical
with the ages of the Biblical antediluvian patriarchs.

Genesis gives the age of each patriarch at the birth of
his eldest son; the Chaldean chronology gives the duration
of each reign. That the two could be easily confused as
they were handed down by tradition must be admitted.

Reckoning the *sarus* at 18 years and six months, we get the following results:

	Year of birth of the oldest son of each patriarch		The reign of the Chaldean ante-diluvian kings
Adam	130	Alorus	185
Seth	105	Aloparus	56½
Enos	90	Almelon	240½
Cainan	70	Ammenon	222
Mahalaleel	65	Amegalarus	333
Jared	162	Daonus	185
Enoch	65	Aedorachus	333
Methuselah	187	Amempsinus	185
Lamech	182	Otiartes	148
Noah's age at the Flood	600	Xisuthros	333
Total for period before the Flood	1,656		2,221

As we compare these totals, the difference is not very great. But it must be remembered that there is a considerable deviation in the different forms in which the Biblical figures have been handed down. And we need not be surprised at this, because figures in Hebrew are peculiarly liable to suffer at the hands of transcribers. Thus we find that according to the Samaritan version the total period before the Flood adds up to 1,302 years, while according to the Septuagint its duration was 2,242. Comparing with this the Chaldean figure of 2,221, we find a discrepancy of only twenty-one years, which is most remarkable, to say the least.[2]

There also appears to have been some connection or confusion between Enoch and Noah. In ancient traditions both are holy men, and Enoch, like Noah, is said to have predicted the Flood. In Genesis, Enoch is translated into heaven without seeing death. In the Babylonian and Chaldean, this is ascribed to Noah. It is also a curious fact that the dynasty of gods with which the Egyptian mythical history begins sometimes contains seven reigns, while others enumerate ten. In one record the same name is found for the seventh and tenth dynasty. The seventh reign is reported as having lasted for 300 years. That happens to be the exact number of years that Enoch, the seventh of the antediluvian patriarchs, lived after the birth of his son Methuselah. The unusual means by which God removed Enoch from this land of the living seems to have left a profound impression upon the generations that followed, and hence it is not surprising that he is at times confused with Noah.

But these traditions are not limited to Egypt and Babylon. The Sibylline books speak of ten ages which elapsed between Creation and the Deluge. The Hindus enumerate nine Brahmidikas, who with Brahma, their maker, are called the ten *Pitris*, or fathers; the Chinese tell of ten emperors who shared the divine nature and reigned before the dawn of historic times; and the Phoenicians also regard ten generations of patriarchs.

Here, as in the case of the Flood traditions, we find ourselves confronted with an impressive array of concordant testimony, gathered from the four quarters of the earth, which leaves no room for doubt in regard to the common ground of the ancient narrative. There are ten patriarchs in the antediluvian genealogy in Genesis, and with a strange persistence this same number reappears in the legends of a great number of nations, especially among those whose history dates back to the very beginning of the human race, as that of Egypt, Babylon, China, and India. Then there is also a strange agreement with respect to the unusual age of this antediluvian generation, though the details have been changed in the oral transmission of these traditions. Finally, there is that remarkable agreement on the fact that the Flood regularly occurs during the reign and the life of the last of these patriarchal kings. One of the Babylonian records closes with these words: "They ruled 241,200 years. The Deluge came upon the land." [8]

Here, then, is another interesting and stubborn fact which must be met honestly, for all these ever-recurring incidents found with so many peoples so widely separated with respect to both time and place cannot be accounted for as a mere accident. These traditions, differing in some of their details, evidently have a common source in the same historical facts.

But there is another tradition found with many peoples in widely separated areas in both ancient and modern times which bears witness to the historical fact of the Flood, even to the extent of pointing to the season of the year in which this fearful cataclysm destroyed the human race. That season is the festival of the New Year, observed at the disappearance of the Pleiades at the end of October or the beginning of November. Urquhart, who reports these traditions, says that a new-year festival connected with, and determined by, the Pleiades seems to be one of the most universal of all customs.[4] It is not only the fact that New Year's Day was observed by so many people at about the same time which makes this significant, but that the observance of this event was always connected with the memory of the dead or was observed as a feast of the ancestors.

The natives of Australia observed this day at about the season mentioned. On this occasion they painted a white stripe over their arms, legs, and ribs, and dancing by the light of the fire appear like so many skeletons celebrating. The same custom is found among the savages of the Society Islands, where the closing of the old and the opening of the new year were celebrated about November. At the conclusion of this celebration each man, returning to his hut, was expected to offer a special prayer for the spirit of the departed relatives.

In the Fiji Islands a commemoration of the dead takes place toward the end of October.

In Peru the new year came at the beginning of November and was called *Ayamarka*, which signifies "carrying a corpse." The festival was celebrated in memory of the dead and was observed with songs and music and by placing food and drink upon the graves of the dead.

The Hindus celebrate their Durga, a festival of the dead, which originally was their New Year's Day and was observed on the 17th day of November.

The Persians called November *Mordad,* that is, the angel of death, and the feast of the dead, which took place at the same time as in Peru, was considered a New Year's festival.

With the ancient Druids the night of the first of November, in which they annually celebrated the reconstruction of the world, was full of mystery. According to a custom connected with this event, the priestesses were obliged at this time to pull down and rebuild each year the roof of their temple as a symbol of the destruction and renovation of the world. If one of them, in bringing the material for the new roof, let fall her sacred burden, she was seized by her enraged companions and torn to pieces. On this same night the Druids extinguished the sacred fire, which was kept burning throughout the rest of the year; and at the signal all the fires in the community were put out, and it was believed that, in the complete darkness that followed throughout the land, the phantom spirits of those who had died during the preceding year were then carried by boats to the judgment seat of the god of the dead.

A strange relic of this Druidic festival has survived in our present Hallowe'en (Hallow Eve) on the last day of October and All Saints and All Souls Days on the first and second of November. In former years the relics were even more numerous — in the Hallowe'en torches of the Irish and the bonfires of the Scotch and Welsh, while in France it was customary to visit the cemeteries and graves of their ancestors at this time.

The Mexicans to this day observe a day of the dead in much the same way and at the same time. They still place food and drink upon the graves of the departed ancestors, as modern travelers in that country have observed.

In ancient Egypt the day of the dead was observed on the 17th day of Athyr, which corresponds to the 17th day of November. On this day the Egyptian priest would place an image of the god Osiris in a sacred ark and launch it into the sea until it was borne out of sight.

Now it must be admitted that the origin of these strange traditions is not as clearly traced as the Flood traditions, and yet there seems to be a connection between these strange events and that great event in the history of the human race.

The date of the festival corresponds to the date of the Flood if, as some hold, the year began in the fall of the year. There are others who question this. All these traditions have in common a remembrance of the dead, which seems to point to a major calamity of the human race. Then there are echoes of a perishing world and the rebuilding of another. Customs and traditions found so widely scattered and with so many people must have their origin in some great experience in the past history of man. There is no common experience of the human race which would so well account for these strange customs and traditions as the Flood. And we may therefore well agree with Urquhart, who in concluding his remarks on these traditions says: "Here the traditions not only unite in bearing down to our own times that awful cry of anguish which once shook earth and sky, but also fix upon the very month and the very day which the Scriptures have recorded." [5]

And, finally, there is the extra-Biblical Flood evidence that has been contributed by archaeology and modern excavations. Organized and scientifically directed excavation activities on sites of ancient civilizations had a modest beginning about a century ago. Since then they have been extended to a great many places in the region once occupied by the ancient Egyptians, Greek, Roman, and the great Semitic, Hittite, and Persian empires of early Bible times. American and European archaeologists have co-operated in these endeavors, and through their joint efforts a great wealth of interesting and important information has been brought to light concerning these ancient people and their civilization which for these many centuries had been buried under great mounds of drifting desert sand. And much to the confusion and embarrassment of the Bible critics, these discoveries have proved again and again that the historical events recorded in the Old Testament are not fables or mere folklore, as they had claimed, but true and reliable history in every detail. This also applies to the Biblical account of the Flood.

Reference has already been made to the Babylonian Flood story discovered by George Smith of the British Museum in the Assurbanipal library of ancient Nineveh. Since then Prof. H. V. Hilprecht of Pennsylvania University has discovered a fragment of still another Deluge story on the site of ancient Nippur. But since the ancient Flood traditions have already been discussed in the previous chapter, further reference is unnecessary.

A French expedition under the leadership of M. Jacques de Morgan carried out a most extensive series of excavations on the mound concealing the ancient city of Susa, the Biblical Shushan of Nehemiah and Esther. In still more recent times a British-American expedition, under the direction of Leonard Woolley, concentrated its efforts on the site of ancient Ur, the original home of Abraham. In both of these cases, discoveries were made which in the opinion of competent archaeologists bear witness to the historical fact of the Biblical Flood.

In the mound which covered all that was left of the glories of ancient Susa, de Morgan found the remains of a number of successive settlements, one lying above the other. The relics of the first settlement, since then known as Susa I, were found eighty-four feet below the top of the mound. In this stratum, representing the first settlement, was found a great quantity of painted pottery, some simple household articles, such as axes made of copper, circular hand mirrors, also made of copper, and some small receptacles which from

172

their size and appearance have been termed cosmetic pots. The pottery found was decorated with delicate artistic designs and reveals an advanced stage of skilled workmanship.

These relics represented the oldest civilization on this site, but the significant fact is that this stratum was separated from the next above it by a layer of five feet of solid deposit containing no relic whatsoever, while above this sterile layer was found an unbroken continuity of settlements to the very top. But this five-foot sterile layer not only interrupted the regular continuity, but also marked a distinct change in the character and workmanship of the relics found, indicating a lapse of time of possibly several centuries.

Since de Morgan's discoveries, pottery of the same character and age was found on a site about eighty-five miles to the northwest of Susa called Tepeh Musyan, and still later the same was also traced to scattered sites in Mesopotamia to the west and eastward as far as Baluchistan. The questions therefore arise: What caused the break in time? What forces of nature deposited the clean stratum separating two distinct civilizations?

It has been suggested that an extended period of drought made the place uninhabitable and led to its abandonment and that the layer of clean soil would accumulate dust and sand carried there by the wind from the arid and barren region round about. But in reply to that it might be said that drought never extended over a period of centuries, but at most over a cycle of a few years or a decade. If the early inhabitants of Susa had been compelled to abandon their homes for a time on account of drought, they most certainly would have returned after a few years, or others would have taken their place, and there would not have been such a distinct interruption in the continuity of the civilization.

War might have been another reason for the abandonment of this site. It is true, war might totally destroy a city or many cities, as it has done frequently in the past, but a war in that early stage of human history would hardly have been able to wipe out completely a whole civilization extending from Mesopotamia to Baluchistan.

For these and other reasons, and because of certain traditions embodied in the list of kings of the first postdiluvian dynasty of Kish in the lower Euphrates, Peake and other archaeologists, including Woolley, have come to the conclusion that the early painted pottery of Susa I and of the regions mentioned represents an antediluvian civilization and that the clean deposit was caused by the Biblical Deluge, which completely wiped out the race that had lived there. Centuries later the same region and the same site were reoccupied by a new race, which developed a new civilization on the graves of a race that had perished in the Flood.

But even more convincing evidence than that found in Susa was discovered by Leonard Woolley in 1929 on the ancient site of Ur. These excavations have already been described with some detail in a previous chapter, and what was said there need not be repeated here. But it may not be amiss to call particular attention here to the fact that in Ur as well as in Susa the first settlement was separated from the next above by a deposit of considerable thickness containing no relics whatsoever, and that, in the second place, this layer not merely separated two distinct settlements, but two distinct civilizations removed from each other by several centuries. In Susa the lowest settlement was found eighty-four feet below the top of the mound, with a layer five feet in thickness separating it from the next above. In Ur the excavation had to go down sixty feet before it reached the bottom, while the layer which separated the first settlement from those that followed was found to consist of clean clay, eight feet in thickness. And while the origin and character of the deposit in Susa was somewhat uncertain, there is no question as to the origin and character of the deposit at Ur. Here it is clear that the stratum of clay covering the earliest settlement was laid down in water; and judging by the thickness of the layer and the area affected, the Flood was of a magnitude far exceeding the dimensions of a local river inundation.

Conditions very similar to those found at Ur were discovered at about the same time at Kish, another ancient city of the lower Euphrates not far from Ur.

It is but natural that these discoveries have aroused much interest and excitement among archaeologists, and a great many theories have been offered as an interpretation. But the men who supervised and participated in these excavations, and were able to examine the deposits and the relics found on the very spot where these cities had been buried, were unanimous in their conclusion that this earliest civilization, represented by the findings in Susa, Ur, Kish, and in the entire area extending from Mesopotamia to Baluchistan, was wiped out by a flood of unparalleled magnitude and that this disaster must be the Flood described in Genesis.

The conclusions of these archaeologists are well summarized by M. E. L. Mallowan in an article in the *National Geographic Magazine* of January, 1930. "The meaning of the stratum became instantly obvious. Our clean bank of clay was the deposit of a great flood that had wiped out the primitive civilizations beneath it.

"The casual observer might argue that such a find was only to be expected in a country whose two great rivers flooded annually, and that our clay bank merely indicated an ancient local flood. True, it was an ancient and a local flood in a sense, but there is every reason to believe that it was something very much more than this: that it was the great Biblical Flood related in the book of Genesis, a flood that afterward came to be regarded not as a local but as a world flood.

"The extraordinary importance of this discovery cannot be overestimated, and it is therefore all the more necessary to point out the salient features to those skeptics who will wish to disbelieve. The point to be considered is this: Does the flood discovered beneath the earliest known remains at

Ur represent a World Flood or does it not? It is well to remind ourselves here that our investigations are only at the beginning, inasmuch as they were made at the very end of last season; but that makes it the more remarkable, in that all the available evidence goes to prove that our flood involved a national and not merely a local catastrophe. Let us summarize what we know about it.

"First and foremost, the remains beneath the flood deposit are the oldest and the deepest ever found at Ur. That is proved from the amount of soil cleared from the surface and from the age of the remains above.

"Secondly, the particular type of civilization obliterated by the flood never again appeared; its outstanding characteristics, in particular the brilliant painted pottery, were wiped out from everyday use.

"Thirdly, above the flood deposit came a new people, the Sumerians, who had just learned to write and whose earliest legends spoke of a great flood. The flood that they described was handed down to later tradition and finally became crystallized in the Genesis account, which corroborates the old tradition in almost every detail." (P. 118 ff.)

When the enemies of Jesus complained that His disciples and even the children had joined in the triumphant song of "Hosanna to the Son of David," Jesus replied that if these were silent, the very stones would immediately cry out. When scholars and churchmen refuse to accept divine revelation and are ashamed to give honor to Almighty God, the stones and the material remains of generations and things that have been must cry out, and the indistinct babbling of humanity's childhood, as recorded in its mythologies and traditions, must bear witness. And strange enough, the very men who so frequently close their eyes and ears to revealed truth of Scripture become the instruments in the hands of God to interpret for their fellow men this testimony and thus, like Balaam of old, unwittingly become prophets of God, confirming the truth as revealed in the Bible.

176

CHAPTER XII

Geological Evidence for a Universal Flood

THE greatest opposition to the Biblical Flood story has come, strangely enough, from the men whose very business it is to observe nature in its wonderful and manifold forms and to search out the mysterious laws that govern it. That is particularly true of the geologist. The science of geology has contributed much toward a better understanding and appreciation of the planet upon which we live. But not all that geology teaches is science or is established as truth by actual measurement, demonstration, or some other scientific method of discovering truth. Much of geology is pure speculation and is as such on the same basis as philosophy, or must be accepted on faith, as the truths of theology. There is no quarrel with this since some truths are beyond scientific demonstration. Or as Thomas Aquinas has so well said: "There is a point, however high it may be, beyond which reason must confess its inability to understand, but it is just at this point that faith comes to the rescue of reason; the mind in matters of faith gives the assent to truth upon the authority of God manifested through revelation and thus man completes the edifice of his knowledge with the structure of supernatural truth. The realm of faith then is not to be conceived in opposition to the realm of natural truth but as the culmination, for in both reign supreme the same divine intelligence." [1] We do not quarrel with modern geology for advancing theories as possible solutions where truths cannot be established by scientific demonstration, but we have a serious quarrel with geology or any other science when such theories are dogmatically presented as established facts and when these sciences are intolerant toward any other view, belief, or theory.

Until the early part of the last century geologists accepted the Biblical Flood as a historical fact and were agreed in tracing to this great world cataclysm many of the phenomena in and on the surface of the earth's crust, which since then have given rise to a great many theories concerning the history, development, and age of our earth and its inhabitants. This change did not occur suddenly or as the result of some important geological discovery, but was a part, or the practical working out, of a large movement of thought known as Rationalism, which gradually spread over all of Europe and the rest of the Western World and touched every phase of intellectual life, such as theology, science, philosophy, literature, and even education. Human reason was made the measure of all things. Whatever could not be harmonized with reason was rejected. Even the Bible was subjected to this treatment. This meant the removal, as acceptable truth, of everything which partook of the miraculous or of any direct interference with the affairs of men or the universe on the part of a personal, omnipotent God.

In biology, Rationalism led to the revival of the ancient Greek theory of evolution as an explanation of the origin of the life that is found in the universe. The Biblical Flood story could, of course, not be made to fit into such a mechanistic scheme any more than the story of Creation as related in Genesis. Hence both the Biblical account of Creation and the story of the Flood were ruled out as unacceptable, and the modern theory of geology, which is evolutionistic in

178

its basic principle, took their place. And yet even modern geology and other sciences have unwittingly contributed much to confirm the Biblical account of the Flood. It is through the untiring efforts of geologists and other scientists that the earth has yielded up physical evidence in great abundance to substantiate the record of Moses concerning a universal flood. The examination of a part of such evidence will therefore next engage our attention in this study.

The first of this type of evidence I wish to submit is what the geologists call "rubble drift and ossiferous fissures." By "rubble drift" is meant a certain type of deposit or sediment consisting of massive, angular unrolled material tumultuously deposited in local pockets and catchment areas, generally full of shattered bones. And by "ossiferous fissures" are meant great fissures or rents in the earth which were formed by some violent contortion of the surface of the earth.

The evidence of such fissures has been found in many places of the earth, some of them measuring from 140 to 300 feet in depth. They were filled with debris which drifted into them soon after they opened. This probably explains why they did not close again. Such fissures have been found in England, France, southern Spain, Germany, Russia, and elsewhere. The interesting feature of these fissures is the debris found in them, for they are filled with the remains of animals, among them those of the elephant, the rhinoceros, the hippopotamus, the reindeer, the horse, the hog, and the ox. The bones found in them cannot be of animals which fell in alive or were buried there, for no skeleton is complete. They cannot have been brought there by streams, for those who have examined them found no signs on them of having been rolled. Neither could the bones have been exposed to the weather for a long time, for none of them show marks of weathering. That water had something to do with depositing them is indicated by the very general cementing together of the deposits by calcite.

Again, it has been observed by such a competent geologist as Prestwich that these ossiferous fissures are usually found upon isolated hills of considerable height, places on which we might expect animals to gather in seeking safety from an approaching flood. Fleeing in terror and driven by the common danger, the carnivorous and herbivorous alike sought refuge on the same elevation, only to meet even here a common watery grave. A very remarkable classical example of such an isolated hill is found in Burgundy, France, in the valley of the Soane. The hill is about 1,030 feet above the surrounding plain, with steep flanks on all sides. A fissure near the top of the hill is crowded with animal skeletons. No skeleton is entire, the bones are fractured, are thrown together in disorderly fashion, and are unweathered and ungnawed. Again we have the strange phenomenon that bears, wolves, horses, and oxen, animals which are ordinarily not found together as peaceful neighbors, scale an isolated mountain only to die and have their remains preserved in a common grave.[2] Such a flood as is described in Genesis offers the most reasonable explanation for this phenomenon.

Another most spectacular example of an ossiferous fissure is found in the isolated little island of Cerigo, near Corfu, off the coast of Greece. This occurs on a barren mountain, in the form of a fossiliferous deposit, a short distance from the sea. It is called the mountain of bones. It is a mile in circumference at the base, and from the base to the summit is covered with bones.[3] The character of this mountain as well as of those already mentioned is such that animals could not have congregated here to feed, but the most reasonable solution for this phenomenon is the rising of flood waters driving them to this elevation. There they perished and were buried by the same flood water.

According to Prestwich, the rubble deposit in England indicates that the country was submerged to a depth of at least one thousand feet, while on the Continent we find evidence of submergence up to three thousand feet.

Equally interesting examples of this kind of deposits are found in the Rock of Gibraltar, where fissures nearly three hundred feet deep and filled with debris similar to that just mentioned have been discovered. Animal remains described are practically the same as those found in the hills of France. These fissures on Gibraltar exist at different altitudes. The highest of them has an elevation of eleven hundred feet. In one of them man-made implements are said to have been found.

Similar deposits were discovered in a cavern near Palermo on the Island of Sicily. An enormous number of hippopotamus bones were found there, some of them so well preserved that they could be carved and formed into ornaments. More than twenty tons of bones were shipped for commercial purposes within six months after the discovery of this cavern. The bones were mostly of the hippopotamus, but there were also found among them those of the deer, the ox, and the elephant. The bones were mixed together without order and were broken and scattered in fragments, but again they are described as showing no signs of having been gnawed or weathered.

A large deposit of bones in a cavity of the calcareous beds of the steppes of Russia was discovered in 1847 near Odessa. In this cavity were found 4,500 bones of bears derived from at least one hundred individual animals; with these were found remains of species of the cat family, hyenas, horses, boars, mammoth, rhinoceros, aurochses, and deer, together with remains of numerous insectivores and rodents, such as hares, otters, martens, as well as wolves and foxes.

At a village near Brunswick, Germany, a collection of tusks, teeth, and bones was discovered piled together in a heap and embedded in diluvial loam. In this heap were found eleven tusks of elephants, over eleven feet long; another fourteen feet, eight inches long and twelve and three-fourths inches in diameter; thirty molar teeth, many large bones, some of them five and six feet, eight inches long.

Mixed with these were bones and teeth of the rhinoceros, the horse, the ox, and the stag, all of them in a confused mass, but none of them rolled or broken.

A bone deposit near Stuttgart in South Germany contained the remains of the elephant, the rhinoceros, the horse, the deer, the ox, and of small carnivores.

Another most interesting fissure was found at Malta, the island made famous by St. Paul's journey to Rome, in which were found in great abundance the remains of birds, especially water birds. With them were mingled sharks' teeth, fish bones, and the remains of frogs, two species of fresh water turtles from one and a half to two feet high, large numbers of small shells; and intermingled with all of this debris were stones of various sizes strange to the locality in which they were found. And, lastly, there were present in this same fissure large blocks of stone, some measuring fifteen feet in circumference, having deep grooves and hollows scooped out of their surface, all of which is irrefutable evidence that the debris found here, together with other circumstances mentioned, was carried here by the action of water. At least no other agent known to man would have been able to deposit and mix these remains in the manner in which they are found.

For an interpretation of the debris found in this Maltese cavern, Howorth quotes Dr. Lester Adams: "The history of the deposition of the contents of the fissure cavern of Muaidra in Malta, read by the light the data produce, appears to me to be as follows: We perceive three distinct kinds of arrangement of the debris in connection with the fossiliferous deposit. First, when water passed down the floor, bearing along pebbles and fragments of bones and teeth of proboscidians, rodents, birds, skulls, etc. Second, a rush of water containing blocks of sandstones from the slope above, together with sand and portions, nay, even entire carcasses of the animals just mentioned; and finally, the scourings of the rock surface and whichever organic remains still lodged thereon, up even to the very level of the plateau on which the fissure opened. Third, the mode wherewith the organic remains and the stones were piled indicated that they had been conveyed, at all events for most part, from the west and north side of the gap for the reason that the debris and remains were piled upon a pile well along the concave eastern wall; the most perfect remains being invariably found towards the interior of the gap, as if they had come sooner to a standstill." [4]

A similar deposit is found at Agate Springs in Sioux County in the northwestern corner of Nebraska. What remains of the hill covers about ten acres. This bone bed was accidentally discovered in 1876. It contains the bones of rhinoceroses, camels, giant wild boars, and other animals, buried together in a confused mass as only water would deposit them. It is estimated that the bones of about nine thousand complete animals are buried on this one hill. Clear signs indicate that the bone layer once extended over a very wide area; hence it is likely that many times that number of animals were brought together at this hill and buried there by the action of water.

This is a fact that is most important. Animals of every kind died in great numbers and were buried apparently almost instantly. With many there can be no doubt that this was so. It has been suggested that ruthless man slaughtered these animals, but considering the number of the remains that have been found, thrown together in great heaps, mixed in great confusion, large and small animals, herbivorous and carnivorous, mammals, and birds, all in one pile, buried in alluvial deposits, intermingled with remains of plants and trees, sea shells and fish, this theory becomes absurd on the face of it. Neither man nor beast could have wrought such havoc in the plant and animal world and buried the carcasses before nature's scavengers devoured and destroyed them, nor could man have buried them in

183

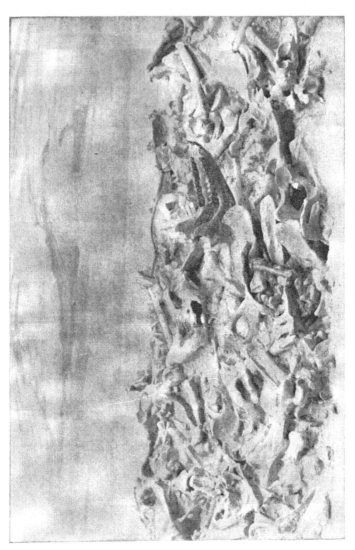

Bones of Rhinoceroses, Camels, Giant Wild Boars Buried at Agate Springs, Nebraska. It is estimated that 9,000 complete animals were buried in one hill

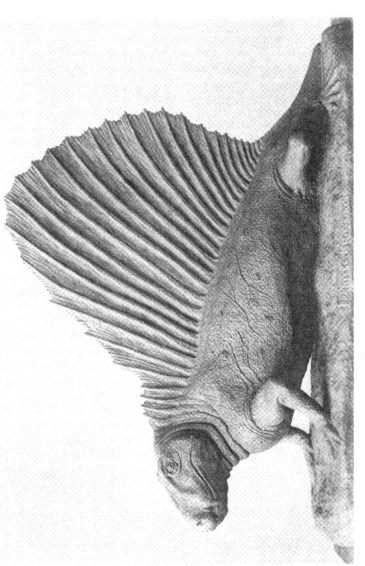

Restoration of the Permian "Sail-Lizard" Reptile, Dimetrodon gigas, on exhibition in the U. S. National Museum. It has since been discovered that the tail of this animal is longer than the restoration shows

such enormous depth and in such places as they are frequently found.

It has also been suggested that some pestilence or common disease may have been responsible for the sudden death of these animals. But what pestilence is known to man which would carry away every kind of animal — the fowls of the air and the beasts of the field, elephants and mice, rhinoceroses and frogs, bisons and snakes, tigers and fish, land snails and insects — all at one time? There may be, and there have been, diseases which have ravaged certain species and nearly annihilated them in a given area, but a pestilence which brought about a universal destruction of animal life is unknown and normally impossible. But even if that were possible, the questions then arise: Who buried these carcasses? Who collected them in these great pits and on the hilltops? When animals are stricken with sudden disease, they are too weak to travel to a common burial ground.

Drought and other causes have been suggested as a means of destruction, but none of them offers a satisfactory explanation. None of them is sufficient to kill, collect, and bury these millions of animals. There is only one known force in nature which is capable of doing just that, and that is water. A great flood of water is the only reasonable explanation for this strange phenomenon. For what else could have driven these animals together on hilltops and caused them to perish in such numbers but the waters of an all-engulfing flood? It does not require an overactive imagination to reconstruct a picture of the scenes which were enacted on those hills and hundreds of thousands of other hills like them in every part of the earth. One can see the terrified and panic-stricken beasts stampeding to higher grounds and to the hilltops before the onrushing Flood. The lion took no heed of the lamb, nor the wolf of the hare; all were bent on saving their own lives. What a horrifying heart-rending cry of despair there must have gone up from the mouths of these uncounted multitudes of terrified beasts of the field and forest! But one by one these mouths were stopped as the waters of the Flood overtook them, until at last even the tallest and strongest succumbed.

Then followed the burial. The convulsions of the earth had provided the graves. The earth opened its mouth and swallowed them, just as they had collected on the tops of these hills. There the bones of the large and the small, the gentle and the ferocious, the carnivorous and the herbivorous, were thrown together in wild confusion in a common grave, and there the Almighty has preserved them for a memorial and a warning that generations of men yet to follow may behold and learn that the Lord, our God, is "a jealous God, visiting the iniquity of the fathers upon the children unto the third and fourth generation" of them that hate Him.

CHAPTER XIII

Glacial and Fossil Lakes, Coal Beds, and Oil Deposits

I N Genesis 8:13-14 we read: "And it came to pass in the six hundredth and first year, in the first month, the first day of the month, the waters were dried up from off the earth: and Noah removed the covering of the ark and looked; and, behold, the face of the ground was dry. And in the second month, on the seven and twentieth day of the month, was the earth dried."

These words need not be interpreted to mean that all the earth in every continent and on every body of land as these are now constituted were dry and appeared then as they do now. The text merely states that land and water were again definitely separated and that the land was now sufficiently dry so that Noah and the animals with him could safely leave the ark to repossess and repopulate the earth. The fact is that the Flood waters had not completely drained to their present basins, and large bodies of water continued to exist for centuries, a few of them even surviving to the present day. In fact, the existence of large inland bodies of water or the remains of such bodies of water as fossil lakes, as they are also called, is further evidence of a universal flood as described in Genesis. At any rate such a flood would offer the most plausible explanation for their existence. If we had no record of a universal flood, we would postulate one to account for the origin of the existing fossil lakes.

The remnants of large inland bodies of water and fossil lakes are found in every continent.

The territory now made desolate by the Gobi Desert in China was, by all indications, at one time a great inland lake as large as the present Mediterranean Sea. The existence of this inland sea of central Asia is attested by the abundant sedimentary deposits about the margin and also by the Chinese historical reference to it as the great Han Hai, or Interior Sea.

According to C. F. Wright, Lake Baikal in Siberia, the surface of which stands more than fifteen hundred feet above sea level, is proof that the whole of Siberia was at one time submerged under a great depth of marine water. In support of his views he advances a number of proofs, among them the fact that there is found in that lake marine life, including an Arctic type of seal, which proves a close relation between this lake and the Arctic Sea. The seals found there closely resemble the seals now frequently found at Spitzbergen. It also seems significant that very similar seals are found in the Caspian Sea. Their remains have been found in the Aral Sea as well.

In India there is a similar well-marked inland basin with clear evidence of having been filled with water at one time. As these inland bodies dried up and the climate became more arid, the region gradually changed into a desert. The Thar Desert in India, east of the Indus, really was traversed in prehistoric times by rivers and contained populous cities and villages. Relics of such cities are now being dug up.[1]

Similar conditions obtained in Mongolia, Turkestan, and Central Asia. Where there was once a well-watered, fertile country, there is now semiarid or desert land.

In the Tibetan tablelands, the highest tableland in the world, averaging sixteen thousand feet above sea level, we find numerous lakes, generally salt or alkaline, scattered over the western and northwestern section. And here, too, the traces left clearly indicate that this high tableland was at one time submerged in a great sea.

In Africa are found dry lakes or shrunken lakes of a similar character. Even the Sahara Desert was not always a desert. The skeleton of a well-marked river system is clearly visible, and, in addition, man-made implements have also been found there in great abundance.

Salt pans or salt licks found in many isolated areas of the Russian steppes and in our own Western prairies, often containing the remains of marine life, are further evidence of such inland lakes.

Here in America, too, there were at one time, as I have pointed out before, great inland bodies of water, such as Lake Agassiz in the North; Lake Bonneville, Lake Lahonton, in the West; and others. One of the most interesting of these ancient lakes is Lake Algonquin, so called after a tribe of Indians inhabiting the region in early historic days, which at one time occupied the present area of the upper Great Lakes, i. e., Lake Superior, Lake Michigan, Lake Huron, and a large area of land north of Lakes Superior and Huron. This magnificent inland body of water is said to have had an area of a hundred thousand square miles and a depth in places of more than fifteen hundred feet. The Algonquin beach has been carefully mapped in the southern parts and is almost as distinct as the shores of our familiar modern lakes. The gravel bars are often used as roads. The ancient shore is usually not far from the present lakes, but stands about twenty-six feet above their level. Its beaches are splendidly displayed on the north shore of Lake Superior, terrace after terrace rising for hundreds of feet at Peninsula and Jackfish Bay.[2]

Lake Iroquois, which at one time occupied the basin of Lake Ontario but extended far beyond its present beaches, was another of these ancient storage basins. Cities like Utica and Rochester in the State of New York and Hamilton and Toronto in Ontario are built upon its ancient shores. Excavations in these old shore deposits have produced fossil remains of the mammoth, buffaloes, and the beaver eighty-three feet below the present surface. And teeth and tusks of the mammoth and the mastodon have been found in a number of places south of this old lake shore.

Still another well-known fossil lake on our own continent is Lake Agassiz, already referred to in chapter 8. This was a large inland body of water surpassing in size even Lake Algonquin. It covered parts of the present States of Minnesota and North Dakota and the Canadian Provinces of Saskatchewan, Manitoba, and Ontario. It drained at different times to the Atlantic through the Mohawk Valley, to the Gulf of Mexico through the Mississippi, and northward to Hudson Bay. Today the comparatively small lakes Winnipeg and Winnipegosis are all that remains of this great inland sea.

Lake Bonneville at one time occupied a part of the States of Utah, Nevada, and Idaho. It had an area of 19,000 square miles, that is, it was nearly of the size of Lake Michigan today, and had a maximum depth of a thousand feet. The present Salt Lake near the city of that name, with an area of only one tenth of its ancestor, is all that remains of this great inland body of water.

Even our Great Lakes may well have had their origin in the Flood. These lakes are unique as great inland lakes and have no rival except in those of Central Africa. They are in the heart of the continent, a thousand miles from an ocean, and yet the basins of four of them dip down hundreds of feet below sea level. These greatest lakes in the world have no important river flowing into them, though a great river flows out. In fact, the main drainage of the region is away from them instead of toward them. The three upper lakes are balanced on the watershed between the three great river systems flowing toward Hudson Bay, the Gulf of Mexico, and the Atlantic. Only a comparatively few miles separate the rivers that flow in these divergent directions. A very slight tilt in either direction might cause these great bodies of water to drain either into the Gulf of Mexico or into Hudson Bay instead of into the Gulf of St. Lawrence.

Geologists believe that the cause of the origin of these lakes is not the same for all. The origin of Lake Nipigon and Lake Superior is ascribed to volcanic action and lava flow, which, it is said, caused a collapse of the underlying strata, thus giving rise to their present basins, while the other lakes are believed to be parts of ancient rivers that were blocked either by moraines or an uplift in the lower valley, thus causing the river to widen into the present lakes. Again, it is quite clear that the forces which may have been operative in bringing about this great change in the geography of our continent were available or active in the Flood. If land could rise or glaciers could form to dam up great bodies of water, the miracles of the Flood, with its catastrophic effects upon our earth, were also possible. But why are people willing to believe the one and refuse to accept the other?

Even geologists who will not admit the possibility of a universal flood agree that some of these lakes are the result of a great inundation which filled up their basins. Others are ascribed to the great continental glacier. Climatic changes and gradual evaporation caused them to disappear or to be reduced in size, leaving certain well-defined traces behind them. Again it must be admitted that the Deluge of the Bible offers a reasonable and the most satisfactory solution for this geological problem. A universal deluge would supply sufficient water to fill their basins, and the earthquakes and other disturbances accompanying this world catastrophe may well have changed the contour of the land and caused old courses of rivers to be changed or dammed and thus giving rise to these great inland bodies of water as described.

Still another most convincing proof from geology for a

flood of a magnitude such as described in Genesis is found in the great coal beds found in all parts of the world.

Geologists are pretty well agreed that the source of all coal is some form of vegetable matter. Sir William Dawson writes: ". . . coal can under the present constitution of nature, be produced only in one way, namely, by the accumulation of vegetable matter, for vegetation alone has the power of decomposing the carbonic acid of the atmosphere and accumulating it as carbon. This we see in modern times in the vegetable soil, in peaty beds, and in vegetable muck accumulated in ponds and similar places. Such vegetable matter, once accumulated, requires only pressure and the changes which come of its own slow putrefaction to be converted into coal.

"But in order that it may accumulate at all, certain conditions are necessary. The first of these includes the climatal and organic arrangements necessary for abundant vegetable growth. The second is the facility for the preservation of the vegetable matter, without decay or intermixture with earthy substances; and this for a long time, till a great thickness of it accumulates. The third is its covering up by other deposits, so as to be compressed and excluded from air. It is evident that when we have to consider the formation of a bed of coal several feet in thickness and spread, perhaps, over hundreds of square miles, many things must conduce to such a result, and the wonder is perhaps rather that such conditions ever have been effectively combined." [8]

Dawson postulates three conditions requisite for the formation of coal. The first is a climatic one and other conditions capable of producing a profusion of vegetation sufficient to account for the great coal deposits of the world today. The question of climate and vegetation in the antediluvian world was discussed at some length in the chapter dealing with the physical world before the Flood. The antediluvian world, with its ideal climate and its luxuriant vegetation, meets all the conditions required here by Dawson. In addition to what was said there regarding climate and vegetation, a quotation from Figuier may find a place here. He writes: "Let us pause for a moment, and consider the general characters which belonged to our planet during the Carboniferous period. Heat — though not necessarily excessive heat — and extreme humidity were the attributes of the atmosphere. The modern allies of the species which formed its vegetation are now found only under the burning latitudes of the tropics; and the enormous dimensions in which we find them in the fossil state prove, on the other hand, that the atmosphere was saturated with moisture.

"Dr. Livingstone tells us that continual rains, added to intense heat, are the climatic characteristics of Equatorial Africa, where flourishes the vigorous and tufted vegetation which is so delightful to the eye.

"It is a remarkable circumstance that conditions of equable and warm climate, combined with humidity, do not seem to have been limited to any one part of the globe, but the temperature of the whole seems to have been nearly the same in very different latitudes. From the equatorial regions up to Melville Island, in the Arctic Ocean, where in our days eternal frost prevails — from Spitzbergen to the center of Africa, the Carboniferous flora is identically the same.

"When nearly the same plants are found in Greenland and Guinea; when the same species, now extinct, are met with of equal development at the equator as at the pole, we cannot but admit that at this period the temperature of the globe was nearly alike everywhere.

"What we now call climate was unknown in these geological times. There seems to have been then only one climate over the whole globe.

"It was at a subsequent period, that is, in later Tertiary times, that the cold began to make itself felt at the terrestrial poles. . . ." [4]

The second and third conditions required for the formation of coal from vegetable matter, according to Sir William

194

Dawson, are: "The facility for the preservation of the vegetable matter without decay or the intermixture with earth substance and the covering up by other deposits, so as to be compressed and excluded from air."

What force of nature could better meet this condition than a flood such as God brought over the first world? Water alone possesses all requirements necessary, first, to uproot the existing vegetation, second, to drift it together in great heaps, and third, to bury it before it rotted. The presence of well-preserved fossil leaves and other delicate parts of plant life seems to prove beyond doubt that the burial must have been very soon after the plant was separated and destroyed.

The probable method of the formation of the coal beds is ably discussed by Price, who writes: "If we care to go into the question of probability of the coal formations, and can picture to ourselves the wide stretch of country clothed for long periods with the most luxuriant vegetation, and if we may suppose that the remarkable atmospheric condition of the ancient world may have absolutely precluded any parching droughts, thus rendering it quite improbable that the accumulated deposits of centuries should ever be burned up by forest fires, we shall have the probable source of materials. If now, in the great world catastrophe which seems to be indicated, these accumulations of many centuries were all washed away, dead and green together, and swept pell-mell into lakes or valleys, somewhat like the great natural 'raft' on the Red River, only on a far more enormous scale, the stumps of the trees would still carry many of their roots with them and would frequently float or stand in their natural upright positions. In this case, too, we would ultimately have the formation of an 'underclay' at the bottom of the bed from the action of the acids generated in the oxidizing mass: and this 'underclay' would naturally contain many roots or something resembling them." [5] Price also points out that mixed up with the coal are found various kinds of marine life, such as crinoids and the clear-water ocean corals, and great quantities of fish remains.

There are two other features characterizing the coal beds which seem to prove that the reasoning of Dr. Price is correct, viz., the well-preserved character of the plant remains and the kinds of plants composing them. With regard to the wonderful perfection with which the plants are found preserved in these beds the geologist Sir Archibald Geikie writes: "Not much is usually to be made out from the coal itself, for the vegetation has been so squeezed and altered that the leaves and branches cannot be recognized. . . . But though the larger plants have usually not been preserved as well in coal, they may be found in great profusion and beauty in beds of rock above or below the coal. . . . Now and then, the plants may be seen lying across each other in wonderful confusion, upon the bottom of the bed of rock that overlies the coal seam and forms the roof of the mine. Though all are squeezed flat like dried leaves in a book, they still retain their original graceful forms." [6]

And speaking of coal deposits of Bohemia, Dr. Buckland writes: "The most elaborate imitations of living foliage upon the painted ceilings of Italian palaces have no comparison with the beauteous proportions of extinct forms with which the galleries of these instructive coal mines are overhung. The roof is covered as with a canopy of gorgeous tapestry, enriched with festoons of most graceful foliage, flung in wild, irregular profusion over every portion of the surface. The effect is heightened by the contrast of the coal-black color of these vegetables with the light ground work of the rock to which they are attached." [7]

Price says: "Most geologists who have written on this subject have bewailed the poverty of our language to convey an adequate idea of the marvelous perfection of the forms laid out to view through the opening of such beds of shale or fine sandstone. But this splendid preservation of the plant remains is a universal characteristic of all the coal-bearing rocks, not alone those of the Carboniferous system, but also those of the Jurassic, Cretaceous, or Tertiary, or even the lignites of the Pleistocene. They are all much alike in these respects: they all contain wood or leaves, flowers, and fruits in a marvelous state of preservation."[8]

And as to the kinds of trees and plants found, Price shows that they are chiefly plants and trees which do not grow in swamps or peat bogs and cannot, by any stretch of the imagination, be supposed to have contributed to the formation of peatlike accumulation in the long ago. For example, we have in the Upper Cretaceous coal such kinds of sassafras, laurel, tulip trees, magnolia, cinnamon, sequoia, poplar, willow, maple, birch, chestnut, elder, beech, elm, with leaves of some palms, and hundreds of others. In the Tertiary of England and the continent we have such trees and shrubs as fig, cinnamon, various palms, varieties of Proteaceae (like those now found in India and Australia), cypress, sequoia, magnolia, oak, rose, plum, almond, myrtle, acacia, with many other genera now found only in America. The Miocene strata of Greenland have yielded great numbers of the same genera.

All this seems to be most convincing evidence, not only of the fact that the world before the Flood was quite different so far as climatic conditions and distribution of vegetation is concerned, but also that this world was stripped of its marvelous and luxuriant vegetation by a flood of unparalleled magnitude, which then floated the debris together into great heaps where the material was covered, sealed, stored, and formed into coal for the benefit of the generations of men who were to follow. And what enormous quantities of this coal there have been stored up for the generations of men that were to inhabit the world that followed the Flood! Coal is found on every continent and on many islands of the sea. Some have more, others less, but there is sufficient coal stored below the surface of our earth to provide man with power, light, heat, and other substances derived from coal for hundreds of thousands of years. Lyell has estimated that the coal deposits in Nova Scotia alone are sufficient to provide a hundred million tons each year for fifteen thousand years, while the coal reserves of Alberta have been estimated at over 673 billion tons. This means that the coal mines of Alberta alone could supply the world with one million tons of coal annually for a period of 673,000 years. The coal deposits of North China are estimated at 150 billion tons. Add to this the coal reserves of the rest of the American continents, of Europe, Asia, and the rest of the world, and our imagination fails even to comprehend the magnitude of the constructive work wrought in the most destructive event in the history of our globe.

There the coal, thus preserved, had been stored many thousands of years. Man either did not know that it was there or did not know what to do with it when he found it. It was not until the eighteenth century, when the steam engine was invented and the Industrial Revolution was ushered in, that coal came into its own and became a means by which a new world order and a new civilization was created.

Huxley, though failing to give due honor to the omnipotent God for this wonderful creation, wrote very eloquently about coal and its meaning: "I suppose that nineteen hundred years ago, when Julius Caesar was good enough to deal with Britain as we have dealt with New Zealand, the primeval Briton, blue with cold, may have known that the strange black stone which he found here and there in his wanderings would burn and so help to warm his body and cook his food. Saxon, Dane, and Norman swarmed into the land. The English people grew into a powerful nation; and Nature still waited for a return for the capital she had invested in ancient club mosses. The eighteenth century arrived, and with it James Watt. The brain of that man was the spore out of which was developed the steam engine, and all the prodigious trees and branches of modern industry which have grown out of this. But coal is as much an essential of this growth and development as carbonic acid is of a club moss. Wanting this coal, we could not have smelted the iron needed to make our engines; nor have worked our engines when we got them. But take away the engines, and the great towns of Yorkshire and Lancashire vanish like a dream. Manufactures give place to agriculture and pasture, and not ten men could live where now ten thousand are easily supported.

"Thus all this abundant wealth of money and of vivid life is Nature's investment in club mosses and the like so long ago. But what becomes of the coal which is burnt in yielding the interest? Heat comes out of it, light comes out of it; and if we could gather together all that goes up the chimney, and all that remains in the grate of a thoroughly burnt coal fire, we should find ourselves in possession of a quantity of carbonic acid, water, ammonia, and mineral matters exactly equal in weight to the coal. But these are the very matters with which Nature supplied the club mosses, which made coal. She is paid back principal and interest at the same time; and she straightway invests the carbonic acid, the water, and the ammonia in new forms of life, feeding with them the plants that now live. Thrifty Nature, surely! no prodigal, but the most notable of housekeepers!" [9]

To this Dawson adds: "All this is true and well told; but who is Nature, this goddess who, since the far-distant Carboniferous age, has been planning for man? Is this not another name for that Almighty Maker who foresaw and arranged all things for His people before the foundation of the world." [10]

We stand aghast when contemplating the awfulness of the punitive justice of God as manifested in the destruction of the Flood. But at the same time we stand in holy wonderment at His mercy and kindness that, in the very act in which He punished and destroyed, He preserved in a most mysterious manner the vegetation He had created and stored in the bowels of the earth, to provide heat and power and a thousand other services to the generations which were to follow. Our God is great in His judgments and in all His wonderful works.

But even more wonderful, if that were possible, than the coal deposits, are the great oil reservoirs stored deep down in the interior of the earth. And, like coal, the existence of oil in certain localities must be regarded as a silent but persistent witness for a world catastrophe such as is recorded in Genesis.

Oil is found in fossiliferous strata and is therefore not an original creation, but a product of organic matter. It came into existence not until life had appeared on our planet and after living organisms had been destroyed and buried on a world-wide scale. The problem of the origin of petroleum has puzzled scientists ever since it was first discovered, and various theories have been advanced in explanation, but none of them offers a solution so completely satisfactory as the one which attributes its origin to a great world catastrophe identical with, or at least similar to, the great Flood.

Petroleum has been known for a considerable time. Through seepage on the coast of the Caspian Sea, and through wells, man became familiar with it, but did not know what to do with it. Gradually he learned to use it for lighting and for medicinal purposes. Not until after the middle of the last century did oil assume its present importance in the industrial and commercial world.

The first oil well in the United States was drilled in 1859. The total oil production for that year was two thousand barrels. By 1931 the total output of oil had grown to 846 million barrels in the United States alone. The world wars increased the demand for oil enormously, and the world output of the precious liquid has reached astronomical figures.

Like coal, oil multiplies man's energy, but it is more concentrated than coal and more convenient for use than coal. Through the use of oil, man has increased to a still greater degree his mastery over the land, the sea, and the air and also over time and space and over other great natural barriers. As an illuminant, petroleum was much in demand, but as a source of energy it has come to be regarded by the great powers of the world as essential to national security and commercial leadership. The possession of coal and iron no longer suffices a nation if it is to maintain its position among the more important powers of the world. Hence it is not surprising that the possession of the world petroleum resources has become a matter of international rivalry and competition. And the world wars were largely fought over the question as to who was to control these great resources of energy and power.

Since the first oil well was sunk in 1859, millions and billions of barrels of this mysterious liquid have been pumped from the bowels of the earth and have been converted into energy and speed. It has made possible the automobile, the airplane, and the armored tank; it has changed man's mode of life in peacetime and has completely revolutionized the science of warfare; it has changed social and economic conditions in the world and has within the short period of one generation completely revolutionized the civilization of the modern world.

The question concerning the origin of petroleum is all the more interesting and important because of these facts. Where does the oil which we pump from the earth come from? How did it get into the earth? In 1923 Dr. J. M. Mac-Farlane, professor of Botany at the University of Pennsylvania, published a notable book of over four hundred pages in which he discusses this question and, in doing so, proposes and defends very successfully the theory that fish are the source of all petroleum. In this book the author makes out a very strong case for the theory that fish destroyed in prodigious numbers somewhere in the distant past constitute the chief source of our oil deposits. Dr. MacFarlane summarizes the results of his investigation as follows: "In review

Oil Well Derricks, West Edmond, Oklahoma

*A Tank Farm; Continental Oil Company,
Ponca City, Oklahoma*

of the evidence of the preceding chapters, the author was compelled to accept that fishes are the source of practically the entire supply of crude petroleum, also of natural petroleum derivatives like asphalt." He says that in these studies he has been increasingly impressed by the apparent recurring cataclysmic cycles which were responsible for the destruction of these myriads upon myriads of fishes.[11]

As to the extent of some of these deposits, he shows that the Oligo-Miocene oil shales can be traced almost continuously for almost 2,500 miles, while the fishes, mollusks, polyzoa, and other organisms recorded from the Caucasian or the Galician centers show a marked similarity to those of Glarus or even of California; and these facts suggest to him that the destruction may have been essentially simultaneous all over this area. And hence he concludes: "It can be definitely said that through all of the geologic formations in which fish remains occur, the large proportion of the remains consist of entire fishes or of sections in which every scale is still in position; every fin is extended as in life attitude; the bones of the head, though often crushed in and broken through subsequent diastrophic strains, still retain almost the normal positions; while near them may be coprolites of the same or some other types of fish in a practically entire state. All of this conclusively proves that when myriads of such fishes were simultaneously killed, their bodies were deposited or stranded within a few hours or a few days at most after death, so that the flesh, the liver, the alimentary canal, and other soft parts were unquestionably enclosed and intact when sediment sealed them up. For numerous experiments that the writer has undertaken prove that even after five or six days dead fishes begin to lose scales, to be attacked and nibbled at by other fishes, by crabs, and by smaller fry, while as yet the flesh and entrails are enclosed, though softened. We unhesitatingly conclude then that a large proportion of the fishes met with in 'fish beds' and oil strata were stretched out and preserved intact by immediate and rapid entombment. So whatever amount of oil any individual or species may have contained, such must have filtered out gradually into surrounding strata." [12]

However, we need not limit ourselves to fishes as the sole source of oil. No doubt all other organisms, containing substances convertible into oil, contributed to the great oil deposits of the present world. As life of every kind, including the myriads of the prehistoric reptiles great and small as well as all other living creatures, was suddenly overtaken, destroyed, and buried, sometimes in great heaps, numbering thousands upon thousands of individuals, the oil contained in these bodies was distilled by heat and pressure and thus stored in sands between impervious strata and there preserved through the ages to the present day.

Concerning the causes for the destruction of these myriads of fishes, MacFarlane writes: "As to the great agency at work in past geologic ages for wide-spread destruction of fish life, the writer would place in first rank the various volcanic and seismic disturbances that have periodically caused local or even cosmic changes of a fundamental nature." [13] The writer then goes on to show that there is evidence of a widespread volcanic activity having occurred somewhere in the distant past, which is again in harmony with what was said in a previous chapter concerning volcanic and seismic activities accompanying the Flood.

We are familiar with the effects of a charge of dynamite or even an ordinary gunshot on fish if this is discharged in the water. It is also well known what destruction may be wrought on marine life by volcanic eruptions or great earthquakes if these occur near the coast or on the ocean floor. The great Flood was, as we have seen, accompanied by great internal disturbances within the earth. The antediluvian seas were filled with an "abundance of living creatures that moved in the water," among them the great whales and leviathans, schools of them, numbering millions and billions; they were killed by volcanic shock and were immediately or soon after buried by great upheavals on the ocean floor, land slides, or falling debris. And there the oil was distilled and stored in the great reservoirs of the earth until man accidentally discovered these unlimited reserves of energy and power kept there for him by the omnipotent and benevolent God who preserved while He destroyed. Further quotations from Price, Buckland, Hugh Miller, and others may well find a place here to show that great geologists of the present and the past agree with this view.

Beginning with Price, we read the following: "If a vertebrate fish should die a natural death — which, of itself, must be a rare occurrence — the carcass would soon be devoured whole or bit by bit by other creatures near. Possibly the lower jaw, or the teeth, the spines, etc., in the case of sharks, or a bone or two of the skeleton, might be buried unbroken, but a whole vertebrate fish entombed in a modern deposit is surely a unique occurrence.

"But every geologist knows that the remains of fishes are, in countless millions of cases, found in a marvelous state of preservation. They have been entombed in whole shoals, with the beds containing them miles in extent, and scattered all over the globe. Indeed, so accustomed have we grown to this state of affairs in the rocks we hammer up that if we fail to find such well-preserved remains of vertebrate fishes, land animals or plants, we feel disappointed, almost hurt; we think that nature has somehow slighted this particular set of beds. But where, in our modern quiet earth, shall we go to find fish deposits now forming like the Cooper-slate of the Mansfield district, the Jurassic shales of Solenhofen, the calcareous marls of Oeningen on Lake Constance, the black slates of Glarus, or the shales of Monte Bolca? — to mention some cases from the continent of Europe more than usually famous in the literature for exquisitely preserved fishes, to say nothing of other fossils. Or we might mention the black Onondaga limestone of Ohio and Michigan; the Green River beds of Arizona; or the diatom beds of Lompoc, California, as a few examples from America of strata packed full of splendidly preserved fishes.

"Buckland, in speaking of the fossil fish of Monte Bolca, which may be taken as typical of all the others, is quite positive that these fish must have 'perished suddenly,' by some tremendous catastrophe.

"The skeletons of these fish," he says, "lie parallel to the laminae of the strata of the calcareous slate; they are always entire, and so closely packed on one another that many individuals are often contained in a single block. . . . All these fish must have died suddenly on this fatal spot and have been speedily buried in the calcareous sediment then in course of deposition. From the fact that certain individuals have even preserved traces of color upon their skin, we are certain that they were entombed before decomposition of their soft parts had yet taken place.

"In many places in America as well as in Europe where these remains of fish are found, the shaley rock is so full of fish oil that it will burn almost like coal, while some scientists have even thought that the peculiar deposits like Albertite 'coal' and some cannel coals were formed from the distillation of the fish oil from the supersaturated rocks.

"De la Beche was also of the opinion that most of the fossils were buried suddenly and in an abnormal manner. 'A very large proportion of them,' he says, 'must have been entombed uninjured, and many alive, or, if not alive, at least before decomposition ensued.' In this, he is speaking not of the fishes alone, but of the fossiliferous deposits in general.

"There is found in all parts of the world a series of strata which used to be called the 'Old Red Sandstone,' now known as the Devonian. In this, almost everywhere we find it, the remains of whole shoals of fishes occur in such profusion and preservation that the 'period' is often known as the 'Age of Fishes.' Dr. David Page, after enumerating nearly a dozen genera, says:

" 'These fishes seem to have thronged the waters of the period, and their remains are often found in masses, as if they had been suddenly entombed in living shoals by the sediment which now contains them.'

"I beg leave to quote somewhat at length the picturesque language of Hugh Miller regarding these rocks as found in Scotland:

" 'The river bullhead, when attacked by an enemy, or immediately as it feels the hook in its jaws, erects its two spines at nearly right angles with the plates of the head, as if to render itself as difficult of being swallowed as possible. The attitude is one of danger and alarm; and it is a curious fact, to which I shall afterward have occasion to advert, that in this attitude nine tenths of the Pterichthyses of the Lower Old Red Sandstone are to be found. . . . It presents us, too, with a wonderful record of violent death falling at once, not on a few individuals, but on whole tribes. . . .

" 'At this period of our history, some terrible catastrophe involved in sudden destruction the fish of an area at least a hundred miles from boundary to boundary, perhaps much more. The same platform in Orkney as at Cromarty is strewed thick with remains which exhibit unequivocally the marks of violent death. The figures are contorted, contracted, curved, and the tail in many instances is bent round to the head; the spines stick out; the fins are spread to the full, as in fish that die in convulsions. . . . The record is one of destruction at once widely spread and total, so far as it extended. . . . By what quiet but potent agency of destruction were the innumerable existences of an area perhaps ten thousand square miles in extent annihilated at once, and yet the medium in which they had lived left undisturbed in its operations?

" 'Conjecture lacks footing in grappling with the enigma, and expatiates in uncertainty over all the known phenomena of death.'

"I will not taunt the uniformitarians by asking them to direct us to some modern analogies. But I would have the reader remember that these Devonian and other rocks are world-wide in extent.

"Surely Howorth is talking good science when he says that his masters, Sedgwick and Murchison, taught him 'That no plainer witness is to be found of any physical fact than that nature has at times worked with enormous energy and rapidity,' and 'that the rocky strata teem with evidence of violent and sudden dislocations on a great scale.'" [14]

The geological evidence thus far advanced is sufficiently convincing to any unbiased person that a universal flood as Moses describes is at least a most reasonable explanation for the phenomena observed, and only one who is prejudiced by obstinate and willful opposition to the Bible, or who lacks the moral courage to accept a view not in harmony with the accepted theories or popular beliefs, can be blind to them. But the very prevailing unbelief regarding the Scriptures on this point is a proof for the divine origin, for this very unbelief was foretold in the same Bible more than nineteen hundred years ago as due to become dominant in the "last days" of our age and to produce the very effects which we find it producing before our eyes today. (2 Peter 3.)

CHAPTER XIV

Fossils in Every Part of the World Evidence for a Universal Flood

ANOTHER and most convincing extra-Biblical evidence for a universal flood as described by Moses is the evidence found in the fossils. By *fossils* are meant the remains, or the cast, or form, of some organism, usually in petrified form. These fossils have been referred to repeatedly in the different parts of this study. They were known to the ancients, were known to the Church Fathers, to Luther, and to early American churchmen. They are found in every country and on all continents in Europe, America, Asia, Africa, and Australia. Fossils of all kinds of animal and plant life both of existing species and of many forms now extinct have been found. There are fossils of land and sea animals, of fish and of birds, of reptiles and of beautiful insects, of giant trees and delicate leaves and parts of plants. They are found in mountain areas, such as the Rockies, the Alps, the Himalayas, the mountains of Greece and Italy. They occur in great numbers on the plains and prairies of Nebraska, Kansas, Oklahoma, Texas, Wyoming, South Dakota, Utah, Idaho, Oregon, and Alberta, but they are also found in the Eastern States and the Eastern Provinces of Canada. They are found on the pampas of South

America and on the steppes of Russia, in Siberia and on the Sahara, on the Gobi Desert and in Greenland. In fact, they are found nearly everywhere. Sometimes they have been discovered in caves or in coal mines, in valleys or on mountaintops, near the surface or deep down in the earth, buried under fifty, sixty, one hundred, even thousands of feet of soil, clay, loess, gravel, sand, and hard stratified rock. In a boring at Oklahoma City a fossil shell was brought up from a depth of six thousand feet.[1]

Fossils are found as individual bones or parts of plant life or with other remains of animal and plant life scattered over a wide area in a given locality. Sometimes countless numbers are heaped together forming whole mountains or quarries of fossil remains. Almost daily new fossils are brought to light in every part of the world. They are discovered by accident as man continues to dig into the surface of the earth, or they are found by the professional fossil hunter, who has acquired a great skill in locating them. Museums and universities and scientific institutions spend huge sums to collect, mount, and classify them. The daily press eagerly brings to the attention of its readers any new discovery made in this field, often in the most extravagant headlines, as some of the following examples, selected at random from my own files, will show:

"Find Mastodon Skeleton, Monster Lived 30,000 Years Ago."

"Five Hundred Thousand Year Old Skull is Discovered in Utah."

"Patagonia Finds Bones of Monster, Each 9 Feet Long; Dinosaur Stood 140 Feet Long in His Stocking Feet."

"That Big Lizard Near Norman. Suppose that you were having a grand swim in some stream in Cleveland County in Oklahoma, and a reptile twelve feet long came swimming ominously towards you."

"Skull of Barosarus has been Found in Wyoming; Strange Creature Believed to have Lived 140,000,000 Years Ago."

"Find Remains of Ancient Forest 1,400 Feet Below Earth's Surface."

"Claims Animal Skull 90,000,000 Years Old."

"Prehistoric lizard found in Manitoba. Believe massive reptile to be 60,000,000 years old. The prehistoric reptile is said to be 60 feet long."

"Forerunner of Mammal. Discovery made in Gobi Desert 2,000,000 to 3,000,000 years older than the age of mammals."

"Monster Proves Colorado Once Under Water."

"Remains of an ancient forest, 1,400 feet below earth's surface, uncovered in oil drilling in California."

"Ancient Skull Discovered in South America. Fossilized Relic of Man Who Lived Millions of Years Ago."

In a previous chapter I called attention to a great deposit of hippopotamus bones found in caves in Sicily; to those great fossiliferous fissures in Gibraltar and other parts of Europe; and to the famous bone deposits of Agate Springs, Nebraska. But there are other famous fossil beds equally important.

At Field, B. C., in the Canadian Rockies, enormous beds of fossil trilobites, an extinct species of the Crustacean family, was discovered. These strange little sea creatures were entombed in enormous numbers. Carloads of them have been removed to the many geological laboratories and museums of the country. Some sudden catastrophe destroyed and buried them at the same time. The material that covered them solidified, and there, enclosed in a solid rock at the very peak of this great mountain range, they have been preserved for us.

Near Lake Onlar the remains of an elephant were found at a depth of sixty feet and buried there with fresh-water and land shells in an unbroken and undisturbed stratum. At other places they are found among large boulders, great beds of gravel, or underneath enormous masses of loess deposits.

212

Near Montreal, Canada, far inland from the ocean and above Lake Champlain, seals have been found several hundred feet above the present sea level.

Remains of several species of elephants are found in all parts of the United States and Canada, from Alaska to the Atlantic and southward to the plains of Mexico. One of these species is said to have attained a height of thirteen feet, six inches. Specimens are found in all the great museums of this country. Fossils of horses from the size of the smallest pony to the modern draft horse, of camels, llamas, of the saber-tooth tiger, of a sloth as large as an elephant, and of the giant boar, as large as a black bear, have been found in different places on the American continent.

The Canadian geologist A. P. Coleman gives a vivid description of the animal life as it once existed in the present state of Iowa. He writes:

"With herds of wild horses, camels, and buffaloes on its prairies, trumpeting elephants of several sorts and sizes in the woods, and the Mylodon and Megalonyx toppling down saplings to feed on their leaves, conditions must have been decidedly interesting in the now peaceful state of Iowa. If paleolithic man then inhabited America, he had game quite worthy of his weapons. Probably, as in Europe, hares or bisons would often fall to his arrows or elephants to his javelins. . . . More than three fourths of the mammals have since become extinct, but nearly all plants and the shellfish, as far as the species have been determined, still survive." [2]

What is true of North America, Europe, and Asia also appears true in South America. According to Howorth, the diluvial deposits containing the fossiliferous remains of animals of various kinds are found in Bolivia, on the plateau, on the great pampas, west of the great mountain range in Peru and Chile, from Caracas on the north to Patagonia in the south. In Argentina they are found close to the sea level, while in Bolivia they are found 12,000 feet above the ocean. Prominent among the fossils found are those of the mastodon, a giant armadillo, the horse, the Megatherium, glyptodon, and other species. And as in North America, so in South America the mastodon appears to have had a geographical range over nearly the whole continent. And not only are fossils of these animals found in every part of that great body of land, but the conditions in which they are found are similar or the same as those in North America, Europe, Asia, or elsewhere. Bones are found in great heaps or individually; they are found on slopes or on plains; they are found near rivers; or they are found far removed from any body of water or swamp, without signs of gnawing or rotting. In fact, the remains that are found indicate that parts of South America, at least at one time, were inhabited by a rich mammalian fauna of which many genera have disappeared entirely.

As to the cause of death of these myriads of animals, the great naturalist Darwin has the following to say: "It is impossible to reflect on the changed state of the American continent without the deepest astonishment. Formerly it must have swarmed with great monsters; now we find mere pigmies compared with the antecedent allied races. The greater number, if not all of these extinct quadrupeds lived at a period and were the contemporaries of the existing sea shells. Since they lived, no very great changes in the form of the land can have taken place. What, then, has exterminated so many species and whole genera? The mind at first is irresistibly hurried into the belief of some great catastrophe; but thus to destroy animals, both large and small, in Southern Patagonia, in Brazil, on the Cordillera of Peru, in North America, and up to Bering Strait, we must shake the entire framework of the globe." [8]

Darwin, though hesitating to accept a theory of a great world catastrophe, has no satisfactory solution. But his distinguished successor d'Orbigny has the courage to draw the inescapable conclusion when he writes: "I argue that this destruction was caused by an invasion of the continent by water, a view which is completely *en rapport* with the facts presented by the great Pampian deposit, which was clearly laid down by water. How otherwise can we account for this complete destruction and the homogeneousness of the Pampas deposits containing bones? I find an evident proof of this in the immense number of bones and of entire animals whose numbers are greatest at the outlets of the valleys, as Mr. Darwin shows. . . . This proves that the animals were floated and hence were chiefly carried to the coast." [4]

And again he says: "This hypothesis necessitates that the Pampas mud was deposited suddenly as the result of violent floods of water, which carried off the soil and other superficial debris and mingled them together. This homogeneousness of the soil in all parts of the Pampas, even in places 200 leagues apart, is very remarkable." [5]

In summing up the results of his studies in South American geology, d'Orbigny says that "it is to the sudden rise of the Cordilleras that he attributes the sudden movement of the sea, which invaded all at once the continent, carried off and overwhelmed the mastodons which inhabited the eastern flanks of the Bolivian Cordillera, the Megatherium, the Megalonyx, and the multitude of animals daily being discovered in the caverns and the fissures of the mountains of Brazil — all the species, in fact, which are extinct." [6]

Even in far-off Australia, New Zealand, Tasmania, and the neighboring islands is found the same evidence of an all-destructive catastrophe which we have found elsewhere. The fossils found are numerous and varied in kind. The most interesting are the remains of the moa, an enormous wingless bird, similar to the ostrich but larger in size. Remains of this bird have been found in isolated spots at places 150 and 200 feet below the surface in beds of gravel and boulders, or they have been found in great caves where the remains of hundreds or thousands of these gigantic birds are heaped together in a confused mass. The occurrence of these masses of bones consisting of so many species of different habits, lying together with their bones intact, unrotted, and unbroken, suggests the same conclusion which has already forced itself upon us elsewhere. It is evident that these birds were driven together to high ground by rising water and finally perished and were buried there under masses of clay, gravel, and other debris. No other cause can offer a satisfactory explanation.

Another type of fossils that might be mentioned here are the petrified forests found in many parts of the earth. Examples of such are celebrated fossil forests near Cairo, Egypt, the huge prostrate trunks in the Napa Valley, California, and the widely known Petrified Forest of Arizona. But probably even more remarkable than any other fossil forest are the petrified forests found in the Yellowstone National Park area.[7] Though the process of petrification is not fully understood, it seems to depend on, or at least is greatly facilitated by, the presence of volcanic and hydrochemical activity. This seems to apply at least to the Yellowstone fossil forest. But whatever the cause may be, the circumstances and conditions under which these rocky trees are found point to an upheaval of the earth's crust so great that only a catastrophe like the Flood would be adequate to bring it about.

Mr. Knowlton observes that in the fossils found in Arizona, for example, the fossilized tree trunks are scattered over many square miles of what is now almost desert. All the trunks show evidence of having been transported from distant parts before they were turned to stone. Most of them are not even in the position in which they were originally entombed, but have been eroded from slightly higher horizons and have rolled in the greatest profusion to lowlands. The appearance this presents is not unlike a so-called log drift that was left stranded by the receding waters.[7]

The Yellowstone Park district has large areas of petrified forests. One such area just outside the park covers about 35,000 acres. One of the largest petrified trunks found there is that of a redwood, still measuring ten feet in diameter. The matrix in which these trees are entombed consists of ashes, mud flows, and breccia, not all of equal texture as to hardness, all of which seems to point to volcanic activity and the action of water.

About 150 kinds of fossils of other plants and remains of trees have been found in the same beds with these fossil trees. Among them are many kinds of ferns, the horsetails, smilax, a broad-leaved bananalike plant, hickory nuts, chestnuts, figs, magnolias, laurels, cinnamon, sycamore, grapes, persimmon, ash, and many others, most of which no longer grow in that latitude or at the present altitude. The destructive agents here seem definitely to point to volcanic activity and water, and both of these great cosmic forces were active in the Flood, as we have seen above.

When gold diggers by the thousands swarmed to the Klondike and Nome, they found the ground frozen to a depth of one hundred feet or more and had to build fires or use steam to thaw their way down. But the gold-bearing gravel was laid down under milder conditions, as is evident from the fossil remains found there fifty and over one hundred and more feet below the surface. Bones of mammals, such as the bison, mammoth, elk, moose, buffalo, horse, caribou, and muskox, have been found in the gravel and in the bottom of the muck, but not in the upper parts. The American Museum of Natural History reported finding mammoth remains with parts of the flesh covered with long black hair still intact and together with them the skull of a lion, similar to the lion now found in Africa.[8]

During the early Klondike days it was not unusual for a miner's pick to strike the skull of a broad-horned bison or of a mammoth, and great tusks were dug up and carved into ivory ornaments and sold in the shops of Dawson City.

Fossil Grape Vine Leaves Found Near Coulee City, Washington

Fossil Leaves of Sassafras

Fossil Dragon Fly

The fossil skeletons of prehistoric reptiles are well known to everyone. Modern oil companies and filling stations have helped to popularize their names. The remains of these ancient monsters have been found on every continent. In America they occur on both sides of the Rocky Mountains for a distance of two thousand miles north and south. They have also been found in East Africa, in the Gobi Desert of Asia, in South America, Madagascar, Australia, New Zealand, and Europe. The best hunting grounds so far discovered are still to be found in Wyoming, Utah, Montana, South Dakota, and Alberta. From the evidence available it seems safe to conclude that in some parts of this continent these grotesque dragonlike creatures were as numerous as the hardy buffaloes on the Western prairie were a few generations ago, but with much more variety of form and species. In point of size they range from the size of a small dog to a monster of over eighty feet in length. Recently a specimen was found in Patagonia, according to press reports, whose length has been estimated at 140 feet. Their habits of life were equally varied. Some were herbivorous, some carnivorous; some flew in the air, others had their abode in the sea, and still others stalked about on the land; some walked on their hind feet alone, some on all fours.

Of the marine reptiles the ichthyosaurs and the plesiosaurs are well-known representatives of the larger species. The ichthyosaur was a sea dragon with a long sharp snout, its jaws armed with sharp teeth, which were set in continuous grooves and not in sockets. It had a short fishlike neck, a large fishlike tail. Remains of the ichthyosaur have been found in great numbers in England and Germany, especially in southern Germany, where hundreds and thousands of these fossils have been taken from the slate quarries of Wuerttemberg. The beds in which they occur are usually strongly bituminous or impregnated with oil; and many huge ammonite shells are found along with them, some of them measuring five and six feet in diameter.

The plesiosaurs, another group of marine reptiles, had a long slender neck and a fairly large body with huge paddles and a tail in proportion to its neck, tapering to a point. One writer describes them as turtles threaded with serpents.

Morosaurs and Tylosaurs are other giant members of this group. Their remains have been found in the chalk bluffs of western Kansas.

But monsters even greater and more ferocious than these once inhabited the mysterious antediluvian seas. One of these was Zeuglodon, or yoketooth. This creature might be described as a cross between a serpent and a whale. In life Zeuglodon was between fifty and seventy feet in length and not more than six or eight feet through the deepest part of its body. The head was small and pointed, the jaws well armed with grasping and cutting teeth. Zeuglodon must have been very numerous in the region now occupied by the Southern States adjacent to the Gulf of Mexico and in southern Europe. At least here his petrified remains are found in great abundance. But Megalodon, the giant shark, must have surpassed even Zeuglodon in size and ferociousness. The length of this fearful sea monster is estimated at seventy to one hundred feet and even one hundred and twenty feet. Its gaping jaws were like a horrible cavern, measuring not less than six feet across, large enough to swallow a small-sized whale.

Possibly the best known of all these ancient reptiles is that large group called dinosaurs. The first dinosaur remains found in America were discovered in 1818 in the Connecticut Valley. Since then their fossils have been found in all parts of the world, in North America in many localities, among the foothills of the Rocky Mountains from Alberta to New Mexico and Texas, with similar beds in the Black Hills in South Dakota and in western Colorado.

To judge by the number of fossils found, the dinosaurs must have roamed in great numbers through the forests and

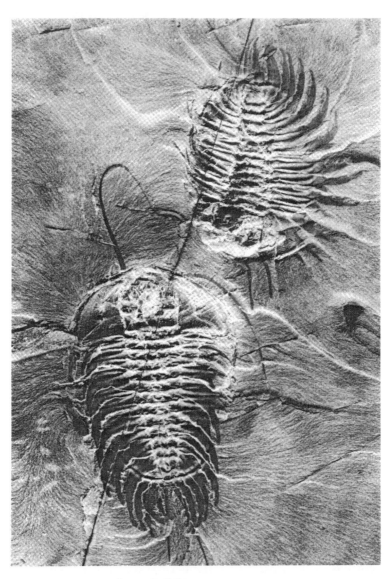

Impressions of Cambrian Trilobites

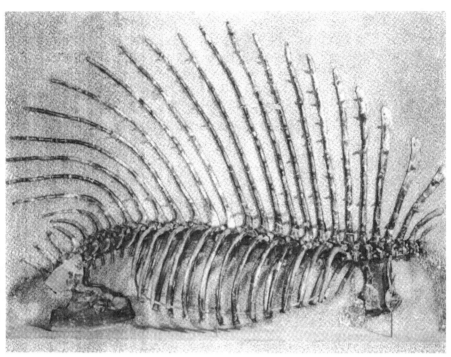

Skeleton of a Finn-Backed Lizard called *Morosaurus Claviger*. Restoration by Osborn and Knight. Collected by Charles Sternberg in Baylor County, Texas. Specimen in American Museum of Natural History

plains of the antediluvian world, particularly here in America. The richest discoveries of the remains of this creature have been made along the Red Deer River in Alberta and in the badlands of our own Western States. They were divided into many separate species and families. Some were herbivorous, others carnivorous. Some lived on land, others in water. Some walked upright, and others crawled about on all fours like the modern crocodile. Still others were equipped with wings and must have looked like flying dragons.

The smallest of the dinosaurs known to us today were little larger than chickens; the largest were monsters of such gigantic size that there is no living thing in the world today, unless it be the whale, that can be compared with them. They were giants not only of their day, but of all time. Our largest elephant today would appear quite insignificant in their presence.

The Brontosaurus, or thunder lizard, measured from forty to seventy feet in length and ten to fourteen feet in height. Their thighbones were five to six feet long. Some of the vertebrae were four and one-half feet high, exceeding even the dimensions of the whale.

This group included Diplodocus and Morosaurus. They were distinguished by a large, though rather short, body, very long neck and tail, and, for the size of the animal, a very small head. Everyone has seen pictures of these monsters on the signboards of a well-known chain of filling stations.

An elephant weighing five tons requires about one hundred pounds of hay and twenty-five pounds of grain for his daily ration. The quantities of food these monsters required must have been enormous. Only a world such as the antediluvian world could have sustained them.

The specimen of Diplodocus in the Carnegie Museum in Pittsburgh is eighty-seven feet in length, and its weight during lifetime is estimated at about forty tons.

224

It is believed that these animals were largely aquatic in their habits and fed on some species of water plants. The long neck would be a distinct advantage to them in feeding on the vegetation of shallow lakes, while their bodies were submerged in the water. Besides that, their long necks would also serve them to scan the surrounding horizon for the approach of an enemy.

Triceratops was another of these antediluvian monsters of the reptile family. He must have been a fearful-looking brute, with three formidable horns on his face and an enormous plated skull which projected backwards over the neck like a fireman's helmet. Over each eye was a massive horn directed forward; a third, but smaller than the others, was perched on his nose. In size Triceratops was second only to Tyrannosaurus, measuring upwards of twenty-five feet in length. His legs were short and massive, resembling those of the hippopotamus. He was invulnerable from a frontal attack, a sort of living, antediluvian army tank. No doubt he was undisputed ruler of his domain, wherever he chose to make his habitat. Fine specimens of these monsters are found in the Royal Museum of Ontario in Toronto, Canada, and in the American Museum of Natural History in New York, and elsewhere.

A close relative of Triceratops was Trachodon. He was not so large as the former, but still of goodly proportion, about twelve feet high as he stalked about on his hind legs. He is also called the Duckbill Dinosaur because of the shape of his head. Trachodon seems to have had a very wide distribution in North America. Many well-preserved specimens have been discovered in various parts of the continent. It is believed that at one time he must have been as numerous in this country as the deer is today.

The counterpart of Trachodon in Europe is called Iguanodon. Twenty-nine specimens of Iguanodon were found in one coal mine in Belgium, 750 feet below the surface.

Among the most bizarre of the dinosaurs were the Stegosaurians, or plated lizards. They were moderately large in size, measuring twenty feet and upward in length. Their natural habitat seems to have been the dry upland away from any body of water. They were vegetarians in diet. They had an exceptionally small head compared with their body. Hence it is believed that they were the most stupid among the stupid reptiles. Their body was protected with heavy armor consisting of a double row of alternating large bony plates running along the back from head to tail. The largest of these plates were two feet thick at the base, tapering down to one inch at the outer edge. The tail was about eight to ten feet long, armed with two heavy spikes measuring eight and nine inches to two feet in length. This must have been a powerful weapon for defense or attack.

Pterodactyl was a flying reptile. It has been aptly called "the flying dragon of the air." Few specimens have been found in America, but it seems to have been very numerous in Central Europe. The pterodactyls varied in size almost as much as the land reptiles. Some were as large as the albatross and others as small as the sparrow. They seem to have been very light despite their great size.

The American representative of this family is called Pteranodon, or Ornithostoma. It was larger than his European cousin, reaching a spread of wings from eighteen to twenty-five feet. It was the largest flying creature in the world and must have appeared like a small airplane when in the sky. What a sight it must have been when a flock of these landed at one place! The fossil remains of this strange creature have been found in greatest number in the State of Kansas.

The recognized king of the reptiles was Tyrannosaurus. He seems to have been the fiercest and most formidable of them all. He walked on his two hind legs, balanced by his huge tail. He measured forty-seven feet in length and stood eighteen to twenty feet high. His enormous jaw was armed

Brontosaurus, the Thunder Reptile. Specimen in American Museum of Natural History. Was found in Wyoming. Sixty feet long, fifteen feet high. Weight, when alive, 30 to 35 tons. The preparation of this specimen required six years of work

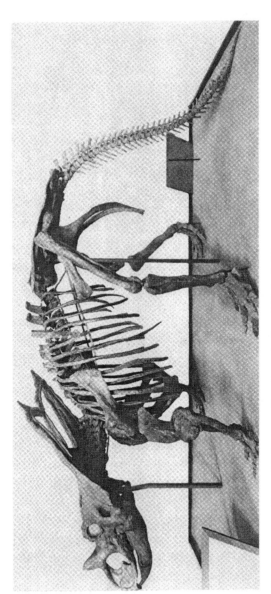

Ceratosaurus – Horned Dinosaur. Specimen in Royal Ontario Museum

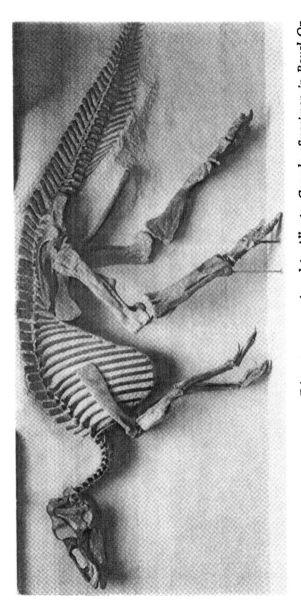

Edmontonsaurus, found in Alberta, Canada. Specimen in Royal Ontario Museum

Badlands Topography of Red Deer Valley, Alberta, Canada, the Great Western Canadian Graveyard of Dinosaurs

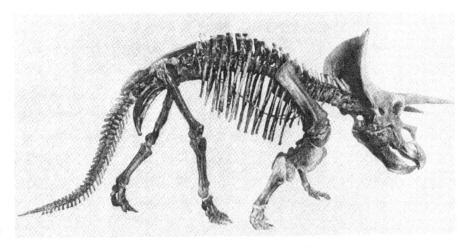

Horned Dinosaur Triceratops as Reconstructed by Charles R. Knight. The specimen in the American Museum of Natural History in New York was found in Montana. Length 24 feet; height 7 feet, 9 inches; weight, when alive, about nine or ten tons, twice the weight of an average Indian elephant

The King of Reptiles — Tyrannosaurus Rex. Specimen in American Museum of Natural History in New York. Found in Montana; 47 feet long; 18 feet, 6 inches high, as shown on picture

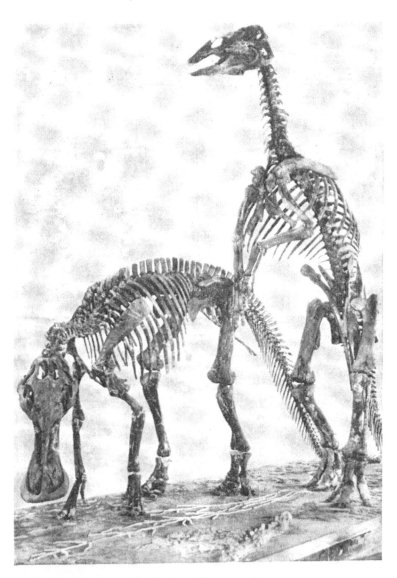

Duck-Billed Dinosaur Trachodon. These specimens are in the American Museum of Natural
History. Found in Montana and South Dakota;
33 feet long; 17 feet, 6 inches high. One of
the most abundant dinosaurs in America

with double-edged teeth three to six inches long. He was a flesh-eating monster and therefore must have been the terror of all his contemporaries.

Such are some of the strange creatures that once inhabited the earth and were found here in America from the Connecticut Valley and the East to the Rocky Mountains and the far Northwest. They were wiped off the face of the earth, and their kind is unknown in the world today except in fossil form. The impoverished world after the flood would not have been able to sustain them, and probably it is fortunate for man and the rest of the animals that they have disappeared.

Some years ago Bert Leston Taylor published the following lines on the dinosaur in his *Chicago Tribune* column:

THE MIGHTY DINOSAUR

Behold the mighty dinosaur,
Famous in prehistoric lore
Not only for his weight and length,
But for his intellectual strength.
You will observe by these remains
The creature had two sets of brains.
One in his head (the usual place),
The other at his spinal base.
Thus he could reason a priori
As well as a posteriori.
No problem bothered him a bit
He made both head and tail of it.
So wise was he, so wise and solemn,
Each thought filled just a spinal column.
If one brain found the pressure strong,
It passed a few ideas along.
If something slipped his forward mind,
'Twas rescued by the one behind.
And if in error he was caught,
He had a saving afterthought.
As he thought twice before he spoke,
He had no judgment to revoke.
For he could think without congestion
Upon both sides of every question.
Oh, gaze upon this wondrous beast
Defunct ten thousand years at least!

Dr. Allen, professor of geology at the University of Alberta, in speaking of the fossil beds along the Red Deer River, once made this observation in his classroom lecture: "These reptiles, whose fossil remains are found in such great abundance along the Red Deer, seem to have been driven together by a common danger and to have perished in the same great catastrophe." And Dr. W. D. Matthew, who is quoted by Price, makes this statement: "The cutting off of this great Dinosaur dynasty was nearly, if not quite, simultaneous the world over." [9] And Professor Lull is quoted as saying in reference to the dinosaurs: "The most inexplicable of events is the dramatic extinction of this mighty race." [10]

How these animals became extinct, why they perished simultaneously over the entire face of the earth, and how they were massed together in huge reptilian cemeteries are inexplicable mysteries indeed. However, a sane and reasonable solution of this mystery is to be found in the universal flood catastrophe as described by Moses. Only water could at the same time destroy and bury them on so wide a scale.

Charles H. Sternberg, a pioneer fossil hunter in Kansas, Texas, Wyoming, and other Western States, wrote an interesting account of his experiences as fossil hunter. In the closing chapter of his book entitled *Life of a Fossil Hunter* (pp. 269—70), Mr. Sternberg says: "How rich are the strata that compose the earth's crust only a fossil hunter can fully realize. Take, for instance, western Kansas, where the soil beneath our feet is one vast cemetery. I know of a ravine in Logan County which cuts through four great formations. The lower levels, of reddish and blue chalk, are filled with the remains of swimming lizards, with the wonderful Pteranodons, the most perfect flying machines ever known, with the toothed bird *Hesperornis*, the royal bird of the west, and the fishbird Ichthyornis, with fish-like biconcave vertebrae, with fishes, small and great (one form over sixteen feet long), and huge sea tortoises. Above are the black shales of the Fort Pierre Cretaceous, thousands of feet of which are exposed in the bad lands of the upper Missouri. In this formation the dinosaurs reign supreme. Still higher are the mortar beds of the Loup Fork Tertiary, where the dominant type changes from reptiles to mammals. Here, in western Kansas, are found great numbers of the short-limbed rhinoceros, the large land-turtle, *Testudo orthopygia*, several inferior tusked mastodons, the saber-toothed tiger, the three-toed horse, and a deer only about eighteen inches high. Higher still, where the grass roots shoot down to feed on the bones, are the Columbian mammoth, the one-toed horse, like our species of today, a camel, like our South American llama, and a bison far larger than the present species."

Discussing the catastrophic destruction of animal life on so vast a scale as evidenced by the "largest bone bed in Kansas," Sternberg writes (p. 131 ff.): "It has always been a problem to account for the number of the animals repre-sented here and for the fact that the bones are so scattered. All parts of the skeletons are mingled in the greatest confu-sion, with no two bones in a natural position. One is of course forced, after an observation of this country, to agree with Drs. Matthew and Hatcher that these bones were de-posited in the flood-plain of a running stream and not in great lakes as was believed by older geologists. But the only sup-position upon which I can account for the intermingling of all the bones of the skeletons on the bottom sandstone layer is that the fine sand through which the bones were distrib-uted, becoming saturated with water, was converted into a quicksand, in which the bones sank until they reached the impenetrable layer below; the heavier bones of course being at the bottom.

"What caused the death of the countless individuals in the Sternberg Quarry, is a question not easily answered. The authorities quoted above believe that during the Upper Miocene Period there were many water-courses separated by slightly elevated divides and broad flood-plains, with possibly here and there small lakes, where the dense vegetation had clogged some sluggish stream. But during a rainy season of unusual duration, the whole region for many miles must have been converted into a series of lakes; and all the animals in the vicinity, after having gathered at the highest points they could find to escape death, must have been finally overwhelmed by some great flood that covered every inch of ground. Then after maceration took place, the bones might have been scattered by other floods." The point to be observed here is that the authorities quoted seem to agree that water was the agent for both the destruction and the burial of these animals.

The great bone deposit at Agate Springs in northwestern Nebraska has already been referred to. Specimens from this deposit are found in all the larger museums of the country. What else but a catastrophe like the Great Flood could have brought together on one spot such an aggregate of animal remains as found there? Either this spot was a high elevation of land in the antediluvian world, to which the terrified animals of the surrounding country took refuge when the waters of the Flood rose higher and higher, or their floating carcasses were carried together by the Flood waters and deposited on this hill when the Flood subsided.

Nor must we overlook the remarkable fact that marine fossils are found on mountaintops hundreds of miles inland from any sea, as in the Canadian Rockies, or buried beneath hundreds of feet of clay, sand, gravel, and other debris. A. P. Coleman, reporting on the evidence of glaciers in East Canada, found marine fossils in the regions of Quebec, Montreal, Ottawa, in the Maritime Provinces, and in Newfoundland. Marine fossils were found underneath boulder clay below Quebec in 1925. Since then similar fossils have been found in many places in Quebec, eastern Canada, and the State of New York. Marine shells were found 340 feet above sea level near the junction of the St. Lawrence and the Champlain Valley. On Ottawa Bay marine shells have been found 510 feet above sea level. Shellfish, crustaceans, sometimes containing well-preserved specimens of the capelin, a silvery little sea fish; and other small species, among them a pair of young seal, were found.

Thus we might continue our discussion on fossils. What wonders of a strange but perished world the fossils reveal! But as we examine them, whether they be found in America, Europe, Asia, or Australia, or any other place on the face of the earth, they all tell one and the same story, and that is a sudden, wholesale destruction followed by an immediate burial. Only one force known to man is capable of accomplishing that, and that force is water. Hence we conclude that the fossils found in every part of the world constitute convincing evidence for the Biblical Flood.

CHAPTER XV

The Mammoth and the Flood

THE most remarkable remains of prehistoric animal life yet recovered are those of the mammoth, found in the frozen tundras of northern Siberia. The mammoth is a member of the elephant family, but was covered with long, coarse hair and was much larger in size. The term *mammoth* is believed to have been derived from the Biblical *behemoth* and was first used by Arabian traders who penetrated far into Russia as early as the tenth and eleventh centuries and traded with the natives in ivory, which was found in the northern part of the country in great quantities. One account says that there had been found a tooth two palms in width and four in length and a skull resembling an Arab hut. Ancient Greek legends and poetry speaks of griffins, strange mythological creatures, with birdlike claws, guarding the gold found north of the Black Sea and in the Ural regions. The bones which those early prospectors found and interpreted to be the claws of a huge birdlike monster no doubt were the tusks of the mammoth, since then found in that region and farther north in such enormous quantities. To ascribe these bones and tusks to monster dragons may have been prompted by more than mere superstition. Tales of ferocious creatures guarding the precious metal against every intruder would keep away the greedy gold stealer and thus leave the mines as a most profitable monopoly in the hands of a few.

The early natives of Siberia were familiar with the bones and tusks of the mammoth. They considered them to be the remains of a giant mole that lived under ground and died as soon as his body was exposed to the light of the sun or the moon. Hence they had a great superstitious fear for this strange monster.

The Jesuit traveler Avril, who traversed Siberia about 1685, says: "The Russians have discovered a sort of ivory which is whiter and smoother than that which comes from India. Not," he says quaintly, "that they have any elephants that furnish them with this commodity, but other amphibious animals which they call by the name of Behemot, which are usually found in the river Lena or on the shores of the Tartarian Sea. . . . Nor are elephants' teeth comparable to them either for beauty or whiteness; besides that, they have a peculiar property to staunch blood, being carried about a person subject to bleeding. The Persians and Turks, who buy them up, put a high value on them and prefer a scimitar or a dagger haft of this precious ivory before a handle of massy gold or silver." And again he says: "Nobody better understands the value of this ivory than they who first brought it into request, considering how they venture their lives in attacking the creature that produces it, which is as big and as dangerous as a crocodile." [1]

Contemporaneous with the mammoth in those northern regions of Siberia were the woolly rhinoceros, the ox, the hare, the sheep, and other animals, some of which are now wholly extinct, while others continue to exist in modern representation. Of these animals the remains of the mammoth are by far the most common. The tusks of the mammoth are found in such enormous quantities that whole islands seem to have been formed by them. A regular trade in this fossil ivory has been carried on for centuries, some of it finding its way eastward to China, some of it westward to Petrograd and to western Europe. The best preserved specimens have been found along the banks of the Ob, Yenisei, the Lena, and their tributaries, where these rivers in flood stage occasionally expose a carcass which has been lying in cold storage underground for uncounted centuries. Where thus exposed, the flesh of these antediluvian giants has been greedily devoured by dogs, wolves, and other carnivorous animals, all of which sounds utterly incredible. However, the facts are well attested. Less perfectly preserved specimens have also been discovered in the frozen soil of northwestern Alaska.

The Siberian mammoth was a member of the elephant family, but must not be confused with the mastodon, another extinct species of this group. The mammoth, when full grown, stood twelve to thirteen feet high at the shoulders. He was covered with a thick coat of long, coarse, black hair. His ears were smaller than those of the modern elephant, his tail was short, and his eyes small. Next to his skin, beneath the hair, was a coat of soft reddish-brown wool. He was armed with a pair of formidable tusks, jutting from his jaws and measuring from nine to ten feet in length along the outer circle and two and a half feet around the base, weighing 180 to 200 pounds apiece. The tusks of the average African elephant today are said to weigh about forty to fifty pounds. On this continent the mammoth roamed between Washington, D. C., and Alaska, and nearly all of Europe seems to have been his habitat. Mammoths used to range freely between Germany and Britain, for there were no Straits of Dover in their day, and the North Sea was a fertile alluvial plain. Quantities of mammoth teeth have been brought up in nets of trawlers, especially off the Norfolk coast. The remains of other animals frequently found together with those of the mammoth are the bones of the woolly rhinoceros, the hyena, the giant stag, and others. Charles Sternberg, on his expedition to the Oregon desert, discovered a mammoth skull on the shores of Silver Lake, and with it he found the bones of the heron, the coot, the swan, the goose, the duck, the grouse, the eagle, the great horned owl, the blackbird, the raven, the flamingo, the llama, the horse, the dog, the otter, the beaver, and the mouse.

It must be noted, however, that contemporaneous with the mammoth there is found another species of the elephant family. Some of the remains have been classified as belonging to the mammoth, but may represent the remains of another species. Whatever the truth may be, the general results will not be changed. The fact remains that one or more now extinct species of elephants roamed over a very large territory now no longer inhabited by any and that contemporaneously with them lived other animals now also extinct.

Though the mammoth or his first cousin lived in all parts of America and Europe, the remains of these ancient monsters are most abundant in northern Siberia, as already indicated. About fifty years ago Sir Henry Howorth published a most fascinating book on the mammoth and his sudden disappearance. The title of the book is *The Mammoth and the Flood,* and it aims to prove that "a very great cataclysm and catastrophe occurred . . . by which that animal, with its companions, was overwhelmed over a very large part of the earth's surface. Secondly, that this catastrophe involved a widespread flood of waters which not only killed the animals, but also buried them under continuous beds of loam or gravel. Thirdly, that the same catastrophe was accompanied by a very great and sudden change of climate in Siberia, by which the animals which had previously lived in fairly temperate conditions were frozen in their flesh under the ground and have remained frozen ever since." [2]

"There is perhaps no inquiry," writes Howorth, "in the whole range of Natural History more fascinating or romantic than that which deals with the mammoth and its surroundings. Even children and unsophisticated people have their imagination stirred when they read how in the dreary and

241

inhospitable wastes of northern Siberia, where neither tree nor shrub will grow, where the land for hundreds of miles is covered with damp moss barely sprinkled for two months with a few gay flowers, and during the rest of the year is locked in ice and snow, and where only the hardiest polar animals . . . can live, there are found below the ground huge hoards of bones of elephants and other great beasts like the horse, buffaloes, oxen, and sheep whose appetites needed corresponding supplies of food. But our interest rises to the highest pitch when we are told that this vast cemetery not only teems with fresh bones and beautiful ivory tusks, but with the carcasses and mummies of the great animals so well preserved in the perpetually frozen soil that the bears and wolves can feed upon them. . . .

"Siberia is a vast territory having a coast line bordering on the Arctic Ocean of over two thousand miles, and having rivers that are equally that long. The whole country is a plain, as level in general as the Dakotas and Montana. With the exception of a few hillocks, practically the only ir-regularities are those caused by the great rivers which wind their way through the broad expanses. As is the vast plain of America's West, so is the immense level waste of Siberia stratified. The strata beneath the surface of Siberia are com-posed chiefly of sand, which would be sandstone if it were somewhat more consolidate than it is. In some places the sand is mixed with layers of clay, and also of gravel. The sands and clays are usually light colored, but sometimes they are browned or blackened by the various forms of vegetation which have been buried in them. On account of the continual cold in Siberia the year around, its strata remain perpetually frozen to an enormous depth, only a few feet of soil on the top thawing out for a few weeks in summer. While the sandy and clayey strata, when dug into, seem dry, they are in fact very moist, the moisture not being apparent because the ground is so hardly frozen. And through the strata of this vast territory, from Bering Strait to European Russia, the remains of many kinds of quadrupeds are so abundantly buried as to astonish everyone who becomes acquainted with the facts."

Starting with the islands in the Arctic Ocean along the coast north of Siberia, Howorth says that every one of them contains in its strata abundant animal remains. There is a group of islands off the coast, in the Arctic Ocean, called New Siberia. Concerning one of these, the Island of Lachov, a small island about fifty miles square, Howorth said its soil is "almost composed of fossil bones." The same is true of another of these islands called Kotelni, which is over a hundred miles long and fifty miles wide. Howorth quotes a visitor to this island named Hedenstrom, who said that so plentifully were elephants buried beneath its surface that, as he walked along on the island for half a mile, he counted ten elephant tusks sticking out of the ground. This general condition existed throughout the whole island. Besides the fossils of elephant, skulls and bones of rhinoceros, horse, bison, ox, and sheep were observed scattered over and imbedded in the earth of the island. Concerning still another island in this group, Howorth quotes Hedenstrom to this effect: "In one island is a lake with a high bank, which splits open in the summer when the sun melts the ice and discloses heaps of tusks, mammoth bones, bones of rhinoceroses and buffaloes. In other parts of the island bones and tusks are to be seen projecting from the ground."

Hundreds of miles to the eastward of the islands called New Siberia is another group called Bear Islands. Here the same condition of abundant fossil remains exists.

Ferdinand Petrovitch von Wrangel, a Russian explorer, was Howorth's authority for saying: "The soil of Bear Island consists only of sand and ice, with such quantity of mammoth bones that they seem to form the chief substance of the island." Found with the bones of the mammoth were also many bones of the bison.

"The sea off the north coast of Siberia, and about the islands, is very shallow, especially the mudbanks barely protruding above the surface of the sea." Whenever there is a storm, says Howorth, fresh supplies of bones are left exposed on these mudbanks. This fact indicates that the strata forming the bottom of the sea off the coast of Siberia is also full of fossils.

"Turning from the islands to the mainland of Siberia, we found the same situation to exist, no matter where we went. The whole coast line has elephant remains embedded in the strata of the shore. The Arctic coast of Siberia is covered nearly all the year round with ice cliffs caused by the freezing of the ocean spray, but wherever the actual shore is exposed beneath the ice cliffs, bones are seen to be plentifully embedded in the earth. Thus the fossiliferous conditions continue as one works his way inland from the ocean into the vast level interior of Siberia."

Siberia being generally level, it is, as a rule, only where the rivers have cut their way through the plain, thus exposing the interior of the earth, that what is hidden there has been discovered. But without exception wherever these rivers are, bones of elephants, rhinoceroses, horses, cattle, sheep, and other quadrupeds are found to be entombed in enormous quantities.

The largest river of Siberia flowing into the Arctic Ocean nearest to European Russia is called the Ob. This river has cut its way through the foothills east of the low Ural Mountains, and in the strata of these foothills everywhere fossil elephants are found in great abundance. The next great river of Siberia emptying into the Arctic to the east of the Ob is the Yenisei. Concerning the buried animals revealed in the strata along the sides of this river, Howorth said: "Pallas tells us that the mammoth bones which fall out of the cliffs . . . are so numerous that on decomposing they form a substance called 'osteocolli' (i. e., bone glue)." The next great river eastward toward Alaska is the Lena. It is

244

a vast stream which twists and turns to make a course of over two thousand miles. The natives who live in the region of the Lena River make a living traveling up and down that river in boats, gathering up the ivory tusks that they see sticking out of the cliffs on the sides of the river and which they find fallen to the edge of the water. This occupation is also followed by those who live along the other streams. The traveler Middendorf, said Howorth, traveled the river Yenisei in a small steamer in 1875 and reported that his boat carried a load of one hundred elephant tusks.

A branch of the Lena is the Vilyui. At the place where the Vilyui and the Lena meet, the bottoms and sides of the rivers are loaded with teeth and tusks of elephants, rhinoceroses, and other creatures which have been washed out of their banks and carried down to that point by the stream. Where the Lena empties into the Arctic, there, too, is found a large accumulation of mammoth bones.

To the eastward of the Lena are two smaller, but nevertheless large streams, emptying into the Arctic. These are named the Indigirka and the Kolyma. Where these two rivers have cut their banks, there is an abundance of bones exposed from their burial places in the strata. Between these rivers there have been discovered places having so many elephant remains that, says Howorth, "the ground might be said to consist entirely of mammoth bones."

"The great Siberian peninsula which almost touches Alaska is called Chukotski Peninsula. It is a high, level plain with enough irregularities, due to small streams and hillocks, to reveal the contents of the strata. All this vast peninsula, according to the same writer, is rich in fossil bones. So plentiful are the remains of animals that the natives use bones, which contain fatty matter, for fuel. Elephants and rhinoceroses form the bulk of the fossils of this region. Alaska, too, has long been known to be the burial ground of many large species. . . .

245

"Mammoths are also found in great abundance in the gravels of the Ural Mountains, in the caverns of the Altai, and elsewhere in Asia. South of Siberia, in the zone stretching from Armenia through Turkestan and China to Japan, in Asia Minor, and Syria, elephants' remains have occurred in sporadic localities. Siberia, where the mammoth has been found in greatest abundance, consists of two distinct zones, one a southern zone, occupied largely by forests and with a more or less broken and mountainous contour; and the other, a northern one, where forest will not grow and where the immense flat wastes are covered with moss and are known as tundras. Beyond these are small islands, in the Polar Sea, in which even more sterile conditions prevail. The remains of the mammoth and its companions occur abundantly in both zones. It is not possible that these animals could have lived under the conditions now prevailing in these regions. The winters in Siberia last ten months of the year. Summer does not begin until July, and winter again starts during the early part of August. From November to March the weather is especially severe. In January the cold registers 65° below zero. The larger portion of North Siberia is now a naked tundra on which nothing will grow, swept by terrible icy winds and covered with moss, sprinkled with a few humble flowers. On such feeding ground it is physically impossible, as has been said, that elephants and rhinoceroses could have existed."

It has been suggested that these animals drifted down the river and that they had their habitat somewhere south in warmer climates, but this is quite obviously impossible. How could these prehistoric remains, or still more, how could entire carcasses of huge animals float down such rocky rivers as the Yenisei for hundreds of miles and retain not only their flesh, but their long hair intact? The remains are found not only on the banks of these long rivers and in the deltas which they form, but perhaps even more abundantly on the very short rivers which fall into the Arctic Sea, such

246

as those between the Kolyma and the Indigirka. They are found not only on the deltas of these rivers, but even more abundantly on their small tributaries. They are found in territories in which there are no rivers down which they could have floated from more temperate regions. Von Wrangel points out that: "The best mammoth bones as well as the greatest number are found at a certain depth below the surface, usually in clay hills, more rarely in black earth. The more solid the clay, the better the bones are preserved. Experience has also shown that more are found in elevations situated near higher hills than along the low coast or on the flat tundra." But even stronger proof than the above is the fact that mammoth remains have also been found on the banks of rivers running south like the Volga and the Ural. Surely these rivers could not have carried carcasses northward.

And finally there is the curious fact that a number of the mammoth carcasses and skeletons found in Siberia were discovered in a standing, upright position in the ground as if they had sunk down where they lived and had been frozen in that position, a position inconceivable in a floating carcass.

Again, it has been suggested that the mammoth and their companions migrated into this region during the summer while they returned southward during the cold season. But this, too, is impossible, because the food found in their mouths and stomachs is not of the kind that is found in that region now. Besides, there are also found shells and remains of plants which occur only in a warmer climate. Shells and plants could not migrate. This proves that the climate and vegetation must have been different in that region and that a change in climate came suddenly and overtook these animals in their natural habitat. There they perished suddenly in some great catastrophe, and they have been preserved in cold storage to the present day.

In summing up his findings on the mammoth in Siberia, Howorth concludes: "Now by no physical process known to

247

us can we understand how soft flesh could thus be buried in ground while it is frozen as hard as flint without disintegrating it. We cannot push an elephant's body into a mass of solid ice or hard frozen gravel and clay without entirely destroying the fine articulations and pounding the whole mass into a jelly, nor would we fail in greatly disturbing the ground in the process. When we, therefore, meet with great carcasses of mammoths with their most delicate tissues, their eyes, trunks, and feet beautifully preserved and lying several feet underground in hard frozen, undisturbed gravel and clay, we cannot escape the conclusion that when these carcasses were buried, the ground was soft and yielding. The facts compel us to admit that when the mammoth was buried in Siberia, the ground was soft and the climate therefore comparatively mild and genial, that immediately afterwards, the same ground became frozen, and the same climate became arctic, and that they have remained so to this day, and this was not gradually and in accordance with some slowly continuous, astronomical, or cosmical changes, but suddenly and 'per saltum.'

"Again, as I have said, the instances of the soft parts of the great pachyderms being preserved are not mere local and sporadic ones, but they form a chain of examples along the whole length of Siberia, from the Urals to the land of the Chukchis, so that we have to do here with a condition of things which prevails and with meteorological conditions that extend over a continent. When we find such a series ranging so widely preserved in the same perfect way and all evidencing a sudden change of climate from a comparatively temperate one to one of great rigor, we cannot help concluding that they all bear witness to a common event. We cannot postulate a separate climatic cataclysm for each individual case and each individual locality, but we are forced to the conclusion that the now permanently frozen zone in Asia became frozen at the same time from the same causes. . . . I see no possible escape from these conclusions, nor have I heard one suggested, by any one of the very numerous sharply critical people before whom they have been fairly placed, and they are in fact the views maintained by the fathers of geology, whose reputation has been put into the shade by more brilliant, but not more judicious investigators."

It is well-nigh impossible to calculate the number of mammoths buried in the sands and muck of Siberia. We may get some conception from the fact that since the year 900 A. D. men have made a business of collecting the ivory tusks of that region and selling them in China, Arabia, and Europe. In a case where a record could be secured, it was found that in one period of twenty years tusks from at least twenty thousand elephants were taken from one Siberian "mine" to the markets of Europe during the nineteenth century. Considering the vast area over which the remains of elephants are scattered, and the numbers in which they are known to exist in many places, it does not seem improbable that five millions or more of these great animals perished in Siberia in the watery cataclysm which caused their end. How any region could furnish nourishment for so vast a multitude of these monsters, to say nothing of the other animals whose bones accompany those of the elephants, is beyond comprehension. But it is equally true that this very fact offers incontrovertible evidence for the grandeur of the world which perished in the Flood.

In 1926 there appeared a most interesting book on the subject of mammoths, entitled *The Mammoth and Mammoth Hunting in Northeast Siberia,* by Bassett Digby, F. R. G. S. The book is a fascinating account of the work done by exploration parties in northern Siberia hunting mammoths and mammoth tusks. It is only by reading the vivid description of an eyewitness, of one who has participated in an expedition and who has experienced the thrill of finding one of these antediluvian monsters, that these mythical creatures become reality and literally reappear in flesh and blood.

I shall limit myself to the description of one such discovery. It was made by a Russian surveyor in 1846. After giving an account of his journey to Siberia and how they came to the place where the mammoth was found, he describes their experience in considerable detail. It was in the early summer of 1846 that the expedition reached the bleak and barren tundras of northern Siberia. The soil over which they had been traveling was a soft, boggy peat covered with a rich profusion of glowing Siberian flowers. The rivers were swollen from the melting of the snow and ice and were cutting deeply into their soft banks. As the party was traveling along one day, their attention was suddenly aroused by a peculiar gurgling and splashing noise. And, as they looked for the cause, they saw a strange black object protruding from the bank and bobbing up and down in the water. As they came closer to the place, they saw before them the head and part of the body of a monstrous elephant still in the flesh, partly washed from the bank and partly holding on, as it were, to save himself from a watery grave. They were, of course, full of excitement because of their discovery, but before they could extricate the body from the sand where it was still held, the bank suddenly gave way and with a splash the monster slipped into the water and was carried away by the turbulent river to the Arctic Sea.

The account of this strange discovery is given in such detailed and vivid description that it will help the reader to get a better picture of the conditions under which these strange monsters have been found in Siberia. And so we shall have this Russian surveyer tell his own story. He writes: "Our patience had been tried, but suddenly a huge black horrible mass bobbed out of the water. We beheld a colossal elephant's head, armed with mighty tusks, its long trunk waving uncannily in the water, as though seeking something it had lost. Breathless with astonishment, I beheld the monster hardly twelve feet away, with the white of his half-open eyes showing.

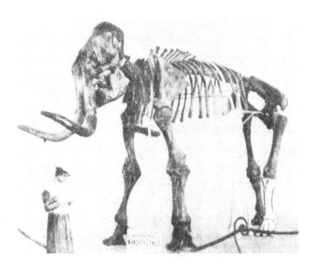

Skeleton of Beresovka Mammoth at Petrograd, Russia. Note the size as compared with the human figure

The Beresovka Mammoth. Found in the flesh in northern Siberia and mounted exactly as found

"The position of the beast interested me; it was standing in the earth, thus indicating the manner of its destruction, not lying on its side or back, as a dead animal naturally would. The soft peat or bog on which it stepped thousands of years ago, gave way under the weight of the giant, and he sank as he stood, on all four feet, unable to save himself. A severe frost came, turning into ice both him and the bog which overwhelmed him.

"Picture to yourself an elephant with a body covered with thick fur, about thirteen feet in height and fifteen feet in length, with tusks eight feet long, thick and curving outward at their ends. A stout trunk six feet long, colossal legs, one and one-half feet thick, and a tail bare to the tip, which was covered with thick tufty hair.

"The beast was fat and well grown. Death had overwhelmed him in the fullness of his powers. His large, parchmentlike, naked ears lay turned up over the head.

"The whole appearance of the great beast was fearfully strange and wild. It had not the shape of our present elephants. As compared with the Indian elephant, its head was rough, the braincase low and narrow, the trunk and mouth much larger. The modern elephant is an awkward animal, but compared with this mammoth he is as an Arabian steed to a coarse, cumbersome dray horse.

"I could not divest myself of a feeling of fear as I approached the head. The open eyes gave the beast a lifelike aspect, as though at any moment it might stir, struggle to its feet, and bear down upon us with a stentorian roar. . . .

"The bad smell of the carcass warned us that it was time to save of it what we could; the encroaching river, too, bade us hasten.

"First we hacked off the tusks and sent them aboard our boat. Then the natives tried to hew off the head, but notwithstanding their efforts this was slow work. As the belly of the brute was cut open, out rolled the intestines, and the stench was so dreadful that I could not avert my nausea and had to turn away. But I had the stomach cut out and dragged aside. It was well filled. The contents were instructive and well preserved. The chief contents were young shoots of fir and pine. A quantity of young fir-cones, also in a chewed state, were mixed with the mass." [3]

Unfortunately the exploration party was not able to save their interesting and valuable discovery. As stated, the river, which had exposed part of the monster, continued cutting into the banks with increased effectiveness, and before the workmen were able to extricate him from his grave and cold storage of many thousands of years, the river had done the work, and the monster who had rested here through the ages began to move, slipped, sank beneath the water, and disappeared. However, another specimen was secured later and safely transported to St. Petersburg, where it has been on exhibit in the museum ever since, unless the ravages of the World War have destroyed it.

As we contemplate this most extraordinary phenomenon of the frozen mammoths in the Siberian north, the questions naturally force themselves upon us: How did they get there? What is the explanation for these strangest of all spectacles? Many solutions have been offered; but every unprejudiced reader will agree with the conclusion arrived at by the English scientist Howorth, who writes: "These facts, I claim, prove several conclusions. They prove in the first place that a very great cataclysm and catastrophe occurred at the close of the mammoth period by which that animal, with its companions was overwhelmed over a very large part of the earth's surface. Secondly, that this catastrophe involved a widespread flood of waters which not only killed the animals, but also buried them under continuous beds of loam or gravel. Thirdly, that the same catastrophe was accompanied by a very great and sudden change of climate in Siberia, by which the animals which had previously lived in fairly temperate conditions were frozen in their flesh under the ground and have remained frozen ever since."

He then continues: "We want a cause that should kill the animals, and yet not break to pieces their bodies, or even mutilate them; a cause which would in some cases disintegrate the skeletons without weathering the bones. We want a cause that would not merely do this as a widespread plague or murrain might, but one which would bury the bodies as well as kill the animals, which would take up gravel and clay and lay them down again, and which would sweep together animals of different sizes and species and mix them with trees and other debris of vegetation. What cause competent to do this is known to us? Water would drown the animals and yet would not mutilate their bodies. It would kill them all with complete impartiality, irrespective of their strength, age or size. It would take up clay and earth, and cover the bodies with it. . . . Not only could it do this, but it is the only cause known to me capable of doing the work on a scale commensurate with the effects we see here in Siberia."

PART IV

The World After the Flood

CHAPTER XVI

Harmonizing Genesis and Geology. The Geological Timetable

THE voice of evidence for the Flood is clear and unmistakable, as we have seen, but modern geology refuses to hear this voice. Instead, it has built up a system based entirely upon organic evolution, which leaves no room for an omnipotent Creator, or a personal God, directing the affairs of men and the universe which He created. The world as it is today is said to be the result of a slow process of evolution which has been going on for millions and billions of years and will continue onward and upward through endless time. This is the accepted view of our age. The writers of our science textbooks propound this theory as truth. The youth of today is brought up on this theory in school and in college. The press, radio, and current literature popularize it, and the uncritical public accepts it as true. Anyone daring to question this theory is considered an obscurantist or a fanatic. But the theory as proposed is irreconcilable with Scripture, and every attempt at a compromise is a surrender of revealed truth in favor of mere human speculation and hypothesis.

As we enter upon the last section of our study, it will be necessary, therefore, to examine these geological theories which contradict the Scriptural doctrine of creation and which become a great stumbling block to the faith of our college-going youth.

Geology may be defined as "a study of the structure, the history, and the development of the earth and its inhabitants as revealed in the rocks" (Scott).

The rocks as they appear on the surface of the earth are divided into three major classes: the igneous, the sedimentary, and the metamorphic rocks.

Igneous rock, also called primitive or crystalline, is the foundation rock of the earth. It is the oldest rock and has its origin in original creation. It is massive, not stratified, and contains no fossils. Granite is the best-known example of this class of rock.

The sedimentary rock is a younger rock. Its origin is quite different from that of igneous rock. It was laid down by the action of water or wind or ice; hence it is also called stratified, from the Latin word *stratum,* meaning that which has been spread out. Each layer of a stratum represents one uninterrupted deposition of material, while the divisions between them are due to longer or shorter intervals in the process or to a change in the substance of the material deposited. A stratum is a collection of layers of the same mineral substances which occur together and may consist of one or many layers. The most common of the sedimentary rocks are the limestones, sandstones, and shales.

By metamorphic rock is meant a rock which was changed into another kind of rock by pressure, heat, or chemical action, such as limestone changed into marble.

According to geological theory, the materials of which these are composed were, in the first instance at least, derived from "the chemical decay or mechanical abrasions of the igneous rocks," and hence they are also called derivative or secondary rocks. The hundreds and even thousands of feet of stratified rock covering the surface of the earth are said to have been formed in this manner, millions and even billions of years being required before the rocky foundation of the present continents of the earth was completed.

Joseph McCabe, a British scientist, gives a very graphic account of this rock-forming process. He says:

"I am taking tonight three aspects of Nature. The first is, in a familiar phrase, the record of the rocks. Suppose we could pass down through this floor on which this hall is built; suppose we could sink about one thousand feet. What should we find? I am not using my imagination, as many of you will know. Several borings have been made within a few hundred yards of this spot. The deepest of those borings goes down about 1,100 feet, and I can tell you what you would find if you sank down under this floor for 1,100 feet. First, the superficial rubbish of the earth, the gravel, and so on. I take no notice of that. Then you would find, as every Londoner knows, a great bed of clay 120 feet thick. What does it mean? It means that during prolonged ages this part of the earth was under water. It means that the finer silt, the finer sediment of the rivers pouring into the sea which covered the site of London, has, age after age, poured its sediment slowly, gradually, peacefully, on the floor of that sea until, with the pressure of millions of tons of over-lying earth, it has been compressed into those 120 feet of clay under our feet. Go lower still, and you find you would pass through 650 feet of chalk. I think most of you know what chalk means. It is a compact mass mainly of the shells of microscopic organisms floating on the surface of a tranquil sea, a warm sea. How many ages do you suppose these tiny little microscopic things, all at least as small as the smallest grains of salt you use at table, were accumulating at the bottom of the sea to give those 650 feet of compressed material which is underneath us tonight? We know today how long — something like 50 million years. Underneath again you have 50 or 60 feet of limestone. Once more, at a still earlier date, this part of the earth was deep under water. It lay at the bottom of a warm semi-tropical sea, a clear peaceful ocean, in which the limestone was laid. Underneath that again you have those famous Old Red Sandstone rocks which you are familiar with in Devonshire. What do they mean? They are the sediment deposited in a lake. Three hundred or four hundred million years ago this part of the earth was covered with a deep lake, and once more, the characteristic is that those grains of sand, colored and cemented by the iron, must have been laid in a prolonged age of tranquil, slow, gradual deposition. There are no convulsions under your feet.

"Now, the crust of the earth is not generally so peaceful. Here we are living on a great ball of iron, its surface corrupted, torn, and ground into soil which has been made into rocks; but it is shrinking. This globe of ours is growing smaller, and at times this crust that seems so solid to us, even masses of rock one thousand feet thick are taken up by these gigantic forces and crumbled as a child crumples a sheet of paper. You have seen yourselves sometimes on the face of a cliff or a mountain-side those solid seams of stone twisted and distorted, while at times in this splitting of the crust of the earth you may even have one of the older strata of rocks thrown over a younger stratum.

"We are accustomed to all sorts of contortions in geology, but we can disentangle them; and as, over the great mass of the earth, those stones are evenly laid, we can interpret them. For a long time it was difficult to say how long it had taken the agencies of the earth to make those rocks. Fortunately, as most of you know, a new science has come to the aid of the geologist. Some years ago, we discovered a wonderful metal called radium, which led to the discovery of an even more wonderful metal called uranium. Uranium breaks up. Its tiny atom is so unstable that once in a thousand years it shoots off parts of its substance and again in another thousand years, until at last the residual substance is a peculiar kind of lead which the chemist can identify. And round that lead sometimes you have the gases that have been shot off.

"It occurred to men of science that if in the rocks under our feet there is a definite proportion of uranium and lead, they have the time when those rocks were deposited. Those volcanic rocks, the molten matter which rushes through the rocks and is deposited at all levels of the earth, contain uranium, and our men of science for the last fifteen years have been examining with infinite patience what is the proportion of uranium and lead in those rocks. I know no physicist in the world, and no professor of geology in the world, who doubts the result. As the Chairman of the British Association said only last week, 'The argument is irrefutable.' The rocks may be older than we say, but at least this chronometrical machine gives us the minimum age of the rocks under our feet, and it tells us that London clay, representing a definite geological period, was laid down 50 to 60 million years ago. It tells you that the older limestone of which I have been speaking, was laid down 250 million years ago. It tells you that these Old Red Sandstone rocks were laid down 350–400 millions of years ago; and the deeper series of rocks cover a period of at least something more than 1,000 million years. Scientific men are agreed upon it, so now we have our older and our younger rocks. And what do they show? They are the catacombs, they are the tombs, of the myriads of living things that have gone before us." [1]

The reader will note well with what positive and dogmatic assurance Mr. McCabe makes his assertion. He is quite sure about all the details of the rock-forming process, and he also knows the exact time required for this process to accomplish a given result. And yet these dogmatic assertions are not based on demonstrated facts, but on a mere hypothesis which has not been verified and is incapable of verification.

That rocks are being formed today, and have been in process of forming ever since the days of creation from "the chemical decay or mechanical abrasions" of older rocks, no one will deny, but to claim that all the sedimentary rocks now existing on the face of the earth had their origin in that manner and were formed at the same rate of time is an unwarranted conclusion.

And yet, on the basis of this hypothesis and the life-succession hypothesis of biology, modern geologists have constructed an elaborate timetable which demonstrates in a very tangible manner the alleged process by which our present world was gradually built up out of a dark and mysterious sea of uncounted ages, until by slow and laborious evolution it reached the present stage of development. A reproduction of this table in simplified outline is found on the following page. It will be helpful for a better understanding of the theory and of the geological nomenclature to spend a few moments with this table.

The names in the first column to the left represent the general periods into which geological time has been divided.

I. *Pre-Cambrian Era.* The groups in this era are at the very bottom of the earth's crust, and they might be called pre-historic time, geologically speaking. The rock of this era is igneous, crystalline, metamorphosed, and some sedimentary. Fossils are very scanty, poorly preserved, or unknown. The Laurentian Shield around Hudson Bay, the Appalachian, or Eastern, protaxis, the Selkirk, or Western, protaxis, and the granite exposures of Ontario, Newfoundland, Wisconsin, and Minnesota are said to date from this era.

II. *Paleozoic Era* represents the next stage of our earth's development. It might be called the ancient history of geological times. It is called Paleozoic because it is claimed that the rock of this period contains the remains of the oldest or most primitive forms of life. The rocks are chiefly sedimentary. They contain a great variety of fossils from sponges, brachiopods, and trilobites in the lowest, to fish, amphibians, and modern insects in the uppermost divisions of this era.

| ERA | PERIOD | ROCKS | DOMINANT LIFE |

ERA	PERIOD		
10,000,000 Years	QUATERNARY		AGE of MAMMALS — PLANTS
CENOZOIC 100,000,000 Years	TERTIARY		
MESOZOIC 200,000,000 Years	CRETACEOUS		AGE of AMMONITES and REPTILES — AGE of SEED PLANTS — MODERN — AGE of SEED
300,000,000 Years	JURASSIC		
400,000,000 Years	TRIASSIC		
500,000,000 Years	PERMIAN		AGE of AMPHIBIANS — ANCIENT PLANTS
600,000,000 Years	CARBON-IFEROUS		AGE of SPORE BEARING PLANTS
PALAEOZOIC 700,000,000 Years	DEVONIAN		AGE OF FISHES and CORALS
800,000,000 Years	SILURIAN		AGE of INVERTEBRATES — SEA-WEEDS
900,000,000 Years	ORDOVICIAN		
1,000,000,000 Years	CAMBRIAN		AGE of
PROTEROZOIC 900,000,000 Years ARCHAEOZOIC 500,000,000 Years	PRECAMBRIAN		RISE of INVERTEBRATES — AGE

The Geological Timetable

The Paleozoic Era is divided into six large divisions or periods, called, in order, from the older to the younger: Cambrian, Ordovician, Silurian, Devonian, Carboniferous, Permian, each comprising a specific geological formation, dated or characterized by the fossils found in them. The oldest rock system of this era is the Cambrian, and the others follow in regular succession in the order given, each system representing millions of years in point of time. Many great events in the history of our earth are said to have occurred during this period. During Cambrian time, for example, the foundation of North America is alleged to have been laid. The beginning of the Appalachian Mountains dates back to the Ordovician. The Silurian is the great limestone-forming period. Fish appear in great abundance during the Devonian. The famous Old Red Sandstone described by Hugh Miller dates from this period. In the Carboniferous age nearly all the great coal deposits of the world were formed, and the Permian is noted for extensive volcanic activity in Europe.

III. *The Mesozoic Era* represents the Middle Ages of geological history and is subdivided into three large periods called Triassic, Jurassic, Cretaceous. The great reptiles ruled supreme during this age, reaching their greatest development during Cretaceous times.

IV. *Cenozoic Era* is the most recent. This age is subdivided into Tertiary and Quarternary, the latter being the most recent period. Birds, mammals, and finally man are said to have appeared during this period.

The names in the second column indicate the separate series in the larger formations. The names are largely selected from the places where these strata were first studied. In the fifth column are found the names of the representative fossils of the period.

This geological timetable, as here briefly outlined, constitutes, without a doubt, one of the most formidable hurdles for our college-going youth. Here he suddenly finds himself confronted with this array of facts arranged and systematized, all endorsed by the world's most noted scientists. The effect is overwhelming. Here are the cold facts. They cannot be denied. The chart shows that the oldest rocks forming the foundation of the earth's crust are at the bottom, and more disturbing still, in them are found the fossils of the lowest or most primitive forms of life. The youngest rocks are at the top. They contain the remains of the highest forms of life, and between these two extremes is found a steady upward, progressive development of plant and animal life. Here is proof written large and indelibly in the very foundation rocks of the earth, and even Genesis, or at least the traditional interpretation of Genesis, cannot efface it. The writer vividly remembers the anguish of soul experienced when suddenly confronted with this problem. And yet — "The Word they still shall let remain," *Verbum dei manet in aeternum.*

At first glance it certainly does appear as though Moses were defeated and the Church proved to be hopelessly out of date, but this is the case only at first glance. The student, when first confronted with this table, believes, of course, that the geologists have actually found these various strata of rocks together in serial order, one following in regular succession upon the other, in one locality where the rock is built up after chart indications. But nothing is farther from the truth. Nothing resembling such a series has ever been found together in one place on the face of the earth. T. C. Chamberlin, the dean of American geologists, admits that "It should be understood that it is not possible to proceed directly downward through the whole succession of bedded rocks, but that the edges of the various beds may be found here and there where they have been brought to the surface by workings and tiltings, or exposed by the wearing away of the beds which once overlay them. The full series of strata is made out only by putting together this data gathered throughout all lands; and even when this is done, an absolutely complete series cannot yet be made out, or at least has not been." In other words, this ingenious geological ladder, with the various series of rocks and species with their oldest fossils, is purely an artificial a priori creation and does not exist anywhere in nature.

Furthermore, the time value of the various parts is purely hypothetical. The claim is made that the fossiliferous rocks made a total of thirty, forty, or fifty thousand and more feet in thickness, but the fact is that there is no place on earth where sedimentary rocks of such enormous thickness have been found. In reality, we never have to go down more than a few thousand feet in a given locality before we strike the bedrock of granite, and below this no fossils are found. Only in a few places have oil wells been drilled to a depth of 10,000 to 16,000 feet without reaching the bottom of sedimentary rock.

The names Cambrian, Devonian, Silurian, or Tertiary, etc., are mere arbitrary labels by which geologists designate certain rocks found in various parts of the earth which happen to contain certain kinds of fossils. The stratified rocks of the earth are not named and classified on the basis of the character of these rocks, but entirely on the basis of the kinds of fossils that happen to be contained in them. It is admitted, of course, that an experienced oil geologist has learned to correlate strata from one well to another, and from one field to another if they are not too distant from one another; but it is generally agreed that as yet there is no safe index or guide to a certain stratigraphic horizon except the index fossil. "In the present state of knowledge," says Scott, "lithological similarity is not a safe guide." [2] The so-called oldest rocks are not always at the bottom as shown in the diagram. Any of these formations are found at the bottom or at the top, as we shall see later. The mineral composition of the rock, or the degree of its hardness, has nothing to do with its age. There are Cambrian and Ordovician rocks which are soft and unconsolidated. Such strata, for example, are found around the Baltic, in Russia, and in the Mississippi Valley. Again, the so-called "young" rocks, such as the Tertiary and Pleistocene, are frequently found next to the granite, and it is by no means uncommon to find them very hard and even crystalline. Examples of this kind are found in California, the Alps, the Himalayas, and other places.

A rock then is called "young" or "old" according to the fossils that are found in it. An old rock is classified as old because it contains the remains of the so-called primitive forms, and it does not matter what this rock looks like or on what level it is found. It may be sandstone, limestone, or shale. And "young" rock is classified as young because of the higher forms of life found in it, such as reptiles, birds, and mammals. In other words, the geological timetable is based entirely on the theory of biological evolution of life developing progressively from the most simple protozoa to the highest and most complex form now existing. But if the biologist is required to produce his evidence for assuming that the lower forms of life are also the oldest or the beginning of all life, he promptly turns to geology and claims that his theory must be true because the simplest or lowest forms of life are always found in the "oldest" rocks. And thus the argument goes on and on in a vicious circle.

We have here a most glaring kind of fallacy, which has completely beclouded the thinking of otherwise intelligent men. The fact is, as Dr. Price says, that "there is no man on earth who knows enough about the rocks or the fossils to be able to prove in any fashion fit to be called scientific that any particular kind of fossil is actually and intrinsically older or younger than any other kind. In other words, there is no one who can actually prove that the Cambrian trilobite is older than the Cretaceous dinosaur or the Tertiary mammal.

Geology is anything but an exact science. A writer in a recent issue of *Bibliotheca Sacra* (June 1939) says: "And whatever has been established beyond reasonable doubt need not in any way be considered as conflicting with the traditional and conservative view of Holy Scripture."

But evolutionary geology is afflicted with other difficulties which make insuperable demands on human reason and can be comprehended only by an act of faith greater than that required to move mountains. One of these problems is the absolute conformity with which so-called "younger" strata overlie "older" strata classified according to their fossil contents as millions, possibly even hundreds of millions of years older, with nothing in the way of erosion or distinction of any kind to mark the hiatus, or the interval, to indicate that many millions of years have elapsed between the laying down of these two sets of strata.

As soon as any mass of rock, whether igneous or stratified, is lifted beyond the surface of the water, as, e. g., the strata which form the present continents of the world, they immediately become subject to the great forces of erosion, such as rain, frost, wind, the action of rivers, lakes, earthquakes, volcanoes, etc. One should therefore reasonably expect that the rocks exposed to these eroding forces for millions of years ought to show evidence of such erosion on the surface. We should expect to find these "older" strata mutilated and cut into irregularities similar to, or even greater than, those found on the surface of the earth today. We ought to expect to find deep valleys, basins, hills, rugged canyons, and the like, but the strange thing is that such evidence is totally lacking. There is nothing of the kind to mark such erosion. Marks of any disturbance of this nature are wholly absent from the time of the contact between the strata supposedly so vastly different in age. In fact, the "younger" strata follow the "older" in perfect conformity, and they appear as though one had followed the other in natural and uninterrupted succession. "Often the two strata appear

268

to be exactly alike, consisting of the same kind of shale or the same kind of limestone, appearing as one formation, and we could not make two formations out of them, except by their fossils." [3] Examples of such perfect conformity are found all over the globe. Price calls attention to a large area near Lake Athabaska in northwestern Saskatchewan where Devonian limestone is conformably covered by Cretaceous beds. This conformity extends for fully 150 miles in one direction and nearly to Lake Manitoba, some five hundred miles to the east, and yet "this vast interval of time which separated the two formations, so far as observed, is unrepresented, either by deposition or erosion," according to the *Canadian Geological Survey Report*.[4]

Another example is to be found at Banff, Alberta, where lower Cretaceous overlies lower Carboniferous without any perceptible break. In fact, the upper beds of the Carboniferous are lithologically almost precisely like those of the Cretaceous above them. The geologist reporting this in the annual *Report* adds this significant remark: "Were it not for further fossil evidence, one would naturally suppose that a single formation was being dealt with." [5]

There are similar examples of such deceptive conformity, as the geologists call this condition, in Kentucky, Tennessee, New York, China, and in a great many other places on our globe.

According to Geikie, quoted by Arthur I. Brown of Vancouver, B. C., "the comformable relations of incongruous strata are repeated over and over again in the same vertical sections, the same kind of anachronistic strata reappearing alternately with others of an entirely different age, i. e., a period repeatedly appearing as if regularly interbedded with them in a series of strata that obviously have never been disturbed." [6]

Evidently we have here simply a natural phenomenon presenting no serious difficulties. I am sure that every fair-minded person whose judgment has not been warped by

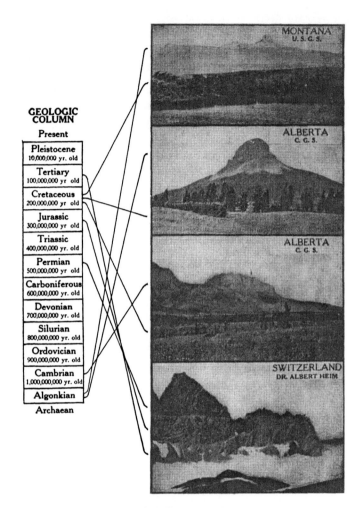

GEOLOGIC COLUMN

Present

Pleistocene 10,000,000 yr. old	
Tertiary 100,000,000 yr old	
Cretaceous 200,000,000 yr. old	
Jurassic 300,000,000 yr. old	
Triassic 400,000,000 yr. old	
Permian 500,000,000 yr. old	
Carboniferous 600,000,000 yr. old	
Devonian 700,000,000 yr. old	
Silurian 800,000,000 yr. old	
Ordovician 900,000,000 yr. old	
Cambrian 1,000,000,000 yr. old	
Algonkian	

Archaean

MONTANA
U. S. G. S.

ALBERTA
C. G. S.

ALBERTA
C. G. S.

SWITZERLAND
DR. ALBERT HEIM

The Double Geological Column as Presented by Byron Nelson in "The Deluge Story in Stone"

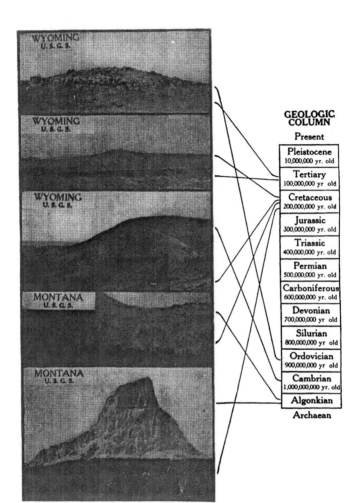

WYOMING
U. S. G. S.

WYOMING
U. S. G. S.

WYOMING
U. S. G. S.

MONTANA
U. S. G. S.

MONTANA
U. S. G. S.

**GEOLOGIC
COLUMN**

Present

Pleistocene
10,000,000 yr. old

Tertiary
100,000,000 yr old

Cretaceous
200,000,000 yr. old

Jurassic
300,000,000 yr. old

Triassic
400,000,000 yr. old

Permian
500,000,000 yr. old

Carboniferous
600,000,000 yr. old

Devonian
700,000,000 yr old

Silurian
800,000,000 yr. old

Ordovician
900,000,000 yr old

Cambrian
1,000,000,000 yr. old

Algonkian

Archaean

any *a priori* theories of dogmatic evolutionary geology will agree with Dr. Price when he writes:

"A plain common-sense view of the matter, which would make such elaborate theories unnecessary, would be to say that these conformities are, like others of this kind, an obvious proof that these strata follow one another in quick succession with no great time intervals in between; because the alleged time distinctions between these two contiguous strata are all a mistake, and no such distinction of age need be taken into account at all. This solves the whole difficulty, and we then take these conformities just as we do any others, at their face value. A wrong theory has made a mountainous difficulty when in reality there is none whatever." [7]

But the faith of the devoted adherents of this theory of evolutionary geology is taxed even more severely by another problem created for them by the rocks that refuse to fit into this life-succession-theory timetable. That is the problem of the so-called "thrust faults." We have seen above that modern geologists calculate the age of rocks according to the fossils found in them and not according to the character of the material composition of these rocks. So long as the rocks accommodate themselves to this theory and follow in proper order, i. e., the "older" rocks at the bottom and the "younger" in succession above them according to the supposed age, all is well; but to the chagrin of evolutionary geologists, this does not always happen — the reverse is at times the case. So-called "younger" rocks are found at the bottom, and rocks supposedly hundreds of millions of years "older" are lying upon them in what looks like a perfectly normal way, without any evidence of violent disturbances. This amazing condition may extend over many thousands of square miles. Such phenomena are called "thrust faults." According to this theory, thousands of square miles, including parts of mountain ranges, were bodily lifted up and pushed over the top of "younger" rocks, thus bringing about this reverse order. Such large scale "thrust faults" are found in the

Canadian Rockies, in Wyoming, Utah, Idaho, in New York, Vermont, Quebec, in the Southeastern States, in the Alps, and in Scotland.

One of the best examples of this upside-down phenomenon is found in the Rocky Mountain region of southern Alberta and northern Montana. The writer is personally acquainted with this region, having lived in the very shadows of the great mountain peaks involved. The district is five hundred miles long north and south, and at least thirty or forty miles wide, including all of Glacier National Park and the famous picturesque scenes around Banff and Lake Louise, the Crowsnest Pass and Kootenay Pass areas, also such majestic peaks as Crowsnest Mountain, Chief Mountain, and others. The entire region comprises an area of about twenty thousand square miles. As a whole the mountains present much uniformity and consist largely of limestone formation classified as Pre-Cambrian in the south and Carboniferous farther north. The underlying rock, however, consists of much younger Cretaceous formation. According to some estimates, the Pre-Cambrian may be a billion or more years older, while Cretaceous is rated as fairly young, being approximately only two hundred million years old.

Here, then, we have a most remarkable spectacle, an area as large as Nova Scotia, including great mountain masses, lifted up bodily thousands of feet after they had been reclining peacefully in their original position for a possible period of eight hundred million years and then pushed over on the top of the more youthful Cretaceous strata. All this happens apparently without any violent revolutions, and it is executed with such marvelous precision that the so-called "older" rock now lies on top, resting "conformably" on the "younger." And apparently the very soft Cretaceous shale below suffered little by the sliding of the limestone over them.[8]

The supposed examples found in Switzerland and elsewhere of similar phenomena of overthrust on such a stupendous scale are equally fantastic. To move a mountain may require only a faith the size of a mustard seed, but to believe all this surely would require a faith many times as great because here a whole mountain range with its surrounding territory is involved. And yet the men who propound this theory sit in judgment over the Creation story as recorded in Genesis and have ruled out the Noachian Flood account as unscientific and impossible!

"There is something fascinating about science. One gets such wholesale returns of conjectures out of such a trifling investment of facts," says Mark Twain. This certainly applies here. I cannot do better than close this part of our discussion with another quotation from Dr. Price. After discussing the theory of "thrust faults" at great length, exposing with relentless logic the absurdity of its claims, he concludes his remarks on this subject with the following paragraph:

"The few examples enumerated of the glaring fallacies to be found in the theory of evolutionary geology will suffice to show that this phase, at least, of modern geology cannot be considered as science, but is a mere theory, an hypothesis, a belief. Its claims cannot be verified by scientific proof, and to say that Genesis has been outmoded by its findings is a false pretense and 'scientific' presumption." [9]

On the other hand, the problem of geology raised by the examples quoted can be solved in a most satisfactory way, without doing violence to human reason and common sense. If it were possible for us today to reconstruct for ourselves an adequate picture of what happened when the great Flood came upon this earth, most of our vexing problems in geology would disappear.

CHAPTER XVII

Other Difficulties Involving
Genesis and Geology

ODERN theories of geology have made it extremely
difficult for a Christian student of this science to
maintain his intellectual honesty and preserve his
faith in the Bible at the same time. It is obviously impossible
to take seriously the Creation story and the account of the
universal flood as recorded in Genesis and also to accept
the current geological theories concerning the origin and
development of the earth. If the Bible is true and infallible
in all matters in which it speaks, then these theories cannot
be true. If, on the other hand, the geological theories are
right, then we must modify our attitude toward the Bible.
The two cannot be harmonized. Even if we extend the six
days of Creation to the unlimited eons of time and ages,
a compromise between these two views is impossible. The
Christian student must realize this and must settle the matter
for himself. If he fails to do so, confusion and skepticism
are inevitable. His faith in the Bible will of necessity be
shaken, and the chances are that he will accept the theories
presented in the geological textbooks of today, or by able
and convincing teachers, and will be led to regard Genesis
as outmoded by modern scientific research. To help such

a student is the purpose of this chapter. I will not attempt to answer all questions that arise from time to time in the struggle through the maze of geological theories, but will confine myself to a few of the most common problems which, next to the geological timetable, are likely to prove to be the greatest stumbling block to the inexperienced student of physical geography and geology.

But before we begin to examine these problems, we must again call attention to the fact that the Biblical record which is of special significance in this study, that is, the story of Creation and the account of the Flood, is extremely brief. The record which deals with the origin of this universe, with all its countless individual creations, comprises one short chapter of thirty-one verses in our Bible. It is a mere telegraphic account of what occurred in those most eventful six days of Creation. The account of the Flood is the other great record of an event which had a most profound effect in shaping the present condition of our earth. Though it is somewhat longer than the Creation story, it is still so short that it must be regarded as a mere summary of what happened in that awful world catastrophe. To give a full account of what occurred in these two great events would require not only a book, but a whole library. These Biblical accounts confine themselves to the basic minimum to satisfy man's desire to know the whence of himself and all things and to reveal to him the omnipotent power of God in the glory of His creative majesty.

In the second place, it may be well to remind ourselves that our mental and spiritual equilibrium need not necessarily be seriously disturbed because some or even many problems of Genesis and geology remain unsolved. There are many things in everyday life which we accept without question and yet do not understand; for example, What is life, life in all its manifold phases — life in man, life in the animal, life in the plant, life in the seed, life in the germ? Man may create an atom bomb, the most horrible agent for the destruction of life, but man cannot create life, not even the life of an insect.

What is death? Every living thing in the world tends toward death. Why? What is death? Who knows the answer to that question?

What is sleep? Why must we sleep? Hymns have been composed about the blessedness of forgetful sleep, and learned essays have been written on the subject, but no one has yet solved the mystery surrounding this most common of life's phenomena.

What is a dream? Oh, yes, the psychologists, particularly Freud and his school, have written much on the subject; but when all is said, there still remain the questions: Why do we dream? What is a dream?

What is matter? Man does not even understand the very substance of which he is made and of which everything that surrounds him is composed.

What is the soul? What is electricity? What causes the Gulf Stream, the river of waters, to keep its course in a sea of water? Why does man grow old and feeble? Why does ice form on the top of the water while cold water sinks to the bottom? And so we could go on and on asking a thousand questions to which the wisest of this world could not give you a satisfactory answer. Why, then, become alarmed if our earth in its structure and form offers problems for which we have no adequate solution? An honest scholar is genuinely humble, and he has learned to say again and again, "I do not know." A beautiful sentence from Henry Beston's Country Chronicle Column in the *Progressive*, June 17, 1947, offers a fitting thought in this connection. He writes: "Among the many things for which I remain profoundly grateful is the fact that so much of life defies human explanation. The unimaginative and the dull may insist that we have an explanation for everything and level at every wonder and mystery of life their popgun formulae. But God be praised, their wooden guns have not yet dislodged the

277

smallest star. It is well that this be so, for the human spirit can die of explanations which do not explain. A world without wonder and a way of mind without wonder become a world without imagination, and without imagination man is a poor, stunted creature. Religion, poetry, and all the arts have their sources in this upwelling of wonder and surprise. Let's thank God that so much will forever remain out of reach, safe from our universe, inviolate forever from our touch." The suggestion of Hamlet to his friend Horatio that "there are more things in heaven and earth than are dreamt of in your philosophy" might well be applied to those wiseacres who try to grasp the infinitude of God and with their puny finite mind attempt to sit in judgment over His revelation and set limits to the omnipotence of His creative and destructive powers.

In the third place, the inexperienced student of geology must keep in mind that when the geologist enters the field of cosmogony, that is, when he attempts to write the history of the universe and deals with the origin and development of this earth, he is no longer in the field of science, but has entered into the domain of metaphysics and theology. He is then no longer operating with demonstrated and established facts, but with theory and hypotheses.

There is of course no quarrel with speculation or the projecting of theories in order to discover truth. The quarrel begins only when such theories are presented either directly or by implication as established facts, or when these theories are in conflict with existing truths either established by scientific proof or derived from divine revelation. As soon as a theory is presented as truth, it has become pseudo science, mere quackery, and is a hindrance to truth.

With these thoughts in mind, we may now approach some of the problems which are bound to disturb the conscientious student in his attempt to harmonize Genesis and geology.

One of the problems is the fact of the stratified rock.

Next to the geological timetable, as this is commonly presented in the geological textbooks used in our colleges today, there is no problem which constitutes a greater challenge to the student's faith in the Creation story of Genesis than this one. In a previous chapter it was pointed out that rocks are commonly divided into three groups — the igneous rock, the stratified rock, and the metamorphosed rock. We learned that by igneous rock is meant the massive unstratified crystalline rock which forms the core and foundation of the earth. Granite is the best-known example of this group. By metamorphosed rock is meant rock which has changed from one form to another through pressure and heat or chemical action. Marble belongs to this class. And by stratified rock is meant that large group of rocks which was laid down in strata or layers by the action of water and wind. They are composed of materials derived from the disintegration of previous rocks. The cement which binds the particles together in the new rock varies. Sometimes it is carbonate of lime, in others it is a clay or a claylike substance, and in still others it may be iron oxide. The firmness of the stratified rock depends upon the character and the amount of cement found in the rock and the degree of pressure to which the whole mass was subjected. The individual strata may differ in material, texture, thickness, and color. Under normal conditions the individual strata lie horizontally, one upon the other. Where they are tilted or bent, the cause must be sought in some geological disturbance which may have been an upheaval or a subsidence of the foundation below.

The individual strata may vary from the thickness of a sheet of paper to layers of hundreds of feet or more. A collection of strata said to have been deposited under similar and uninterrupted conditions is called a formation. The most common of the stratified rocks are limestone, sandstone, and shale. Other forms are gypsum, chalk, marl, and clay.

The problem of Genesis and geology arising from the sedimentary rocks concerns their origin. Sedimentary rock, as stated above, is a secondary rock. Its material was derived from some previous form of rock. This original rock was disintegrated through the action of water, wind, frost, cold, heat, plant life, and other forces. The disintegrated particles were carried away by wind, water, and ice and redeposited in separate layers. The cementing substances, mentioned above, bind them together to form a new rock. This sedimentary, or stratified, rock is found everywhere, with only a few areas excepted. It encloses nearly the entire earth with its mantle, measuring in some places hundreds or even thousands of feet in thickness. And this brings us to the very heart of the problem. If all the existing sedimentary rock, which forms the crust of the earth, had its origin in a slow process of rock formation as just described, then what becomes of the six days of Creation, or what about the traditional age of the earth? It is obviously impossible to harmonize the two. To wear down the hard basic igneous rock by erosion and to form the enormous masses of stratified rock enclosing the earth from these disintegrated particles would require eons of time, each comprising millions or billions of years, making the six days of Creation or the traditional six thousand years of the earth's history appear ridiculous.

But the problem becomes even more perplexing when one considers the origin of the very minerals which compose these rocks. Many of the minerals, like the rocks themselves, are of a secondary origin. They are derived from previously existing minerals, through the agency of weathering, water containing carbon dioxide or acids, through radio activity and forces produced by certain organisms, minerals are changed to form new ones. Gypsum, chalk, iron ores, lead, and others, are examples. This process of change is like the disintegration of rocks, inconceivably slow, yet the quantities of these secondary minerals now found in the crust of the earth are enormous. The time required to produce them can be conceived only in years of astronomical figures. And again we find ourselves in irreconcilable conflict with the Biblical conception of the origin and the age of the universe.

To escape from this dilemma, both theologians and geologists have resorted to a re-interpretation of Genesis. Some have tried to solve the difficulty by placing a period of immeasurable time between verse one and the rest of the first chapter of Genesis; others, after verse two and the rest of the chapter. Still others have changed the six days of creation into six periods each numbering millions or billions of years. The well-known German scholar and Bible student Bettex belongs to the first group. He says: "With the words 'In the beginning, God created the heaven and the earth' begins and closes the first section, one might say the first chapter of the Bible. With the words 'The earth was without form and void' begins the second chapter. Between the 'in the beginning' and 'the earth was without form and void' was a great epoch and pause in the Biblical narrative." [1]

Dr. Chalmers, a noted English divine, says: "The writings of Moses do not fix the antiquity of the globe. It teaches that between the first account of Creation which evoked out of the previous nothing the matter of heaven and earth, and the first account of the first day's work recorded in Genesis, periods of vast duration may have intervened." [2]

Hugh Miller, a famous English geologist and firm believer and defender of the Bible, quotes Chalmers approvingly and adds: "Such are a few of the geological facts which lead me to believe that the days of the Mosaic account were great periods and not natural days." [3]

Dr. Kinns, another English Bible student and scholar, says: "The word *day* (*yom*) signifies an indefinite period of time in the first chapter of Genesis" and then proceeds to prove his point from many Old Testament parallel passages in which *yom* evidently does not mean a day of 24 hours each. Even Origen, one of the early Church Fathers, held a view similar to those just quoted. He says, "A whole age is a day." [4]

The well-known German church historian Kurtz viewed the Biblical account of Creation as a prophecy in reverse, that is, he holds Moses saw the great event of Creation, which had occurred in the past and in the absence of any human witness, as other prophets foresaw the events lying in the future long before they had occurred; and Moses recorded his prophetic vision in prophetic language, choosing for that words familiar to those for whom he wrote.

It is not our purpose here to discuss the various attempts that have been made by theologians or geologists to harmonize Genesis and the modern theories of science, nor is it part of our task at this time to enter upon a linguistic examination of the Hebrew word *yom* and its use in the Old Testament. That the first and common meaning of *yom* is "day" in the sense of a day of twenty-four hours is known by every student of the Hebrew language, but that it may also mean "day" in a wider sense, equivalent to a period of time, and that it has been so used in the Old Testament, is also admitted. But even when *yom* is used in this latter sense, it is never used for an epoch of unlimited time. Whether *yom* is used in the sense of a period of time in the first chapter of Genesis is quite another question. The Bible's own interpretation seems to point quite definitely to a day of twenty-four hours, and this also has been the interpretation of conservative theologians until the theories of modern geology were advanced about 125 years ago. However, a careful study of the first two chapters of Genesis in a proper perspective and in full comprehension of the world's greatest catastrophe, the Flood, and a clear understanding of the principles which underlie the evolutionary theories of modern geology, will obviate such concessions. It is because we never get beyond our early childhood conception of the days of Creation and of the Noachian Flood that the Creation theories involving millions and billions of years of slow evolution frighten us.

But now what light can be obtained from the first chapter

of Genesis and from the account of the Flood to help us solve this dark and perplexing problem of stratified rock and secondary minerals?

In the first place, it must be admitted that in the world of today new rocks and new minerals are being formed according to the processes described above, and it is also admitted that this process, though ceaseless, is exceedingly slow. The "everlasting" mountains which seem to be the only permanent thing in this world are neither permanent nor everlasting. Heat and cold, snow and ice, frost and water, wind and earthquake, plant life, and other forces of nature are forever gnawing away at their structure and tearing down their substances, transporting the material to distant locations, where new soil and new rocks are formed from the decay of the old. Huge masses of rock are reduced to boulders, boulders to pebbles, pebbles to gravel, and gravel to sand by the forces of frost, ice, running water, and by the action of tide and wave along the shores of oceans and lakes. The wind carries away the fine sand and deposits it again in huge sand hills or wandering dunes, or it is packed down by the weight and action of the water and solidifies where it was created to form new rocks as different from the old as igneous is different from stratified rock. This process of change is ceaseless, irresistible, but imperceptibly slow. Just as we speak of a process of anabolism and katabolism in living organisms, so there is a corresponding change in the inorganic world about us. Πάντα ῥεῖ [panta rei], everything is in a flux, said the ancient Greek philosopher, and so it is.

Now, while all this is quite true, new rocks and new minerals are in a perpetual process of formation, it does not follow that all secondary rocks and all secondary minerals found in the crust of the earth today had their origin by this slow and timeless process. When God created this world, He created a complete world, a world as it was to be to the end of time. It was here as it was in the case of the first man.

When God created Adam and Eve, they were complete and perfect human specimens in every detail. They possessed all the parts, limbs, and organs of normal human beings. Their organs, mental faculties, and normal drives were ready to function from the moment that the breath of life was breathed into their bodies. They were in every respect perfect models and protoypes of what God wanted man to be. But once this first pair had come into being, God fixed a definite law by which the race of man was to perpetuate itself; and now human beings no longer come into existence as did Adam and Eve, but only through the operation of this unalterable law. The process of man's development now is slow and gradual, requiring almost one third of his life before he has reached maturity. And what is true of man also applies to animals and plants and even to the inorganic creations. God in His wisdom created a world of constant change, a world which, once set in motion, would continue to recreate itself until the end of time.

The world which God made was complete in every detail. That world had from its very beginning land and corresponding water segments. There were hills and valleys, rivers and lakes, open and wooded lands, but there were also rocks and soil, clay, sand, and gravel, igneous rocks and rocks which were the equivalent of our stratified rocks of today, lead and uranium, chalk and limestone, and all the other minerals. But once this world had received this form and the divine approval because of its complete perfection, God set in motion the machinery of the universe like a magnificent clockwork. He fixed definite unalterable laws by which this world was to perpetuate itself in keeping with its original pattern, just as He had done with men and the rest of the organisms created.

And now old rocks crumble and disintegrate, and new ones are formed. Rocks become clay, and clay is converted into productive soil. Minerals are transformed, and new ones emerge. Organisms produce chalk and limestone, and running water converts boulders into the finest sand. But because this law is now operative, it does not follow that all rocks classified as sedimentary, and all secondary minerals now found in the crust of the earth, had their origin by this process, just as it would be absurd to maintain that the first human being was conceived and born as his descendants are conceived and born today.

We accept this view of the original earth because a correct interpretation of the Creation account in Genesis compels us to do so. But here, as in so many other instances, we are not exclusively dependent upon Genesis or other parts of revelation for our information, but geology itself comes to our aid and produces the physical evidence for this view.

At the very bottom of the geological timetable there is a group of rocks known as pre-Cambrian rock. It is found in every part of the earth. In fact, it constitutes the very basement rock for all succeeding series. This pre-Cambrian rock is fundamentally different from all other formations. It contains no fossils in its lowest series. It is more highly metamorphosed than any other formation and has been subjected to greater transformation than other strata. Hence it has been a puzzle to the geologist ever since it was first studied. A very recent textbook on geology describes these rocks as follows: "The pre-Cambrian rocks essentially lacking the record of life (fossils) cannot even be correlated very accurately. In addition, because they have suffered deformation in all the earth's great periods of orogeny since the time of their origin, it is obvious that they must in general be more highly metamorphosed than any of the younger strata. In fact, the pre-Cambrian rocks are so badly altered and show such wide variations in composition and structure that it has been well said that they are only homogeneous in their heterogeneity. Little wonder that the early geologist called these beds of rock Primary, or Primitive, and dismissed them as too complicated to be deciphered." [5]

These strange primitive and highly metamorphosed formations, which are found in every continent and form "the basement complex, since all younger rocks rest on them," may well include the original sedimentary rocks created by God when the foundation of the earth was laid.[6] They have been deformed by "the earth's periods of orogeny and are highly metamorphosed." A correct understanding of God's creative work on the third day and of the cosmic revolution which accompanied the Flood and affected every part of the earth may well account for that. These rocks are rich in minerals of every kind; gold, silver, copper, iron, and nickel are found in them, in every continent, and even this harmonizes with Gen. 2:12.

However, all that has been said offers only a part of a solution to the great problem of sedimentary rocks and the secondary minerals. For a more complete answer we must turn again to the great Flood of Noah and try to reconstruct a picture of the ravages that were wrought on the surface of our earth in that great catastrophe.

The Flood was a world revolution of such stupendous magnitude that the human imagination is incapable of forming an adequate conception of what happened in that most catastrophic flood year in the history of our earth. For forty days this planet was twisted and torn in ceaseless convulsions; its foundation was shaken by earthquake and volcanic eruption, the bottom of the sea rising to take the place of land and mountain areas, while continents and other land masses subsided to become the abyss of the sea. And all the while torrential rains such as the world had never seen before or after were pouring from the heavens, and the fountains of the deep were belching forth the water of the sea. Tide and wave swept away in wild confusion forest and mountain, living things, boulders, and sand and carried them into the deep, while the sea gave up its secrets and intermingled them with the wreckage of the land barriers that had set bounds for it. The destructive force of the walls of water set in motion by the revolution accompanying the

Flood is beyond calculation. But the work of the Flood did not cease at the end of the forty days of revolution, rain, and ruin. We are told in Genesis "that the waters prevailed upon the earth an hundred and fifty days" (Gen. 7:24). For a period of five months the enormous weight of water, measuring hundreds, and in places possibly thousands, of feet in depth, rested on the debris and wreckage of that first world. This was the beginning of the new rock-forming process. Soft materials not sufficiently buttressed on the sides would give way under the pressure, causing the underlying strata to bend or break. The same would happen when great masses of vegetation had been buried. For a year and ten days the water of the flood remained on the face of the earth, before Noah was permitted to leave the ark with his human and animal cargo. During all this period the laws of nature governing water, tide, and waves were active, and the processes wearing down what remained of the antediluvian mountains and hills, or the protruding land masses exposed by the receding waters, continued.

As the water moved to and fro in its periodic change of ebb and tide, it wore down these elevations; and as it returned with its load of debris, layer after layer of the soft churned-up materials were laid down, and stratum after stratum was built up in regular succession to grow into the great formation of sedimentary rocks which now so perplex the geologists.

That fossils are found in these rocks is natural because that first world had an abundance of animal life in keeping with the abundance of vegetation and food supply. And the strange phenomena that the fossils of land and sea life are frequently found mingled together in the same rock, and that the remains of whales and other sea monsters, small and great, are found far removed from the sea and even on mountaintops, or that trees have been found in a semiupright position, piercing several succeeding strata, as in the Cragleith Quarry in England, where a trunk of a tree was found

287

intersecting ten or twelve successive strata of limestone, find a most reasonable explanation in the Flood as described in Genesis.

The texture, color, and character of the materials of these rocks or even of the individual strata in a given formation would naturally differ according to the locality from which the material was moved or where it was deposited. Sometimes it would measure but a few feet in thickness and at other times hundreds or even thousands of feet, depending upon the depth of the basin to which it was carried. Sometimes the material consisted of clay, soil, or the ooze of an uplifted ocean bed, at another place it may have been volcanic ash, loess, boulders, gravel, and sand. Sometimes it was hurled together in wild confusion, just as that happens in floods of much smaller proportions today; at another time it was carefully assorted in homogeneous strata.

This process of rock formation continued long after that fateful year of the Flood, for we must not imagine that all the continents and islands were already in existence in their present topography and that all the earth was completely dried up when Noah and his animals left the ark. There are many regions on earth which have all the evidence showing that they were submerged under large bodies of water until fairly recent times. The great fossil lakes of this and other continents have already been referred to. But besides these there are many other regions — now far removed from bodies of water or now are even arid or semiarid wastelands — where ancient shore lines and beaches are clearly discernible. A very good example of this is found just south of Cheyenne, Wyoming. Dr. Price describes this territory as follows: "Throughout all this region one cannot fail to be impressed with the visible evidence almost everywhere of a vast mass of water as it stood here for a short time forming real sea beaches, still so clearly marked, and was gradually drained from off these lands, and this vast mass of water must have been here at no very remote period; otherwise the many

288

visible signs of the retreat of the water would long ago have been obliterated. These marks are as fresh looking as if the water had been here only a few centuries ago. The marks of the Romans over much of the Island of Great Britain are less distinct than the handwriting of the ocean in its retreat from off the great plains region at the foot of the Rockies.

"The evidence is various and cumulative in character. For example, if we face southward and travel from Cheyenne, say twenty or thirty miles toward Denver, we notice some low-lying mesas on the west, with still lower ones on the east. These mesas were once left as islands during the last of the retreating water. At one point it is only about a mile between these erosion remnants, the intervening plain being almost horizontal. Following farther to the south in the line of this old drainage channel, one notices a mass of rocks in the middle of the channel, wide and deep depressions being still visible on either side of these rocks where the increased rapidity of the water swirled around them. About one mile still farther south we come upon the upper end of a modern ravine made by the head of a modern little stream as it cuts backward into the soft alluvium.

"This particular assemblage of phenomenon might be duplicated a hundred times all up and down the front of the Rockies from the Gulf to the Arctic. Similar phenomena occur on a smaller scale among the mountains of the eastern part of the continent and in similar situations all over the world." [7]

However, the effect of the Flood in its strata-forming potentialities was not limited to the period of the rising waters or even to the 150 days during which the water apparently remained stationary, but it extended also to the 150 days that followed when the waters abated and the earth again became dry land.

One of the great problems of the Flood, as we have seen, was the question concerning the source of the water. Whence came the water which was sufficient to submerge the entire face of the earth with its highest mountain? We answered that question in a previous chapter.

But a problem equally perplexing is: What became of the water when the Flood began to subside and land and water were again separated?

Some of the water no doubt was absorbed by the atmosphere, from which part of the Flood had come, as the reference in Gen. 8:1 to the wind passing over the earth implies. But it is inconceivable that all the waters were disposed of in that way, as even Moses seems to indicate. He writes: "And the waters returned from off the earth continually" (Gen. 8:3). The Flood subsided when the waters continued to return to the great basins, the original source of most of the Flood waters. When the Flood began, the barriers that had been fixed by the Creator on the third day of Creation to separate the water and land segments had been removed, and water and land had again returned to the original chaos, which had existed before the third day of Creation. When the "waters returned continually" after the Flood, a miracle similar to that performed on the third day of Creation was repeated. Land and water were again separated, and dry land once more appeared. The enormous mass of water which covered the entire globe and which had been stationary for 150 days was suddenly set into motion in a specific direction. The force required to move a body of water was the same then as it is now. That force is gravity. This means that when the waters returned continually, there occurred a series of major disturbances upon the surface of the earth. The great diastrophic movements of the third day of Creation were repeated, and great land masses rose once more out of the water, while the bottom of the sea dropped to corresponding lower levels. The word "continually" would seem to indicate that these two movements of the earth were not simultaneous in every part of the earth, but that the process was gradual, covering a longer period of time, possibly many months or even longer. Think of the enormous volume of water rushing on with ever-increasing speed toward the new lower levels as the bottom of the sea slowly gave way and great land masses were forced up and new mountain ranges were being born. The eroding, transporting, and stratifying force of such masses of water in motion is beyond calculation. Imagine a supergiant lifting up the basin of the Pacific Ocean on its western shore and pouring its water over the American continents in one great splash. Nothing could withstand the force of the on-rushing waters of such a flood. Mountains would be leveled and hills be moved; valleys would be filled up and rocks and boulders, gravel and sand, be scattered abroad over miles and hundreds of miles of territory; and changes would be effected in the surface of the earth which under the normal operation of the laws of nature would require millions of years to accomplish.

To get the full significance of the effect of the receding water, we must remember that these waters were rushing on toward the newly created basins over the soft churned-up debris and the wreckage of the world that had been subjected to a continuous convulsion of forty days and to a flood which had lasted for more than a year. Volumes of water of such proportions, set into torrential motion, laden with rocks, gravel and other debris, rushing over the newly deposited materials not yet solidified and confined to places of narrow channels because of the rising mountains, could easily scoop out a Niagara Gorge, a Grand Canyon, and similar channels, or build up a Mississippi delta measured by thousands of square miles in a matter of days and weeks instead of the fantastic millions and billions of years commonly ascribed to that process.

A striking example of erosion by running water is furnished by the Simeto River on Sicily. Wallace reports that this river cut a deep channel through a solid bed of lava, which was laid down in a volcanic eruption in 1603.[8] In 1828 Sir Charles Lyell visited this scene and found that this comparatively small river had cut a channel several hundred feet wide and forty to fifty feet deep through the solid mass of volcanic rock.

Travelers tell us that gorges measuring hundreds of feet in depth are cut in the loess deposits of China by a single flood of a comparatively short duration. But all the floods of a century, or ten centuries for that matter, of the Yangtze and Mississippi Valleys do not add up to the one great Deluge that destroyed the first world.

The second 150 days of the Flood were therefore a second great orogenic period in the history of our earth. The first mountains were "brought forth" when God caused chaos to take form and when He separated the water from the land on the third day of Creation. These original antediluvian mountains were subjected to the fearful ravages of the Flood. Some of them probably collapsed as a result of earthquakes and volcanic activity accompanying the Flood. The remnants of these broken, twisted, metamorphosed, and tilted strata bear a mute and eloquent testimony to the forces that were released in that awful world destruction. Others were probably uprooted and broken up by the same forces and their wreckage strewn as boulders and erratics over hundreds of miles in the surrounding territory.

In 1903 occurred the so-called Frank slide at Frank, Alberta, Canada, where part of Turtle Mountain broke off the top and crashed down the mountainside into the valley beyond, covering several square miles with the debris of crushed rock and boulders, some as large as moderate-sized houses. The amount of rock that slid from the mountainside was estimated at forty million cubic yards. The town of Frank was completely buried under fifty to seventy feet of debris, and the course of the river was directed into a new channel. The cause of the slide was believed to have been the action of frost and water in the crevices of the mountaintop, the weakening of the foundation through coal mines far under the mountain, and a slight earth tremor, which probably was the immediate cause. But if the combined influence of these factors could cause a mountain to break in two and spread its wreckage over large areas below, what, then, might have happened in that great flood when the greatest forces of nature — volcano, earthquake, and water made their combined attack on the antediluvian mountains? The wreckage of boulders and erratics in various parts of the earth, often piled up in wild confusion, is the answer.

Still other mountains were probably blown into atoms by volcanic explosions like Krakatoa in 1883 and their substance scattered over thousands of miles, settling as volcanic ash or loess or other volcanic products.

The second period of mountain building began when the waters abated, when the bottom of the sea dropped to new levels and the continents of the modern world were pushed upward out of the water. All the great mountain ranges of the present world came into existence during this period. The fossils found in strata are an indisputable proof that they came into existence long after life had appeared on earth, and the fact that fossils of marine and land organisms are often found closely associated is evidence that their substance was laid down in a great flood of water. However, we need not assume that all the present mountain ranges were born simultaneously in every part of the earth. The drying-off process was slow and gradual and continued long after Noah had left the ark. The physical evidence of the existence of large bodies of water until fairly recent times in regions now arid and semiarid would seem to warrant that conclusion. Hence the geologist's conception of the ancient North American continent, with its Cordilleran and Appalachian trough and other features quite different from the present profile, may well be regarded as possible. But the millions of years usually ascribed to the process that brought about the changes become absurd in the light of the cosmic forces that were at work in the Flood and in the period immediately after the Flood.

Another factor not to be overlooked in trying to solve the mystery of our earth's surface is the force of wind and weather erosion. After the flood waters had subsided and large areas had again become dry land, it must have required many years in some localities before the land was sufficiently covered with vegetation to protect it against the action of wind and weather. The revolution on the earth had been so violent and the destruction so complete that the large areas of plant life must have been covered under hundreds and even thousands of feet of earth, sand, lava, volcanic ash, and other debris or have been completely destroyed and washed away by the water. In other areas the bottom of the sea was raised and became dry land and was therefore wholly devoid of all plant life. In these areas years must have elapsed, possibly even decades or centuries, before grass and weeds and small shrubbery had covered the barren, devastated surface, while more centuries were required for the reforestation of the mountainsides and the woodlands. But soil unprotected by vegetation is extremely unstable. Wind and rain may produce tremendous changes on its surface in a comparatively short period of time. One need but observe the effect of a heavy rain on the barren hillside or along the slopes of newly plowed fields of light and sandy soil. A bar of sand and clay six feet deep was washed into one of the St. Louis streets during a single heavy rain during August of 1946. In another street a car was nearly buried in clay and mud by the same rain. On the experimental farm of Wisconsin University at La Crosse, Wisconsin, it was found experimentally that land erosion by rain amounts to seventy tons an acre in a single rainfall of four and one-half inches on a sixteen-per-cent slope of the land. Anyone familiar with our Western prairies knows that a single cloudburst frequently scoops out gaping gullies tens of feet in depth and of equal width, carrying the soil down the hillside to the valley below. The next shower to follow continues the destructive work. In a very few years the

The Sahara Desert

An Example of Moving Sand. A Resurrected Forest. After burying and killing the forest, the sand was blown away, exposing the dead **trees**

topography has undergone a radical change, and new and heavy strata of clay have been laid down in the plains below. An amusing story about the alleged time required to lay down the delta deposit of the Mississippi is told by Dr. Graebner in *God and the Cosmos*. It appears that some human remains had been discovered deep down in the delta deposit near New Orleans, Louisiana. The age of these remains was estimated at 57,000 years, but a short time later a piece of wood at Port Jackson was found at a still greater depth, and an examination of this wood proved it to be from the gunwale of a Kentucky flatboat. The impressive 57,000 years thus shriveled to a very modest 200 years or less.

And what the action of the wind can do to the topography unprotected by vegetation was vividly demonstrated in the destructive dust storms of the early thirties in the dust-bowl regions of our Western States. Mountains of sand were literally moved over hundreds of miles during these dry and dusty years. A single dust storm produced banks of sand and clay ten to twenty feet high, covering trees, farm implements, and even buildings. It was estimated that a single dust storm moved forty to eighty tons of soil an acre from its original place to localities far removed. Many of the magnificent cities of the ancient Babylonian Valley, the Chicagos, Londons, and Liverpools of bygone days, lie buried under mountains of sand and silt carried there by the wind from the surrounding deserts. Nineveh was one of the greatest cities of antiquity, but when Xenophon passed the site about 200 years after its destruction, he did not even recognize the place where the city had stood, so completely was it covered by the drifting sands from the desert.

There must have been large areas in the postdiluvian world which remained barren for many decades before vegetation had spread to cover them and had gained sufficient foothold to hold the soil. The effect of uninterrupted wind and weather erosion on these regions is beyond calculation. Deep ravines and gorges, valleys and lake bottoms, were filled up by the moving soil. There it solidified to form masses of sandstone, shale, and clay deposits or other forms of sedimentary rocks. What might have required millions of years by the slow, normal process of rock formation was thus accomplished in a few years, or decades, or centuries at the most.

To recapitulate in conclusion our findings concerning the question raised at the beginning of the chapter, we might say that the problems of sedimentary rocks, secondary minerals, the great gorges, the age of the earth, and the many other phenomena of our earth are difficult indeed and that, as in the case of many other mysteries of everyday living, we have no complete or altogether satisfactory answers for them. The solutions for these problems commonly found in the textbooks of our schools today are not demonstrated science, but mere theories and hypotheses. They are an attempt on the part of groping men to find an answer.

There is no fault in proposing an hypothesis as a point from which to start in search for truth, but the fault in this case lies in the fact that these hypotheses and theories are presented as assured facts, as so many of our schoolbooks for the grades, textbooks for physical geography and geology, guides in our National Parks, and much of our popular literature on the subject sufficiently prove. The writers of these books and articles sit in judgment over the Biblical account of Creation because only "through faith we understand that the worlds were framed by the word of God" (Heb. 11:3). It is not that phase of geology which is based on actually demonstrated facts which is in conflict with the Bible and which confuses the young Christian student, but these hypotheses and theories presented as established truth.

No, the answer to these difficult questions is not found in these theories. The most reasonable solution to all these problems is still to be found in God's own revelation concerning the origin of the universe and in His account of the destruction of the first world in the great, universal flood.

CHAPTER XVIII

The Glacial Theory
and the Flood

ABOUT 125 years ago a Swiss engineer conceived a new
idea, which, he hoped, would explain more satisfactorily certain phenomena and difficult geological
problems found on the surface of the earth. This theory is
the so-called glacial theory. A discussion of the Biblical
Flood would be incomplete without a careful examination
of this theory.

By the *glacial theory* is meant a belief, now generally
held by geologists, according to which the greater part of
North America, one half of Europe, and large portions of
other continents were at one time in the distant past covered
with an enormous sheet of moving ice, similar to the glaciers
found today in Greenland, the Antarctic, and in other regions
of the earth. Geologists hold that there were at least four
or five, or possibly even more, glacial periods in the history
of our planet, lasting for many millions of years. During
these periods the tropical or semitropical climate that had
prevailed was superseded by a severe cold, and the greater
part of our continent as well as other parts of the earth was
changed into a desolate, icy waste. For reasons unknown
the climate again changed, the ice melted, the glaciers re-

ceded, and the earth again bloomed forth in all its spring-like glory — but only to be destroyed once more by the cruel, irresistible force of ice. And thus the struggle has been going on through eons of time. Another ice age is approaching, so we are told, but we are assured that this will not overtake us until from two to two and a half million years hence. After that, however, a permanent glaciation of the earth can be expected. But for the time being we need not be seriously worried about this approaching catastrophe. We are assured by other prophets that it is not scheduled to occur before five or six million years from now. Others give our earth even eighty million years of respite before this awful evil will overtake us. And we are told that we need not take a pessimistic view concerning the future of our race, for we are informed: "It will make no difference to man. His command over matter will have reached such a pitch that he will be able to live without corn fields and cows."[1]

Others are even more reassuring than that. Thus Prof. A. P. Coleman, formerly of Toronto University, writes: "Some believed that this calamity (the approaching ice age) was due within a few thousand years. More recent studies in astronomy and geology have banished this gloomy fore-boding and changed from the rather moderate ups and downs of the earth's climate during the billion and half years of its geological record" to a more optimistic view. For according "to the latest views of the physicists concerning the sun's resources of heat, we may anticipate the continuance of life on the earth for a time that is practically endless from the human point of view, reaching into the hundreds or even thousands of millions of years. Thus mankind may proceed with its low and halting upward movement, free from haunting dread of an approaching extinction of the race."[2]

The glacial theory became a recognized working hypothesis about a hundred years ago. About that time a number of eminent writers in the field of geology had taken notice of the remarkable phenomenon so common in Scandinavia, Russia, Germany, and Switzerland, of large detached rocks or boulders, found often in great abundance, of immense size and of a kind that did not appear *in situ* in the district where found, but had been transported there from some remote locality, sometimes over a distance of hundreds of miles. The generally accepted reason for this phenomenon was that these rocks had been moved there by the force of water and that some great continental flood or floods had swept them from the original source to their present location. There remained certain difficulties hard to explain by this so-called diluvial theory, but there was no other known agent to account for this phenomenon. But there were those even then who doubted that water alone could account for these scattered boulders and the enormous deposits of gravel and clay intermingled with them, found in regions as just described. But no further light was thrown on the problem until 1822, when a Swiss engineer by the name of Venetz made some interesting studies concerning the existing glaciers in the Swiss Alps and their effects upon the mountains and valleys over or through which they had traveled. He reported his observations in a paper read before the Helvetic Society of Natural History and urged that glaciers were responsible for the erratic blocks which had so persistently puzzled the diluvian theorists. Others followed the clue given, the most prominent among them being Louis Agassiz, later professor at Harvard University and generally known as the Father of Natural Science in America. Agassiz soon became the most ardent advocate of the glacial theory and has thus gained the name of being the originator of the modern school of glacialists. Since then the study of glaciers and their work has been pursued by many noted geologists, and today the glacial theory is generally accepted as the only plausible explanation for the phenomena mentioned and the most reasonable explanation for many of the perplexing geological problems.

*Louis Agassiz, the Father of Natural
Science in America*

That glaciers now exist in many parts of the earth, such as Greenland, the Antarctic regions, Iceland, Scandinavia, and in many of the great mountain ranges, is admitted, and that these glaciers leave certain well-defined marks wherever they are found is also granted; but that in some distant past these glaciers extended far beyond their present limits, covering the greater part of North America, large areas of Europe and of other continents, is not an absolutely demonstrated fact, but based on inferences drawn only from our present-day knowledge of glaciers.

At first glance the glacial theory offers a simple and a most beautiful explanation for many of the puzzling geological problems found on the surface of our earth. But a closer examination of the theory reveals insurmountable difficulties which are overlooked entirely by the average writer on that subject. But before we examine the theory as a whole, and its relation to our study of the Flood in particular, it will be helpful to review the essential facts known about glaciers as they exist in the world today.

A glacier is a mass of ice so situated and of such a size as to have motion. The force giving rise to its motion is gravity, just as it is in the case of running water. The higher the source of running water and of the moving ice, and the greater the pressure of the source, the greater will be the inherent driving force. The rate of motion will therefore depend upon these two factors. Some Alpine glaciers observed during the summer months moved at the rate of thirty-seven inches a day, while the rate in winter was only about one half as great. Others move at a rate much slower. On the other hand the great Jacobshaven Glacier of Greenland has been observed to move at a rate as high as sixty-five feet a day at the foot where it enters the sea. The movement of glaciers has been fittingly compared to the slow forward-rolling movement of molasses or tar in winter or with the slow rolling movement of molten lava.

Glaciers are formed from snow where the annual snow-fall is in excess of the melting power of the source at that point. Through the influence of pressure, melting, and occasional rains, the snow is gradually transformed into ice. In the polar regions, glaciers are formed at an altitude of 6,000 feet or over. In other parts of the world they are formed only where mountains are high enough to rise above the snow line. This is true even under the equator in the heart of Africa and South America, so that all peaks that rise above 16,000 or 17,000 feet bear glaciers.

Like running water, moving ice is a powerful agent in transporting rocks and other debris. But owing to the difference of ice and water, there are great differences in their modes of transportation. As the glacier moves along between the walls and peaks of mountains, rocks are plucked from the sides, or earthy material or boulders fall down upon it from overhanging cliffs and banks or are deposited upon it by landslides of greater or lesser extent. As this material comes to rest upon the surface of the glacier, it at once begins to partake of its motion. Other material is added, and thus the load is carried down the mountain side and deposited where the glacier begins to melt. Such a line of debris is called moraine. When it is formed along the edge of the ice, it is called a lateral moraine. If it is deposited at the foot of the glacier where the rate of melting is equal to its movement, it is called a terminal moraine. Sometimes the earthy material carried by the glacier is so enormous in quantity that the terminal moraine covers large masses of ice and protects them from melting for a long period of time. Sometimes even forests may thrive on the debris covering such masses of ice. When the ice finally melts away and removes the support from the overlying debris, this settles down in very irregular manner, causing deep depressions which from their shape have been given the name of "kettle holes." Where glaciers enter directly into the ocean, as on the coast of Greenland and in the Antarctica, they give rise to icebergs, while Alpine glaciers provide an inexhaustible source of water for mountain torrents and the great continental streams. If it were not for the glaciers, the water supply of the earth would gradually accumulate and be permanently stored in the polar regions and in those elevations where the melting of snow and ice no longer occurs. The largest ice fields today are found in Greenland and in the Antarctic. In Greenland the ice sheet covers an area of over 700,000 square miles and on the Antarctic Continent the area of 5,000,000 square miles, or an area twice the size of continental United States.

On the facts thus gathered from existing glaciers the glacial theory has been evolved to account for certain phenomena found on the surface of our earth. The most important and most perplexing of these phenomena are the following: (1) moraines and glacial drifts, (2) rounded and smooth rocks, (3) striated, carved, and furrowed rocks, (4) erratics, perched rocks, and boulders, (5) peculiar topographical formations as drumlins, kames, etc., (6) glacial lakes.

1. *Moraines and Glacial Drifts.* We have already seen how glaciers may collect and transport large quantities of debris, such as boulders, clay, gravel, and sand, and deposit these materials in various forms called, by a general term, moraines, or glacial drift, when spread over a wide area. The distinguishing feature of glacial deposits are: (1) the composition of glacial deposits consists of a mixture of various materials, such as boulders, large fragments of rocks, clay, sand, and gravel. (2) As a rule, these materials are not separated or stratified, but indiscriminately mixed together without any particular order. Wherever deposits of this kind are found lying on strata of a different character, such deposits are believed to have been subjected to glacial action. In North America the so-called glacial areas comprise roughly all of Canada; in the United States, the mountain region to the Pacific coast and southward to California,

and, east of the Rocky Mountains — following roughly a line parallel with, but somewhat west and south of, the Missouri River — from southern Alberta to a point just below St. Louis and then extending eastward, again roughly following the Ohio River to below Cincinnati, and then east to a point below the City of New York.

In New England the glacial deposits have an average thickness of from ten to twenty feet. West of the Alleghenies, in New York, Pennsylvania, and Ohio, glacial drift reaches a thickness of from 150 to 200 feet.

One of the most puzzling glacial phenomena in the Mississippi Valley is the driftless area, two hundred miles long and over one hundred miles wide, which occupies the southeastern part of Minnesota, the southwestern part of Wisconsin, and the northeastern corner of Iowa. This area is surrounded on every side by the characteristic marks of glaciation, but it itself is free from any glacial evidence. Its rocks preserve no scratches and are not covered by glacial deposits or by foreign boulders. No completely satisfactory reason for this phenomenon has yet been found, though different theories are advanced. A similar driftless area has been observed in Russia near Orel, a place which has figured prominently in the war news during World War II.

2. *Rounded and Smooth Rocks.* Rounded and smooth rocks found only in certain areas are believed to be further evidence for the glacial theory. Every glacier carries with it, imbedded in its under surface, a great number of rocks and stones, which during the slow but unceasing motion over beds of rocks crush and grind down all rocky projections, thereby producing gently rounded or flattened surfaces even on the hardest and toughest of rocks.

3. *Striated, Grooved, and Furrowed Rocks.* By striated, or furrowed, rocks are meant rocks with deep grooves cut into them, apparently by other rocks slowly moving over them under tremendous pressure. This is a perplexing phenomenon, and the glacial theory is believed to be the

most reasonable explanation for the striated rocks. Such striae have been observed in many places. An excellent example is found near Sandusky on Lake Erie. The portion of the striated rocks preserved there is thirty-three feet below a line extending from rim to rim. But less spectacular striation marks are found in many places on the earth.

4. *Erratics, or Perched Rocks.* By erratic rocks, or perched rocks, are meant large isolated masses of rock far removed from their original source and deposited in areas where the same type of rock is not found. Erratic blocks were among the phenomena which first attracted men of science and caused them to question the diluvial theory. Large masses of granite and hard metamorphic rock, for example, which can be traced to Scandinavia, are scattered over the plains of Denmark and northern Germany. Some of these blocks are of an immense size, weighing thousands of tons. The same phenomenon is found here in America in the New England States and in New York, Pennsylvania, Ohio, Michigan, Wisconsin, Minnesota, Iowa, in eastern and western Canada, and elsewhere. These erratic rocks are found sometimes in great numbers and piled up in irregular masses forming hills of granite boulders, which are often covered with great forest trees. In many cases the distance over which they have been transported is very great, and sometimes they are found at an elevation apparently much higher than their source.

Professor D. F. Wright found an enormous accumulation of boulders on a sandstone plateau in Monroe County, Pennsylvania. Many of these boulders were granite and must have come either from the Adirondacks about two hundred miles north or from the Canadian highlands still farther away. On the Kentucky hills about twelve miles south of Cincinnati conglomerate boulders containing pebbles of red jasper can be traced to an outcropping of the same boulders to the north of Lake Huron, more than six hundred miles distant. Surrounding the shores of Lake Okoboji, in northwestern Iowa, are great heaps of granite boulders carried there from the nearest possible source two hundred miles or more away. But the most remarkable example of boulder transportation is found on the summit of Mount Washington, over six thousand feet above sea level. The boulders found consist of gray gneiss, the nearest outcropping of which is at Jefferson, several miles to the northwest and three thousand to four thousand feet lower than Mount Washington. The largest known glacial erratic in North America is on the great plains of western Canada, at Ohkotoks, near Sheep Creek, Alberta. The boulder is of quartzite and apparently was transported at least forty miles from its source. It is eighty feet long, forty feet wide, and thirty feet high and is buried about five feet in the ground.[3]

5. *Topographical Formations, like Kames, Drumlins, etc.* By *kames* are meant mounds and widening ridges of sand, gravel, and fragments of rock, resembling an artificial rampart across the country. Sometimes they are several miles in length. They vary in breadth and height, some of the more conspicuous ones being upward of 400 to 500 feet broad at the base and arising to a height of sixty feet above the general surface of the ground.

By *drumlins* are meant lenticular-shaped hills composed of glacial material and containing, interspersed through their mass, numerous scratched stones of various sizes. They vary in length from a few hundred feet to a mile and are usually about two thirds as wide as they are long. In height they vary from twenty-five feet to two hundred feet. The region around Boston is noted for drumlins.

6. *Glacial Lakes.* It is a well-known fact that regions generally believed to have been covered with continental glaciers are noted for their great number of lakes. Minnesota, Wisconsin, Ontario, Manitoba, northern Alberta, and other regions are striking examples of this. Geologists believe that these lakes had their origin in the action of ice once moving

over this area, scooping them out, damming up streams and filling them with water.

These and many other factors and geological problems have led modern scientists to the glacial theory as the most reasonable explanation to these problems.

A study of a world catastrophe such as the Flood would not therefore be complete without a careful examination of this theory.

We may begin by saying that if anyone feels constrained to accept the glacial theory as the best solution for the geological problems mentioned, he may do so without fear of conflicting with the Biblical cosmogony or of violating his faith in an infallible Bible. This does not mean, however, that he may substitute the glacial theory for the Flood. The Flood of Noah's times is an historical event recorded as such in the Bible and therefore must be accepted. But the Bible says nothing for or against an ice age as taught by modern geologists. The fact that the Flood was accompanied or followed by a sudden and radical change in temperature and that a severe and rigorous climate settled upon a certain region of the earth has been stated at greater length in a previous chapter. And that this cold period lasted for a long time in the regions affected is quite possible and even probable. It is also granted that huge masses of ice may have floated down from the polar regions before the diluvial waters had fully subsided and the continents had taken their present form. Nor is it denied that this floating ice may have been an effective agent of the Flood waters in changing the topography of the earth. It is quite conceivable that these diluvial icebergs left indelible traces on the surface of our earth as they moved along protruding islands and mountain peaks or when they finally were stranded in the shallow subsiding waters of the Flood. There where they landed, these mountains of ice may have remained for ages, blocking streams and courses of water and causing other great changes. However, that is something quite different from the accepted glacial theory. Nor can we allow on the basis of Scripture that millions of years were involved. For though there may be some reasonable doubt about the exact chronology of the Old Testament, especially in the period between Noah and David, the difference is not a matter of many thousands, much less millions, of years, but at most a question of centuries or possibly a few millennia. With Moses, the history of our earth begins within the scope of human reckoning; and with Luke (ch. 3) or St. Paul the two great historical events in history, man's fall and man's redemption, are not separated by years numbered in astronomical figures, but are within the scope of normal human history. With these limitations, the belief in a continental ice age does not conflict with Genesis or any other part of the Bible. But it is quite another question whether the proposed theory is the real answer to the difficulties encountered and the solution to the problems in question. It is true that practically all recognized geologists today accept the glacial theory as a fact, but such acceptance itself is not yet decisive, nor need it disturb us. The glacial theory is a human opinion and not a fact which has been demonstrated. It is based on inferences, not on demonstrated proof, and the history of human thought has established one fact beyond a doubt, and that is the truth of the familiar Roman dictum *Errare humanum est.*

It is not so long ago when the most noted and recognized scientists and experts accepted La Place's theory of the universe as the solution of the *Weltraetsel* or Darwin's theory of evolution as the answer of the question concerning the origin of the species. But no reputable scientist today will subscribe to either of these theories as propounded by these two specialists in their respective fields. Again it must be remembered that the conclusions of the glacial theory are arrived at only by inferences and not by actual demonstration. For glaciers as they now exist on the mountainsides, in Greenland, or in the Antarctic regions, carrying their

*Childs Glacier, Alaska. A huge valley
glacier fed by many tributaries*

*An Erratic of Quartzite Sandstone of Rocky
Mountain Origin. Fifty feet long and 35 feet
wide; 25 feet high above the surface. Northeast of Glenwoodville, Alberta, Canada*

A Basalt Boulder Hurled High into the Air by New Mexican Volcano. Note the size in comparison with man

debris down the valley or into the sea, are one thing. That glaciers, covering the greater part of our continent and other continents, existing in regions which normally have a semi-tropical or even tropical temperature, that such glaciers moved hundreds or even thousands of miles from the centers of their sources — creeping over plains and mountaintops, scooping out great troughs for lakes and rivers here and spreading a glacial drift to a depth of thirty, sixty, one hundred and fifty, and two hundred, or even more feet over millions of square miles — is quite another matter. Before subscribing to all that the glacialists tell us, it may be well for us to inquire whether the proposed solution actually solves the problems in question or whether it raises new problems even more difficult than those it claims to solve. In other words, we had better make sure that the cure prescribed is not worse than the disease itself.

The very first question that presents itself for an answer is: "What caused the change in the climate to bring about a world-wide glaciation?" The fossil remains prove that before this alleged ice age overtook the existing world, our earth had enjoyed a tropical or semitropical climate, or, as one writer puts it, a uniform and springlike climate. What caused the change? What caused this cosmic change to repeat itself four or five times in succession? A great many theories have been proposed, but every geologist knows that the final answer to this question is still to be given. The Canadian geologist A. P. Coleman admits: "Until more is known of the causes of glacial periods, accounting for these alternations of cold and warm climate, no positive answers can be given to such questions." [4]

To bring about a world-wide glaciation as proposed would require the suspension or at least a most radical change in the laws governing the universe. True, the Flood, as described in Genesis, was brought about by divine intervention in the laws of nature. But to cover the world with a flood of ice to a depth of more than fifteen cubits over the highest mountains required a miracle or a series of miracles greater than that necessary to bring about the universal flood. A sufficient quantity of water necessary to submerge the entire face of the earth was and still is available, and it did not require some cosmic miracle to create it and thus make possible a universal flood. Even the forces necessary to spread the existing water were already in the universe, and all that was needed was the release of these forces. To cover the earth with ice, however, far greater changes were required. The sun had to be blotted out over certain areas for millions of years, while it continued to send forth its heat and rays of light over the remaining parts of the earth in the same latitude of the globe. And though the Hudson Bay and the northern waters far beyond are said to have been covered with ice, yet it is claimed that evaporation continued to produce quantities of snow for these regions unprecedented in the history of our earth. All of this is so utterly contrary to the process of the laws of nature, as we know them, that a miracle greater than the Flood would be required to account for such changes. It is folly therefore to assume that the glacial theory simplifies the problems of geology, or that it removes them beyond the sphere of the miraculous. The violent change in, or the suspension of, the laws of nature necessary to bring about the alleged ice age are in their very essence a miracle, and a stupendous miracle at that.

Coleman admits that the problem is almost "insoluble." Writing on the glaciation of Labrador, he raises the question: "Why should a low tableland, too far from the sea to furnish any evaporation, except Hudson Bay, which it presently filled and obliterated, become one of the continent's greatest glacial centers?" This problem, like that of the even more remarkable Keewatin in the very heart of the continent, seems almost insoluble. The region probably stood higher than now at the end of the Pleistocene, perhaps to the extent of two thousand feet, but it was far below the snow

313

line under present conditions of precipitation. Even the tableland of the Torngats, which reaches four or five thousand feet, has no permanent snow and nourishes only a dozen little cirque glaciers, less than twenty-five miles from the sea at present, though it is winter two-thirds of the year and snow falls in almost every month of summer. However improbable it may seem, an ice sheet covering at least 1,500,000 square miles and thick enough near the margin to bury the Appalachian Mountains centered in Labrador, and it is usually taken for granted that this happened three times, with two intervals of deglaciation. The evidence for these statements, however, is drawn almost wholly from the southern fringes of the glacial theory, and no detailed study of the drift of the interior has ever been made.[5]

I should like to call special attention to these words of this recognized geologist: "However improbable it may seem, an ice sheet covering at least 1,500,000 square miles. . . ." That is not the language of demonstrated science. That is the language of faith. If the theologian makes a statement based on the Bible, he is ridiculed as naive and credulous and as one still clinging to outmoded beliefs or myths. But when a geologist makes a wild claim, lacking the authority of the Bible, then it is repeated as absolutely true, and no one dare question it. It is evident that the theologian by no means has a monopoly on faith and dogmatism.

The second question which the glacial theory forces upon us is: "Why would the glaciers arise and move out from the specific centers generally ascribed to them?" According to the accepted theory, there were three chief centers on this continent from which the ice radiated over all of Canada and a great part of the United States. The first of these is the Labrador ice sheet, with a center between Labrador and Hudson Bay. The second is known as the Keewatin ice sheet, with a center northwest of Hudson Bay, near the Great Slave Lake. And the third is known as the Cordilleran ice sheet, with a center in north British Columbia.

From these centers the ice is said to have pushed out, covering over four million square miles or the greater part of the continent. If the glacial theory is to offer a reasonable explanation for certain phenomena on our earth, there must be some reasonable cause for the origin in the geographical areas assigned to them. If present-day glaciers are to be the criteria and exemplify the law involved, this continental ice sheet could not have originated in the centers assigned to them. Glaciers today are found only on mountains or plateaus and never originate below an altitude of six thousand feet even in the Arctic region.

Referring to this phenomenon, Russell A. Wallace writes: "It is a very remarkable and most suggestive fact that nowhere in the world at the present moment are there any extensive lowlands covered with perpetual snow. The tundras of Siberia and the barren grounds of North America are all clothed with vegetation, and it is only where there are lofty mountains or plateaus, such as in Greenland, Spitzbergen, and Grinnell Land, that glaciers, accompanied by perpetual snow, cover the country, and descend in places to the level of the sea." [6]

The altitude of the alleged Labrador and Keewatin ice sheets is comparatively low, not rising much over a thousand feet above the sea level, and possibly lower, while the Cordilleran source at places only rises to about three thousand feet. If the work of the glaciers as observed in the mountains today is to be applied on a continental scale, then surely it is only fair to apply the law that governs the formation of glaciers today. And according to that law no glaciers could have originated in the areas assigned to them. If, on the other hand, a general rise of half of the continent is postulated, we require again such a violent change for which there is no satisfactory explanation. In fact, the enormous weight of the alleged mountains of ice should have caused the land to sink rather than rise.

*The Extent of Glaciation in North America
During the Ice Age*

But the problem of the glacialists becomes even more involved. While glaciers are formed in North America and on this side of the pole, there is no evidence of similar glaciations on the opposite side of the pole in northern Siberia. "It is a familiar fact," writes Howorth, "that there are no traces of glaciation in northern Asia, but, on the contrary, there is the most complete and consistent evidence that no such traces are to be found either on the flat tundras or on the higher ground." [7]

And again he writes: "We find, roughly speaking, that by the fortieth meridian of east longitude, passing through the White Sea, and the one hundred sixtieth of west longitude, passing through Alaska, but separated by the Atlantic Ocean, is included the portion of the northern hemisphere which presents us with proofs of that abnormal extension of ice which we styled the Glacial Epoch. Great as this extension of the glacial episode was, it is only fair to point out that from the Kola Peninsula in fortieth east longitude to Bering Strait, the vast tundras of Siberia, extending through one hundred fifty degrees of longitude, do not appear to present any traces of that abnormal ice episode which is so remarkably impressed on northwestern Europe and the northern part of America. . . . There is consequently no evidence for assuming that during the extension of the glacial episode on Scandinavia, Great Britain, and North America the climate of Siberia differed very greatly from what it is now. Presumably it must have been warmer, for the land at that time supported vast herds of mammoth, rhinoceros, and other large mammals whose remains are found in the tundras of Siberia and the more northern New Siberian Islands." [8]

This is a most astounding fact indeed! An Arctic winter and an icy waste on the one side of the pole; on the other, in the same latitude or extending even farther north, a warm and pleasant climate suitable to sustain land animals of various kinds. In this case evidently the sun did not shine alike on the just and the unjust, for while Siberia was bathed in summer sunshine, America, in the same latitude, was shrouded in polar darkness and shivered in perpetual ice and snow — a solar blackout on one side and a brilliant summer sun on the other. Most people would call that a most astounding miracle, surpassing in uniqueness even that of Joshua. Evidently the matter is not so simple as the average textbook on the ice age would try to make it.

But there is a third problem even more serious than the other two, and that is the question: What was the force that caused the ice to move over the greater part of North America, Europe, and other regions of our earth? As stated above, the three centers from which the ice moved outward were: the Labrador, the Keewatin, and the Cordilleran protaxis. The ice flow that reached St. Louis and beyond seems to have had its source in the Keewatin area west of Hudson Bay. This means that the ice was pushed onward over a distance of from 2,000 to 2,400 miles. As with water, so there is with ice only one force which could cause it to move or flow, and that one force is gravity. Where gravity cannot operate, that is, where there is no pressure, either from the glaciers or weight acting on it en masse, or acting differentially on the particles in consequence of the ice having a sloping surface, it will not move, but will remain as stationary as ice in a lake or pond. We are told that water will flow on a slope of six inches to a mile. Glacial ice is a more or less viscous body which moves partly en masse in its bed and partly by differential motion among its particles, that is, in a sort of rolling movement, the top falling over its front, as in the case of molasses, pitch, or lava. From the very motion of ice, it is evident therefore that it requires a very steep slope before it will become mobile. Ice, on a level surface, is a dead, immobile mass which can be piled up to a considerable height, like so much rock or so many bales of hay, without causing the slightest movement. It would require a Pikes Peak piled on the Himalayas and a steady slope from Keewatin to St. Louis to provide sufficient gravity to cause such a mountainous sheet of ice to move over this area. But the fact is that the source of the glacier which is said to have reached St. Louis has an elevation of less than one thousand feet above sea level and sloping northward rather than to the south, and the whole region from Keewatin to St. Louis is an area of comparatively low altitude without an appreciative slope southward. It would mean, therefore, that the original glacier had to overcome gravity and move contrary to all laws of nature upgrade until it had reached the transverse watershed at an elevation of about two thousand feet and, after that feat was accomplished, push on for two thousand miles southward over a territory in which the slope is so gentle that it can be called a flat country.

Prof. G. W. Dawson, speaking of the ice sheet that is supposed to have moved over western Canada (quoted by Howorth), writes: "I have not found either in the Laurentian region or over the area of the plains, or in the Rocky Mountains, any evidence necessitating the supposition of a great northern ice cap or its southern progress. . . . To reach the country in the vicinity of the forty-ninth parallel, a northern ice sheet would have to move up the long slope to the Arctic Ocean and cross the second transverse watershed; then, after descending to the level of the Saskatchewan Valley, again to ascend the slope amounting to over four feet in a mile to the first transverse watershed and plateau of the lignite tertiary. Such an ice sheet, moving throughout over broad plains of soft and unconsolidated cretaceous and tertiary rocks, would be expected to mark the surface with broad flutings parallel to the direction and to obliterate its transverse watershed and valleys. . . . If it be supposed that a huge glacier, seated on the Laurentian axis, spread westward across the plains, the difficulties are very serious. The ice, moving southward after having descended into the Red River trough, would have to ascend the eastern escarpment of soft cretaceous rocks forming its western side, which in one place rises nine hundred feet above it. Having gained the second prairie steppe, it would have to pass a third over the sloping surface, surmount the soft edge of the third steppe without much altering its form, and finally terminate over seven hundred miles from its source and at a height exceeding the present elevation of the Laurentian axis by over two thousand feet. The distribution of the drift negatives the theory which would oppose the passage of an immense glacier across the plains." [9]

The problem of the Labrador glacier is even more serious. The glacier moving down from that center had to cross lakes and river beds and ascend mountain peaks three and four thousand feet higher than its source. Nowhere today do we find glaciers overcoming such formidable obstacles and moving hundreds and thousands of feet above their source. Both Greenland and Antarctica, the two regions where continental glaciers are found today, consist of high plateaus and mountain ranges, from which the glaciers move down to the sea but not up.

Even A. P. Coleman, an ardent glacialist, is somewhat perplexed about this glacier and writes: "When one remembers that the St. Lawrence Valley rises little above sea level and that the Labrador glacier center, three or four hundred miles north of Quebec, is on a tableland scarcely two thousand feet high, it is evident that advance of an ice sheet from that gathering ground towards the coastal plain would encounter a very serious obstacle before reaching New England and southeastern New York. Is it possible that it could surmount this mile-high barrier and spread over the plains on the other side?

"Much less is known of the glacial history of the mountains than of the lowlands on each side, and there are conflicting views on the subject. Some authors, doubting that they were ever crossed by the ice, others believing that only one glaciation covered them and that they stood up as nunataks above the later ice sheets, while a few geologists seem to hold that two or even three ice invasions passed over them without trouble." [10]

But if it is claimed that there was a general uplift of the continent in the regions concerned, providing the necessary slope for the glaciers, we still have failed to solve the difficulty. If, for example, the elevation of Labrador stands at four thousand feet at the time of the ice age, as is claimed by Coleman, the altitude is still too low to push glaciers over the tops of mountains to the south several thousand feet higher. But more than that: If there was an uplift, we must have an explanation for such an unusual phenomenon. The arguments are all against an uplift and rather in favor of a subsidence because of the enormous load of ice piled upon this area if the glacial theory is to stand.

Again we find that the solution offered is more difficult than the problem it aims to solve. To accept this solution would require a faith large enough not only to move mountains, but a faith so strong that it would create supermountains, plane them down to a normal level, or cause them to disappear in the bowels of the earth, only to repeat the same process over and over again. Surely no unbiased person would claim that this is less miraculous than the Flood of Noah's day.

But others argue that gravity was furnished by the mountain of ice itself, that is, it is claimed that the sheet of ice grew to such an enormous height from the continued addition of snow that a mountain of ice was formed high enough to provide the necessary gravity and that the upper strata of ice moved over the lower strata down the mountainside and eventually over the entire continent. That the upper strata may move over the lower is not doubted or denied. This phenomenon can be observed in existing glaciers, where the upper strata have been observed to move more rapidly than the lower, which are retarded by dragging along on the surface. But if this is granted, then new questions are raised with new and more difficult problems.

The first question is: How, in the first place, could a glacier originate in a region which was nearly level with the sea or had an altitude of less than one thousand feet above sea level? The fact is that nowhere today are glaciers found at sea level either in the Arctic region or anywhere else. There are no glaciers in the Arctic below an altitude of six thousand feet. The mountains of Greenland reach an elevation of from six thousand to eleven thousand feet, while the plateau of Antarctica has an elevation of ten thousand feet, the average being six thousand feet.[11]

In the second place, it must be remembered that ice sliding over ice could not gather such material as boulders, clay, sand, and the like, which is usually described as glacial drift. Glaciers can pick up a lot of debris only by plucking it out from the mountainside, or by catching this material as it falls onto their sides from higher elevations, or by picking it up or pushing it along at the base. None of these possibilities could have occurred with a glacier sliding along over ice from a mountain of ice.

But there is still another problem connected with this supposed mountain of ice. It certainly raises the important question: What is the natural limit to the thickness to which ice can accumulate before it will melt as a result of its own weight? The pressure of thousands of feet of ice would be so enormous and the friction of the molecules of ice so great that thousands of feet of ice would cause the bottom to melt at a rate more rapid than it could accumulate on the top. The fact is that existing ice fields today do not reach such fabulous thicknesses as are postulated by the glacialists. The ice sheet on Antarctica is estimated not to exceed two thousand feet in thickness and is described as generally much thinner in other places, while the ice sheet in Greenland, on high ground, is about a thousand feet in thickness.[12]

In short, in whatever way we view this theory, it involves new physical problems so enormous that it must be ruled out as a possible solution of the phenomena it claims to explain. Only by resorting to the miraculous, or to the assumption of direct divine intervention, could the ice have accomplished the things that are ascribed to it.

But the glacial theory raises many other serious questions, so that one wonders how straight-thinking scientists can continue to propose it as a solution to the problems they aim to solve.

One of the claims made for the glacier is that it has been a great erodent agent, scooping out U-shaped valleys and eroding lake and river beds out of the solid rock. One would not necessarily object to this claim if it were not assumed that the glacier scooped out and spread glacier drift at the same time. That a glacier can pick up ground material or that it can transport other material is not denied, but that it can erode, pick up, and spread out the material at the same time over hundreds of thousands of square miles and to a thickness of many hundreds of feet, as is claimed for some places, is quite a different matter. It is inconceivable, to say the least, how an ice sheet could be an excavating instrument sufficiently erodent to be able to scratch and furrow rocks and to excavate lakes and river beds and to carry blocks of stone for hundreds of feet up to maintaintops and at the same time deposit a soft bed of material on the surface over which it moves. If an ice sheet had sufficient energy to traverse deep basins like the Great Lakes, the Baltic, and the North Sea and to carve out deep glacial grooves, it is hard to understand how it could avoid sweeping away every trace of soft material from the area over which it moves.

Moraines found with existing glaciers today, whether they be lateral, medial, or terminal, are something quite different, and by no stretch of the imagination can such moraines be converted into a continental glacier drift. We do believe that the existence of the so-called glacial drift covering hundreds of thousands of square miles of level country cannot be accounted for by the action of glaciers. There are too many difficulties to make this seem plausible. Furthermore, glaciers are entirely incapable of separating the drift into separate beds of sand, gravel, clay, and the like, as actually occurs in the glacial drift. The debris of the moraine is mixed and heterogeneous and never separated and sorted, as is the case in the areas covered by the so-called glacial drift.

Again it is claimed that glaciers are the only plausible explanation for the presence of erratics, already mentioned in an earlier chapter. The phenomenon of erratics is quite common. They are found here in America, in Europe, and elsewhere. The classical example usually referred to are the erratics of North Germany carried there over hundreds of miles from their original source in Scandinavia. But an even more remarkable example is found in our own country in the boulders of gray gneiss found on the summit of Mount Washington. The composition betrays their origin. They were carried there over a great distance, but what is more, from the source allegedly three to four thousand feet lower than their present elevation. It is readily admitted that it is difficult to conceive of any agent moving huge blocks of stone weighing many tons over hundreds of miles and depositing them on an elevation higher than their original source. An attempt to find a reasonable solution for this problem gave rise to the glacial theory. But we shall see that the glacial theory is not the answer to this problem. That glaciers are able to transport boulders and other material is not denied. This has been observed over and over again on existing glaciers moving down the mountainside. Glaciers move rocks downgrade, but moving rocks upgrade is a different matter. The force that pushes glaciers on is gravity, as we have seen before, but gravity moves only in one direction and that is downward. There is no more inherent power in ice to move uphill than there is in water to flow upgrade. The laws of gravity control the movement of both. How far an a priori theory can blind able and competent scientists and lead them to jump to unwarranted and unscientific conclusions is shown by A. P. Coleman. After admitting the impossible barriers that a glacier would have to encounter when expecting it to rise a mile above its source, this noted and careful Canadian geologist continues: "The climber who spies a bit of foreign stone on the top of Katahdin, Washington, or White Face, should look on it with interest as evidence of strange events. It was picked up probably hundreds of thousands of years ago on the lowlands of the north, was lifted a mile in the grasp of a vast glacier, was released on the summit of the mountains, and has survived the attack of frost, rain, and sun, even serving to be a part of the geological record of the Pleistocene." [13]

This is not science. This is faith, simple faith, in a theory. Moving these events back into the dark past by hundreds of thousands of years does not change the laws of gravity. If those boulders were lying somewhere on the lowlands a hundred thousand years ago, they were held there then by the same force of gravity that holds rocks in their position today. And there is no mysterious power in ice to neutralize the force of gravity. If glaciers move over mountaintops, their sources must be higher than the tops over which they move. A glacier rising in the lowlands cannot move uphill over mountaintops any more than water will flow over ridges higher than its source. But if the sheet of ice was so thick that it covered the surface over which it moved with thousands of feet of ice, elevating its top high above the highest mountaintop, how then could it pick up boulders or rocks on the surface and carry them to the top of the mountains to deposit them there? Glaciers can receive their load only from rocks which they plucked from the mountainside or which fall upon them from peaks higher than the glacier. The rocks on the surface over which the glacier moves cannot work upward through the glacier or by means of the glacier. In fact, rocks that are deposited on the upper surface of the glacier will tend to work down as the glacier moves along, especially when great crevices are formed at an abrupt decline.

And there is still another problem connected with the erratics for which the glacial theory has no satisfactory answer, and that is the question of the mixture of rocks in one locality brought there from sources lying in opposite directions. This phenomenon has been observed in several places of the earth. One of them is in Saxony, where rocks are found lying together of which some had their source in Scandinavia in the north, while others were carried there from some source in the south. A similar phenomenon has been observed on Prince Edward Island, on our own continent, where rocks from Nova Scotia, New Brunswick, Cape Breton, and Laurentian rocks from Labrador are found together in the same place. Moving ice cannot accumulate boulders from opposite directions and deposit them together at one place. An ice sheet moves only in one direction and spreads its debris along the course of its movement. It cannot accumulate boulders and other debris from opposite directions.

But there are still other problems that the glacialists will find hard to explain. What about the fossils found in the so-called glacial drift? If the glaciers ground the hardest rocks to clay and mud and left deep furrows and grooves in the rocks over which they moved, how does it come that fossils of various kinds, fragile shells and other remnants, escaped this grinding process without injury? Not only are these fossils found uninjured, but fresh and salt water shells are mixed together at the same place. How would an ice sheet accomplish this feat? And thus we might continue to raise other questions which are left unanswered by the glacial theory. Either the geological problem remains unsolved by this theory, or the solution offered raises new and more difficult problems than those which it claims to solve. Whether or not there was a period following the Flood which might be called an ice age is a question about which opinion may differ, but that the ice was responsible for the great changes on the surface of the earth ascribed to it is quite a different matter. Only by injecting into this theory a miraculous element is it conceivable that glaciers could have operated on a scale as suggested or could have wrought the changes on the surface of the earth ascribed to them. That God could have suspended the laws of the universe for the time being and enshrouded the earth with a vast sheet of ice is not denied, but that He did so is nowhere told. The evidence adduced by the glacialists is not convincing. However, the Bible tells us of a great world catastrophe which brought to an end the world which He had created. This was a catastrophe of water and not of ice, and we shall see that this universal flood as described in Genesis is sufficient to account for most, if not all, of the phenomena upon which the glacial theory has been built.

CHAPTER XIX

The Flood the Most Reasonable Solution for the Glacial Theory Phenomena

THE glacial theory, as we have seen, is based on phenomena found on the surface of the earth which have been enumerated in the previous chapter. These phenomena are extremely perplexing in their very nature and point to some extraordinary force in action or to some radical change and revolution in our earth. But we have also seen that the glacial theory is an insufficient and unsatisfactory answer to these problems. It solves some problems but creates new ones more difficult than those it aimed to solve. But there is a reasonable answer to all of these questions, and that answer is to be sought in the great world catastrophe which brought the first world to an abrupt end in the great universal flood described in Genesis.

In a previous chapter we have pointed out that there is only one force in nature known to man which offers a reasonable explanation for the sudden destruction and burial of the vast herds of mammoths that in some distant past inhabited the northern plains of Siberia. There is only one force of nature capable of destroying and at the same time burying those great creatures of prehistoric times. There is only one force which can best account for the existence of the great coal beds in the various parts of our planet and the huge basins of oil now found in the bowels of the earth. And likewise there is only one force in nature known to man that will meet most satisfactorily all the requirements necessary to account for those phenomena upon which the geologists have constructed their glacial theory. That one force is water.

Water in a volume sufficiently great and sufficiently disturbed by great upheavals, such as might be caused by earthquakes, volcanoes, and great storms, is capable of becoming a force so cosmic in proportion that it is quite able to accomplish most or all of the changes ascribed to the action of great mountains of moving ice. People who minimize the effect of the Great Flood or attempt to supplement it by other forces fail to comprehend, in the first place, that this was a flood of global proportions and, in the second place, they fail to take into account the great forces of nature by which this flood was brought about and which accompanied it in its destructive work. It must be remembered that the Biblical Deluge was a world convulsion in which heaven and the whole earth were involved. It was God's intention and purpose to destroy that world which He had created for sinless man, and so all the latent forces of nature were unleashed to accomplish this greatest upheaval of all time. These great forces of nature — earthquakes, volcanoes, wind, and water — formed a terrible alliance for a universal destruction. These forces, when combined, are capable of developing an agent for destruction and transportation so enormous that it is beyond human calculation. Even local floods caused by the rising of a single river or river system have at times changed the topography of a given area beyond all recognition. But such local floods, and even the greatest of them known in history, must be multiplied ten thousand times ten thousand to give a picture of that disaster which overtook the first world.

In describing the Dayton flood of 1913, an eyewitness of that disaster wrote as follows: "No boat could live a moment in the rushing current which took houses, bridges, railway tracks, telegraph poles, everything in its overwhelming sweep. I saw the levee, which protected the entire west side and which was described as strongly built of gravel with an average height of twenty feet and thirty-five feet broad at the base, suddenly melt into the river. The great Pennsylvania four-track right of way, part of the finest road-bed in America, melted away like salt. The track on the west side looked like a handful of tangled string thrown into a puddle. One could only get an idea of the strength of the raging flood when the great bridge, weighing hundreds of thousands of pounds, floated downstream hundreds of feet before sinking out of sight." [1]

Another eyewitness, describing the same flood as it affected Peru, Indiana, wrote: "We saw the Broadway Bridge go out and the wreckage rush down with the flood against the interurban bridge, a concrete structure. The wreckage was hurled with such force against the concrete pier that it snapped like a match and was lost to view in the swirl of water." [2]

One of the most catastrophic floods in the history of America was the Johnstown flood of 1889. An eyewitness of this disaster wrote: "For several days towards the end of May the rain had fallen steadily. The creeks were swollen, the rivers full. The enlarged lake became a receiving basin for all the excess water of that region in the Alleghenies.

"Suddenly, with very little warning, the huge dam gave way.

"A solid wall of water forty feet high splurged down the mountain, sweeping everything in its path. Six small villages were practically picked off their foundations and their wreckage hurled with terrific force full upon the people of Johnstown. Few had any chance to escape. They were picked up with their houses and smashed down against

330

the hapless town. The accumulated ruin of eight small villages was carried full force against the stone bridge at the foot of the valley." [3]

Railway cars, trees, wreckage of houses, were thrown together in a great turmoil. Great trees were uprooted, hurled into the air, and pushed through large buildings as one pushes an ice pick through a cardboard box.

Another disaster of a magnitude which appalled the entire nation occurred in September of 1900 in the city of Galveston, Texas. This tragedy was caused by the water of the ocean sweeping over the city. A great storm had arisen, blowing in from the sea over the ill-fated city. As time went on, the wind increased in velocity, growing into a raging hurricane and reaching a velocity of 120 miles an hour. The waters of the Gulf were literally lifted by the fearful wind and hurled with destructive force against the city. The houses crumbled as though made of cardboard, and the raging waters of the sea crept higher and higher into the city. Large buildings collapsed; people and animals perished by the hundreds. "Wreckage," writes an observer, "was thrown with the force of a catapult against the houses which had successfully offered resistance to the storm. In the cemeteries the dead which had been buried for years were washed from their graves and carried across to the mainland. Loaded and empty freight cars were thrown into the bay. Miles of track were twisted and torn like that much tinsel." [4]

In the great flood of the Mississippi in 1927 new channels were cut, and at one place near South Pass a stony whirl scoured the bed of the great river in a few days from a depth of thirty to one hundred and four feet.[5]

The Yellow River in China is notorious for its record of destruction and change. In 1324 it cut a new bed for itself hundreds of miles from its original channel. It continued its course in this new bed for 530 years, but in 1854 it again left its course to turn above Shantung, five hundred miles away, and no one is able to predict with certainty how long it will follow its present course.

Thus we might continue to show that even local river floods have throughout history greatly changed the geography of our globe and altered the face of the earth. But what is a flood of a single river or river system, even in its most destructive magnitude, compared with the universal flood of Noah's days?

In the Biblical Deluge the water continued to rise for forty days and for forty nights, which means that water, storm, earthquake, volcano, and tidal wave were in fearful destructive action for nearly six weeks without interruption. And after the fury of the elements had abated, the earth did not immediately return to normalcy, for we are told that the water remained upon the earth for nearly a year without much change. During this entire period the existing forces of nature, such as wind and tides, continued their normal activity. The winds stirred up this universal ocean and drove its water with relentless force against the mountain peaks. The tides were active then as now, with the only difference that their destructive forces were increased manifold. And it is reasonable to assume that even earthquakes and other disturbances which had occurred during the first forty days continued for some time because of the dislocations that were caused in the foundation of the earth during the Flood and because of the enormous weight of water spread over areas which had not previously been subjected to such a pressure.

Even after the Flood had subsided sufficiently for Noah to leave the ark, the waters did not completely disappear from the surface of the earth at once, but continued over certain areas for centuries, possibly even for thousands of years. Gradually they disappeared, and what had been the bottom of these great seas and lakes became dry land, leaving behind the sea bottom as dry surface.

Again we must bear in mind that the Flood itself changed the balance between water and land masses. Many areas that had been sea in the antediluvian world were elevated to become dry land or even mountain ridges, while some of the prediluvian continents and islands subsided and became bottoms of the sea. If we thus view the Biblical Flood in its real perspective, we find in it a combination of the greatest forces latent in nature, so enormous in their totality that no additional agents or forces are required to bring about those physical changes which the glacialists are wont to ascribe to the mythical moving continents of ice.

The phenomena which have disturbed the geologists of the earlier part of the last century and which gave rise to the glacial theory have been enumerated. The foremost of these problems were the moraines and the so-called glacial drifts, the striated rocks, the rounded boulders, and the erratics. All of these phenomena can best be accounted for by an action of a flood such as described in the Bible.

The moraines and the glacial drifts consist, as we have seen, of large fragments of rock, clay, gravel, and sand. These materials are found in various conditions. Sometimes they are stratified and separated according to their separate elements, and sometimes mixed together without any order. The very fact that the materials of these moraines are frequently separated and stratified seems to be strong evidence that they could not have been laid down by the action of ice. Only water can separate and stratify these materials. The action of water corresponds exactly to the condition in which these materials are found. The heavier materials are deposited first, while the lighter are sifted out and carried greater distances and deposited in the order of their specific weight. Swiftly running currents will deposit less in shallow water, where the velocity is highest, and deposit more in the deep water, where the current is retarded. Moreover, it would be in these deeper waters where the finer materials are deposited. Thus we can account for clay pits in one area followed by sand and gravel bars in close proximity. An examination of any flood plain will demonstrate the correctness of this contention.

Again, the action of water in flood condition seems to be absolutely necessary to explain not only the way in which the material of the drift is spread out over the level plains, but also the manner in which it covers the irregular and broken topography of the country. Drift sometimes occurs up to great heights on the slopes of hills, either in a continuous spread or in a detached mass, where evidently it was arrested by some projection or it filled up some hollow. In many cases it ranged in terraces along the flanks of the hills, leaving its high-water marks.

Furthermore, water, not ice, will best account for the presence and the mixing of marine and fresh water shells and the bones of seals and whales, mammals and saurians, and other fossils, with the drift.

And, finally, those peculiar formations known as kames and eskers can well be accounted for as the result of the meeting of raging waters which carried a mass of heterogeneous materials that remained in disturbed suspension until the turbulence subsided, when the material was gradually deposited in various patterns. A great flood of water entering at both ends of a strait or a crooked or tortuous channel, would break into or meet other waves, and at the place where the collision occurred the kames and eskers would naturally form. Such a flood of water would also account for the variations in depth of many deposits in various areas, piling them up like drifted snow where a sheltering nook or some obstacle prevented the water from having its proper denuding effect. The enormous depth of the drift found in some places cannot be accounted for by ice, but can well be accounted for by the action of water. In the valley of the Clyde the drift deposit is said to reach in some places a thickness of 355 feet. In certain areas of Germany such a deposit has been estimated to exist in a thickness of over three hundred feet. And Coleman speaks of a till in the Vancouver and Puget Sound region having the thickness of a thousand feet. Similar depths of drift have been found in many other places. Again the action of water is the only reasonable solution to account for this phenomenon.

Another phenomenon that contributed very greatly in confirming the geologist in his belief in a continental glacier is the so-called glacial striation. These striae, or grooves and scratches, found on the rocks in many places of the earth are a most remarkable phenomenon indeed. The deep furrows cut into the rocks along Lake Erie have already been referred to. It is evident that they were produced by a sharp-edged, hard stone or by a number of such stones moving over the surface of the softer layer of the rocks below them. Any hard angular rock moving over softer material with sufficient force and pressure will scratch, cut, and carve such a rock as certainly as a carpenter running his plane over the surface of a piece of wood will achieve these results on the material on which he is working. But this fact does not prove that the propelling force of the carving and cutting instrument was a moving sheet of ice thousands of feet in thickness and thousands of square miles in area. It has been demonstrated that water in sufficient quantity and propelled with sufficient force is capable of moving, rolling, and pushing large masses of rock along on the surface over long distances. The volume of water that was agitated and the forces that were active in the Great Flood would have been quite sufficient to account for this phenomenon. The grooving tool would be the same whether the agent moving it was ice or water, the only difference being that in the one instance the tool is held in the grasp of a slow-moving sheet of ice, while in the other it would be pushed and propelled by a volume of rushing water.

In addition, it is also quite possible that some of the striae were produced by floating masses of ice on the great bodies of water that remained after the Flood, referred to earlier in this chapter. Rocks and stones on the shores and banks of large bodies of water are affected by the action of ice in this manner, as can be observed. The same forces were active for decades and possibly centuries on these large inland bodies of water which have now disappeared and left their debris behind.

And, finally, there are the boulders and the erratics, which seem to be the greatest problem of all and really represent the trump card of the glacialists in the support of this theory.

At first glance it really seems difficult to meet the argument of the glacialist at this point. That ice is capable of carrying rocks must be admitted, and that the boulders and erratics which represent these phenomena were removed from their original source and carried to elevations far above the altitude of the parent rock must also be admitted. But the glacial theory is not the answer to this problem, as we have already seen, because of the many other difficulties involved and the new problems it raises. But here again water, if found in sufficient quantity and sufficiently disturbed by the forces of nature already described, is quite capable of accomplishing this seemingly impossible feat. And, again, floating ice, not glaciers, might have been an effective agent of the Flood waters to accomplish the impossible.

The earthquake in Sicily in 1908 caused a tidal wave forty feet high, sweeping with irresistible fury everything before it and wiping out everything that had not been destroyed by the earthquake.

I have already referred to the tidal wave caused by the eruption of Mount Krakatao in 1883, which moved huge blocks of rock, some of them weighing as high as thirty to fifty tons, two to three miles inland.

A similar transport of huge masses of rock occurred as a result of the eruption of Mount Pelée in 1902. Similar evidence could be accumulated in great quantity to prove the enormous transporting power of water in a flood stage.

Howorth, discussing the carrying power of water, quotes Hopkins on the subject as follows: "If a stream of ten miles an hour would move a block of a certain form of five tons weight, a current of fifteen miles an hour would move a block of similar form of upwards of fifty-five tons, and a current of twenty-five miles an hour would, according to the same law, move a block of 320 tons." [6]

And, again, Professor Prestwich, discussing the same problem in a paper read before the Geological Society on the effects of the Holmsferth flood, which was caused by the bursting of a large reservoir, writes: "The weight of the material swept away from the embankment and scattering in gradually decreasing quantity for a distance of half a mile could not have been much less than forty to fifty thousand tons. Where the valley was narrow, the water tore up the surface to a depth of ten to twenty feet and carried away large masses of rock to considerable distances. When the breadth of the valley increased from thirty to fifty yards to one hundred to two hundred, the force of the flood abated. Still the meadows were covered to a depth of from one to two feet with masses of rock mixed with sand and gravel. The bulk of the debris consisted of angular fragments not exceeding one or two feet in diameter. But among them a few large rounded blocks stood out in prominent relief. One of them measured seven feet in extreme length but five feet in breadth and two and one half in depth and weighed probably from five to six tons and was transported for half a mile. Near it was another mass almost the same size. A third block, rather near the reservoir, measured twelve feet by six and one half feet and two feet deep and probably weighed seven or eight tons. The most remarkable block, however, lay in the middle of the valley near upper Digley Mill and at a distance of one third of a mile from the present rock. It was twenty-two feet long, six feet broad, and three and one half feet thick and probably weighed about twenty tons. Although the greater part of the valley was covered with debris, there were places where its surface had been torn up from four to five feet. A stone post at the entrance of the churchyard was broken in two, and one part six and a half feet long by one and a half feet square was found one hundred and fifty yards lower down the valley. All the slabs on the tombs were moved from fifty to two hundred yards, and this occurred where the waters, having spread out a good deal, had lost much of their force. . . . The fields were covered with gravel and fragments of rock, not large, but some from one to two tons in weight. Large iron boilers were carried considerable distance. That of Digley Mill, weighing from fifty to one hundred twenty tons, was found more than a mile down the valley." Dr. Prestwich concludes his account with these words: "If such are the remarkable effects of the temporary flood caused by a body of water comparatively so small and along a valley where its powers could not be maintained, we may form some conception of the enormous power which a more continuous flood with more sustained action would possess."

In 1916 the reservoir of the city of Winfield, Kansas, broke, causing a sudden destructive flood. The reservoir is located on a high elevation about one block east of St. John's College. A small leak had developed which weakened the structure and caused it to break with unexpected suddenness. The torrent of released water roared down the hillside and over the campus of St. John's College toward the city, carrying boulders, gravel, and other debris in wild confusion with it. Large and tough bars of steel were literally twisted around the large maples along the street. A large boulder weighing many hundreds of pounds was rolled down the hill and over the campus and driven into one of the large basement windows of Baden Hall. It required considerable effort to remove it later. The volume of water which caused this flood was comparatively small, because the reservoir stores water for a city of not more than ten thousand population, yet the havoc wrought on the surface over which the

338

water traveled and the number of the boulders, rocks, and other debris scattered over its course was enormous. There are no limitations to water when in flood condition.

A description of the great flood in the Devon Valley, which occurred in August, 1877, and is quoted by Howorth in *The Glacial Nightmare*, reads as follows: "A river four feet in depth was running as a brach from Dollar Burn down the railway. The bridge had become blocked, and the water coming against the obstruction rose in the air as from a volcano, tossing trees and boulders about like straw. . . . The water was perfectly thick with sediment and darkened color, while every now and then mighty boulders were brought into collision with a noise like distant cannon. . . . I now reached the special scene of this disaster, viz., the washing down of the houses. These houses were of stone and were swept away by being undermined. . . . I noticed the cornerstone of one of the houses hurry past me and wondered where it would be carried. Later in the day I found this stone about a third of a mile further down, settled upon the railway; one of its diameters measured three feet and the other two feet four inches. Where the houses fell, an area of three hundred yards in length by forty feet in average breadth and six feet in depth was swept out. Here, then, at least five or six thousand tons of material were removed, much of it being large stones and boulders, some of the latter weighing from ten hundredweights to a ton. . . . The water, laden with its boulders, must have been shot out of the glen as from the mouth of a cannon, for, instead of following the usual course, it went straight over its bank and deposited mighty boulders over a large area twelve feet at least above the present level of the burn. Several of these boulders were a little short of three tons in weight, and many weighed from one to two tons. Some of them alighted with such precision and force that they were shattered into several fragments. A little lower down the water again broke away at a tangent and strewed a similar deposit over a large

area, but the boulders were, on the whole, not quite so large.
. . . As the water lost its transporting power, it filled up its
own channel in its lower levels with pebbles and boulders
to the extent in some places of four or six feet, so that the
burn at the later part of the day ran at a higher level than it
had formerly done. . . . Coming once more to the railway,
we found an immense heap of boulders, some being half
a ton in weight, blocks of stone from the ruined houses, trees,
and shattered furniture, with smaller stones and sand in
abundance. From the surface of the railway that goes over
the burn, three thousand tons were drawn away and from
the burn itself three thousand tons more, while a similar
quantity has since been rolled away by the burn and taken
out by the railroad company. Here also a considerable piece
of land was denuded. . . . Still lower down the water broke
through an embankment and strewed an immense quantity
of boulders in sand and clay upon several fields."

Add to this the possibility of floating ice, then consider
the lifting and carrying power of such floating masses of ice,
and a reasonable solution for the problem of erratics high up
on mountaintops seems possible.

I might continue to add further evidence concerning the
carrying power of water when in flood condition, and the
latent force in water raised to a flood condition to alter the
face of the earth beyond recognition. But what has been
said on the subject is sufficient to show that the Noachian
Flood, when viewed in its real perspective, is the most
reasonable explanation for all the phenomena upon which
the glacial theory has been constructed.

Geology is a most fascinating and valuable science. It has
contributed much to make the physical world about us
more intelligible. It opened secret treasures of the earth
that had been withheld from the knowledge and the use of
man for uncounted generations. We appreciate the service
this science has rendered to the general advancement of the
human race. But when the speculations of geology come

into conflict with God's own revelation concerning the origin of His universe and concerning that great judgment by which the first world was destroyed and the face of the world completely altered, we will correct geology and not God's revelation.

A humble and unbiased investigator of the available evidence on the crust of our earth cannot lightly brush·aside the Biblical accounts of Creation and of the Flood. After all, our Bible has stood the test of time despite the countless attacks made against it through the ages. If men would only approach this sacred record in the same spirit as when in search for truth in the research laboratory, they could not but agree that the Biblical account offers a sane and reasonable solution of the many difficult problems which confront the student of geology. And if some questions remain for which even then there is not found a satisfactory answer, even that fact need not unduly disturb us, because heaven and earth about us are full of mysteries for which man, with his finite limitations, has not found, nor ever will find, a satisfactory answer. For our final answer we cannot get beyond the wisdom of the Psalmist when he reverently, with awe and wonderment, says: By the word of the Lord were the heavens made; and all the host of them by the Breath [Spirit] of His mouth. He gathereth the waters of the sea together as an heap; He layeth up the depth in storehouses. Let all the earth fear the Lord; let all the inhabitants of the world stand in awe of Him. For He spake, and it was done; He commanded, and it stood fast. (Ps. 33:6-9.)

The Last Judgment, by Doré

CHAPTER XX

The Flood a Prototype of the Final Judgment

T HE Flood is the greatest single event in the history
of the earth since the days of Creation. It is the
most satisfactory solution for most of the problems
which perplex and confuse the Christian student of geology
and physical geography.

But the Flood has more than a geological significance.
The basic cause for this great world catastrophe was not
geological or cosmic, but ethical and moral. Because of the
wickedness of man God destroyed that world of superb
perfection which He had created for an habitation of man.
A study of the Flood would therefore be incomplete without
a reference to the moral depravity of that generation which
was responsible for the destruction of the earth and without
some application to the world of today.

According to Jesus and the Apostles, the Great Flood was
a prototype of the final Judgment awaiting the present
world. St. Peter writes (2 Pet. 3:5-7): "For this they will-
ingly are ignorant of, that by the word of God the heavens
were of old, and the earth standing out of the water and in
the water, whereby the world that then was, being overflowed with water, perished. But the heavens and the

earth which are now, by the same word are kept in store, reserved unto fire against the Day of Judgment and perdition of ungodly men."

And Jesus says (Matt. 24:37-39): "But as the days of Noe were, so shall also the coming of the Son of Man be. For as in the days that were before the Flood they were eating and drinking, marrying and giving in marriage, until the day that Noe entered into the ark, and knew not until the Flood came and took them all away; so shall also the coming of the Son of Man be."

For those who are able to read the signs of the times it is evident that we are now living in those days described by Jesus.

As in the days of Noah, so the world today has reached an unprecedented stage of material and technical progress. There never was a time in the history of man when physical advantages, comforts, luxuries, and leisure were so widely distributed as in our age. We harnessed the forces of nature and have compelled them to do our bidding. We have gone up into the heavens and brought down lightning, no longer the terror of man, and have forced it to bear our burdens, to run our errands, and to furnish us with amusements in our leisure hours. We have gone down into the bowels of the earth and have brought up its treasures, liquids and solids, that they might minister to our needs, pleasures, and comforts. The arts and sciences flourish among all the civilized peoples. Superstition, ignorance, and illiteracy are rapidly disappearing. Human suffering is being alleviated, life is prolonged, and men even speak of the time when death will be abolished.

But there is a counterpart to all this material progress. As of the first generation, so must it be said of the great masses today that they are flesh. They are no longer governed or guided by the Spirit of God. Our age is an age of worldliness, or carnal-mindedness, and secularism; violence and wickedness abound. The philosophy of the average

344

man is decidedly a this-world philosophy. Godlessness stalks about with a brazenness as never before. In Europe the Christian Church has collapsed and seems to be on the way out to make room for atheistic Communism, a way of life worse than paganism. The political and social chaos caused by the war, the famine, misery, and bitterness which have followed the war, are accelerating the process of moral and religious disintegration.

Atheism and a purely materialistic view of life are even finding their way into the pagan world. The temples of the heathen are decaying. The gods are crumbling or are being thrown into the rubbish heap. Atheistic Communism has overrun all of China and is finding its way into India and Africa. It is no longer a question of what god or gods, but it is no god at all.

And what about America? According to the last religious census, less than half of the adult population of the United States is connected with one of the Christian denominations. This means that at least seventy million in our country profess no religion. They are not pagans in the common meaning of that term. They are indifferent to all religions, are unconcerned about God and God's revelation; in other words, they are godless. This means that seventy million Americans are practical atheists! And that in a country which boasts of the superiority of its religious and moral standards. To millions of our people, the Bill of Rights, guaranteeing freedom of religion, stands for a freedom from all religion. Democracy has become our fetish, and in the minds of many it supersedes in importance even religion and God. In our seats of higher learning, the colleges and universities of our country, where the leaders of the next generation are being trained, the authority of the Bible has been completely eliminated. The Creation story and the Great Flood are ruled out as impossible. What remains of the Old Testament is relegated to folklore or is placed on the level of mere poetry. The miraculous elements of the entire Bible, the deity of Christ, the atonement of Christ, the resurrection from the dead, in fact, most of the fundamental articles of our Christian faith, are either questioned or openly denied and even ridiculed. What the Bible calls the Moral Law of God is placed in the categories of taboos and social mores, and sin has been reduced to a mere maladjustment, the result of frustration, or is merely termed a form of anti-social living.

The college graduate of today is the teacher of the grade and high school of tomorrow. He is the future textbook writer, the editor of our magazines, the newspapers, and other publications. He will hold all the influential places in the society that will follow ours, and thus the unbelief and skepticism which is dispensed at the fountainhead of knowledge today will gradually penetrate down through all the strata of society of tomorrow.

But that is not all. Even within the Church, unbelief has become rampant. Unbelief has found its way into the very sanctuary of the Church itself. A study made a few years ago revealed the following distressing facts: 64 per cent of the ministers in one of the larger Protestant denominations in America deny the Trinity; only 25 per cent of the pastors of the same denomination believe in the Virgin Birth; 85 per cent of pastors in the same group no longer regard the Bible as an infallible revelation of God. Fewer than 47 per cent of all Protestant ministers accept the Genesis account of Creation as reliable, and only 64 per cent of all Protestant ministers questioned believed in the efficacy of prayer.[1]

It is again a case of the godly being influenced by the ungodly, or the children of God looking with lustful eyes on the daughters of man. They are concerned about the material things and the carnal pleasures of this world.

The descendants of Seth had the greatest men as their teachers and guides, men who had walked and communed with God, such as Adam, Enoch, Methuselah, Noah, and all the great patriarchs, and yet the godly were overcome by

346

the ungodly. They were merged with them. No doubt the form of the earlier Church remained, and a pretense of religion was preserved among them until the day that Noah entered the Ark. But it had lost its power, and as a result the world perished.

And so it is today. We are building bigger and better churches. We are more artistic in the forms of our services. We are even spending more for missions. The Church speaks much about Christian education, but no longer understands the term spirituality. The Church is more and more ceasing to be a salt and a leaven in this ungodly world. The Church is less and less a city on a high hill and a light to guide others.

The *Pictorial Review* of some years ago characterized the conditions in the modern American Church in a rather striking manner in an article entitled: "Has the World Conquered the Church?" It wrote as follows: "The church has been wedded to the world, and the world is now her married name. She is now truly the church of the world, as formerly she was the church of God. She is far more influential socially and politically. She can elect you to a high office and does it. If you contribute enough to her support, she may move you in the worst and highest society. She keeps up with the Dives crowd. She will yet buy grand opera for her choirs. She gets money not merely as she did formerly from her own church collections, but from her husband, the world at large. She would be in bankruptcy if it were not for the union she has contracted with the world. The church is not gaining the world. The world is gaining the church. More money is being spent by the church for religious purposes than ever was spent in the history of mankind, and never before have men and women been so indifferent to the teaching of religion. You may join the church and still remain entirely of the world in your life and character. Preachers must be produced suitable for this church of the world. They do not lead their flocks, the flock leads them. They are intelligent, entertaining speakers, but they do not speak with authority. Some of them are sensational preachers, but with all the fuss they make, with all the publicity they get from the press, they come woefully short of the stature of these older preachers of the word. The reason is that they have themselves no convincing sense of the Gospel they preach. The trouble is this. The church has become rational and is growing less spiritual. The church is losing the vision and is engaged more and more in the purely secular salvation of man. There is a decadence of faith. And the fear is, what kind of rabid faith will take the place of this sublime and simple faith which had inspired the greatest churches, the bravest deeds, the monuments and motives of mankind?"

Such are the conditions in the Church and the world about us, and the tragedy is that we have grown so accustomed to the situation that we are no longer disturbed. It is evident that we are approaching a time such as existed in the days of Noah. The line of demarcation between the godly and the ungodly is being wiped away. God's supreme and absolute authority is no longer recognized. His Word is being rejected. The Law of God has been set aside, and men no longer fear God or fear to transgress His commandments. But where there is no fear of God, there is no respect of man. All restraint has been removed. Lawlessness and license, violence and corruption, have followed in the wake. Remember how often the words "corruption," "violence," and "wickedness" occurred in the description of the generation of Noah. If we were to characterize our age today with two words, these words would be "violence" and "corruption." Our newspapers and radio are the daily records of the violence and oppression, the corruption and wickedness, in our world, such as have not been known in the history of man. Human life is the cheapest thing today in a world of rising prices. Never have men been so callous to human suffering and misery. Murder is committed by men and women, by young and old, by individuals and gangs, by whole communities and nations. The men and women of our generation who are past middle age have lived through two horrible and wicked wars. Ten million human lives were destroyed in the First World War, and twenty million more died as a result of that war. And in less than a quarter of a century we were at it again. The Second World War is said to have destroyed 65,000,000 human lives, and the bloody business continues on a global scale. All the natural and human resources of the civilized nations of this earth and all the creative ingenuity of man were harnessed for a wholesale destruction of men, women, and children in nearly every part of the world. The perverted genius of man has succeeded in creating such instruments of torture, barbarism, and destruction that even Satan and his legions in hell must have been surprised. Our press and radio commentators report with glee the results of this work of hell, and our godless generation applauds. Even the Church has become callous to this fiendish orgy of murder and violence; to a deplorable degree the Church has ceased to contend for righteousness and justice and finds it more expedient to become "patriotic" and more convenient to sanction the horrible, bloody business as a holy war.

In Genesis we read: "There were giants in the earth in those days . . . the same became mighty men of old, men of renown." The Hebrew word means more than what we understand by the term "giant." It means those that fall upon others, brigands, thugs, tyrants. These *nephilim* were famous in that world. They had made a great name for themselves through their acts of violence, lawlessness, and corruption. They were known by all, and their statues were probably found in the antediluvian shrines of honor.

There are *nephilim*, or giants, in the world today. They are the men who rule this world. They hold their councils in secret. They dispose of countries and millions of human beings as so many figures on a chessboard. They confiscate property that does not belong to them and condemn millions of innocent people to a horrible death of misery and starvation. They blot out whole cities of men, women, and children, with hell-born missiles of death, but they are applauded as great men and renowned, and their portraits and statues are given a place of honor in the halls of fame in our world today. This is a blind and wicked generation, led by blind and wicked men.

Such is a picture of the world today. In the chapter which gives the reasons why God brought the world-wide flood upon the first world, we read: "And God saw that the wickedness of man was great in the earth and that every imagination of the thoughts of his heart was only evil continually. . . . The earth also was corrupt before God, and the earth was filled with violence. And God looked upon the earth, and, behold, it was corrupt, for all flesh had corrupted his way upon the earth." (Gen. 6:5, 11-12.)

This description most certainly fits our own generation. The world is ripening fast for its final judgment. It would be well therefore that we heed the warning of Peter when he says: "The Lord is not slack concerning His promise as some men count slackness; but is long-suffering to us-ward, not willing that any should perish, but that all should come to repentance. But the Day of the Lord shall come as a thief in the night, in the which the heavens shall pass away with a great noise and the elements shall melt with fervent heat, the earth also and the works that are therein shall be burned up. Seeing, then, that all these things shall be dissolved, what manner of persons ought ye to be in all holy conversation and godliness, looking for and hasting unto the coming of the Day of God, wherein the heavens, being on fire, shall be dissolved and the elements shall melt with fervent heat! Nevertheless, we, according to His promise, look for new heavens and a new earth wherein dwelleth righteousness. Wherefore, beloved, seeing that ye look for such things, be diligent that ye may be found of Him in peace, without spot and blameless." (2 Pet. 3:9-14.)

Appendix

Since the publication of THE FLOOD the author has been asked repeatedly (1) why he did not say something about the new science of radiocarbon dating, and (2) how he would harmonize the Biblical chronology of the Flood with the findings of this new science.

The answer to the first question is: The book on the Flood appeared before Dr. Libby had published his treatise on radiocarbon dating.

The following is offered as an answer to the second question:

a. The radiocarbon dating technique is still a very young science and the future will tell whether there will be a further development or a modification of what has been achieved so far.

b. The radiocarbon dating technique is based on the assumption that all forces and processes of nature had always through all times been as they are in the world today. In 1911 it was discovered that cosmic radiations are effecting a corresponding change in the gases composing our atmosphere. When these gases, caused by this change, are absorbed by the plants, the plants become to that extent radioactive and when the animal eats this plant, the animal in turn also becomes radioactive. So long as the plant or animal remains alive, a constant equilibrium is maintained, each one constantly taking in some radiocarbon and constantly losing an equal amount as the radiations are given off. But when the animal or plant dies, the two-way process is stopped because from that moment the dead animal or plant ceases to absorb but continues to give off these radiations. Since the rate at which radiocarbon loses its intrinsic character is known, the length of time since death occurred can be ascertained by a type of test which has been evolved. But, apparently, great skill and precautions are necessary to secure even the moderately accurate results that have been achieved thus far.

Furthermore, the method employed involves the burning of the object tested, so as to reduce it to gas. The gas is then tested. It is obvious that because of this fact many objects cannot be tested by this method. Animal bones are found not to be good specimens. Shells are rated very low as test material, while charcoal and well-preserved wood rate very high. To make the test possible, there must be enough of the substance to be tested to produce a certain quantity of carbon dioxide gas when burned.

As already stated, this method is based on the assumption that the forces and processes of nature have always been exactly as they are now. Dr. Libby, one of the pioneers in this new science, writes in his book, *Radiocarbon Dating*:

> If the cosmic radiation has remained at its present intensity for 20,000 or 30,000 years, and if the carbon reservoir has not changed appreciably in this time, then there exists at the present time a complete balance between the rate of assimilation of new radiocarbon atoms for all material in the life cycle. (P. 8)

But this very "if" assumption seems to allow legitimate reason to question the accuracy of this testing method when ages are involved that would go back to the period before the Flood. We know that the Flood brought about great changes in our universe. There were, for example, several radical changes in the climate, changing it from a universal springlike climate to the present zones of extreme heat and cold. That such changes took place can be demonstrated by the fossil remains found in all parts of the world. But if there was a radical change in the climate of our world, then it is also reasonable to assume that there was a corresponding change in the atmosphere; and that again would mean that the cosmic radiation was not the same that it is today. If the cosmic radiation was not the same before the Flood as it is today, then this system of dating will not be reliable for any dates which go back beyond the date of the Flood.

Notes

CHAPTER I

1. Sir John William Dawson, *The Meeting Place of Geology and History*, pp. 36 ff.
2. Alfred Russell Wallace, *Studies Scientific and Social*, I, 277.
3. Idem.
4. Ibid., p. 276.
5. B. Jowett, tr., *The Works of Plato*, pp. 377 ff.
6. Wallace, op. cit., p. 277.
7. Sir Henry Howorth, *The Glacial Nightmare and the Flood*, II, 427.
8. Alfred Russell Wallace, *The Geographical Distribution of Animals*, I, 277.
9. F. H. Knowlton, *The Fossil Forest of Yellowstone National Park*, pp. 28 f.
10. George McCready Price, *The New Geology*, pp. 652 ff.
11. Johannes Riem, *Neue Christoterpe*, pp. 193 f.
12. Frederic A. Lucas, *Animals of the Past*, pp. 24 ff.
13. Wallace, *The Geographical Distribution of Animals*, I, 150, 151.
14. "Wyoming," *The National Geographic Magazine*, August 1945, pp. 153 to 188.

CHAPTER II

1. Edward Hitchcock, *Religion of Geology*, p. 122.
2. E. A. Ross, "The World Trends in Population," quoted in *Birth Control*, by Adolph Meyer, pp. 62 ff.
3. Hugo Obermaier, *Fossil Man in Spain*, pp. 279 ff.
4. Sir Henry Howorth, *The Mammoth and the Flood*, p. 226.
5. G. Fredrick Wright, "Scientific Confirmation of Old Testament History," *Bibliotheca Sacra* (1913), p. 346.
6. For a more detailed account of the discovery of ancient human remains in North America see: *Ancient Man in North America*, by H. M. Wormington.
7. Harold Peake, *The Flood, New Light on an Old Story*, pp. 95 ff.
8. Bassett Digby, *The Mammoth and Mammoth Hunting in Northeast Siberia*, pp. 39 ff.

9. Dawson, *The Meeting Place of Geology and History*, pp. 36, 37.
10. Frederic A. Lucas, *Animals of the Past*, p. 164.

CHAPTER III

1. Willis Mason West, *A Short History of Early Peoples*, p. 1.
2. C. Leonard Woolley, *Ur of the Chaldees*, pp. 42 ff.
3. Ibid., pp. 75 ff.
4. Martin Luther, *Works*, I, 475.
5. Woolley, op. cit., p. 38.

CHAPTER IV

1. *Legends of Babylon and Egypt in Relation to Hebrew Tradition*, pp. 80 ff. — The word *kuffah* is also employed for a large basket. Cf. Ex. 2:3-5.

CHAPTER V

1. B. C. Nelson, *The Deluge Story in Stone*, pp. 156 ff.
2. George McCready Price, *The New Geology*, pp. 60 ff.
3. *Journal of the Transactions of the Victoria Institute*, LXII, 86.
4. *Bulletin of the Lutheran Academy for Scholarship*, October 1943 (Mimeographed form).
5. John Cunningham Geikie, *Hours with the Bible*, I, 170 f.
6. Quoted by Dr. Ludwig Diestel, *Die Sintflut in den Flutensagen des Altertums*, p. 8.

CHAPTER VII

1. Quoted by John Cunningham Geikie, *Old Testament Characters*, pp. 7 ff.
2. Diestel, *Die Sintflut*, p. 11.

CHAPTER VIII

1. Price, *The New Geology*, p. 242.
2. *Face of the Earth*, I, 17 ff., quoted by Price, op. cit., p. 244.
3. *The National Geographic Magazine*, October 1923, pp. 447 ff.
4. Howorth, *The Mammoth and the Flood*, p. 353.
5. Price, op. cit., p. 220.
6. *Journal of the Transactions of the Victoria Institute*, LXI, 98 ff.
7. Pliny has left us a graphic description of the eruption of Mount Vesuvius which occurred A. D. 79, during which the cities of Pompeii and Herculaneum were destroyed and the elder Pliny lost his life. A very vivid account of the eruption of Mount Pelée on Martinique in May 1902, in which 30,000 people lost their lives, is found in the *National Geographic Magazine*, July 1902, p. 248.
8. In this description of the eruption of Krakatoa the author is following rather closely the account as given by Sir Robert Ball in the *National Geographic Magazine*, June 1902, pp. 200 ff.
9. William B. Scott, *An Introduction to Geology*, pp. 30 ff.
10. Sir Archibald Geikie, *Textbook of Geology*, I, 483.
11. A. P. Coleman, *The Last Million Years*, p. 34.

CHAPTER IX

1. James Geo. Frazer, *Folklore in the Old Testament*, pp. 46 ff.
2. William Wundt, tr. Edward Leroy Schaub, *Elements of Folk Psychology*, pp. 391 ff.
3. Johannes Riem, *Die Sintflut in Sage und Wissenschaft*, pp. 7 ff.
4. "Unter allen Sagen aber ist keine, die so allgemein waere, so überall auf der Erde vorkommend, und so sehr geeignet, zu zeigen, was aus ein und demselben Stoff je nach der Gemütsart eines Volkes werden kann, wie die Sage von der Sintflut. . . . Lange und eingehende Besprechungen mit Herrn Dr. Kunike haben mich zu der Überzeugung gebracht, dass er offenbar recht hat, dass die *Tatsache der Flut zuzugeben ist*, denn allen Mythen, vor allem den Naturmythen, liegt ein wirklicher Tatbestand zugrunde, dass aber eine spätere mythenbildende Zeit dann sich des Stoffes bemächtigt und ihm die nun vorliegende Form eines Mythus gegeben hat."
5. Richard Andree, *Die Flutensagen, ethnologisch betrachtet*, passim. See also Leonard King, *Legends of Babylon and Egypt in Relation to Hebrew Traditions*, and Harold Peake, *The Flood, New Light on an Old Story*.
6. Hugh Miller, *The Testimony of the Rocks*, p. 284.
7. *Mythology of All Races*, X, 222.
8. Lowell Thomas, *Hungry Waters, the Story of the Great Flood*, pp. 188, 189.
9. J. S. Bartlett, *History of Wyoming*, I, 62.
10. Richard Andree, *Die Flutensagen*, pp. 73 ff.
11. Miller, *The Testimony of the Rocks*, pp. 286 f.
12. *Buffalo Courier Express*, February 22, 1942.
13. Howorth, *The Mammoth and the Flood*, pp. 444 ff.
14. Diestel, *Die Sintflut*, p. 31.
15. Thomas, *Hungry Waters*, pp. 184 ff.
16. Peake, *The Flood, New Light on an Old Story*, p. 15.
17. Ibid., p. 16.
18. Miller, *The Testimony of the Rocks*, p. 290.
19. John Urquhart, *Modern Discoveries and the Bible*, pp. 173 ff.
20. Howorth, *The Mammoth and the Flood*, pp. 421 ff.
21. Urquhart, pp. 175 ff. Urquhart assumes that the year began in the fall, but it is impossible to determine this with absolute certainty.
22. Peake, *The Flood, New Light on an Old Story*, pp. 18 ff.
23. B. Jowett, tr., *The Works of Plato*, IV, 387, 388.
24. Ovid, *Selected Works*, pp. 134 ff.

CHAPTER X

1. William Wundt, *Elements of Folk Psychology*, p. 392.
2. Sir John William Dawson, *The Historical Deluge in Relation to Scientific Discovery*, pp. 4 ff.
3. Hugh Miller, *The Testimony of the Rocks*, p. 297.

CHAPTER XI

1. George Smith, *The Chaldean Account of Genesis*, VI, 290.
2. John Urquhart, in *Bible League Quarterly*, October—December 1931, pp. 181—83.
3. Peake, *The Flood, New Light on an Old Story*, pp. 54 ff.
4. Urquhart, *Modern Discoveries*, p. 186.
5. Ibid., p. 191.

CHAPTER XII

1. Pierre Marique, *History of Christian Education*, I, 169.
2. Howorth, *The Mammoth and the Flood*, p. 216.
3. Ibid., p. 217.
4. Ibid., p. 218.

CHAPTER XIII

1. C. S. Scrivivasachari, *A History of India*, p. 5.
2. A. P. Coleman, *The Last Million Years*, p. 156.
3. Dawson, *Some Salient Points in the Science of the Earth*, p. 253.
4. Cited by Samuel Kinns, *Moses and Geology*, or *The Harmony of the Bible with Science*, p. 166.
5. Price, *The New Geology*, p. 465.
6. Quoted by Price in *The New Geology*, p. 467.
7. Quoted by Price in *The New Geology*, p. 467.
8. Price, *The New Geology*, p. 467.
9. Dawson, *Some Salient Points in the Science of the Earth*, pp. 252 f.
10. Ibid., p. 253.
11. J. M. MacFarlane, *Fishes, the Source of Petroleum*, p. 14.
12. Ibid., p. 400.
13. Ibid., p. 14.
14. Price, *Evolutionary Geology and the New Catastrophism*, pp. 235 ff.

CHAPTER XIV

1. It is in the possession of Mr. Ben Theimer of that city.
2. Coleman, *The Last Million Years*, p. 56.
3. Howorth, *The Mammoth and the Flood*, p. 351.
4. Ibid., pp. 352 ff.
5. Loc. cit.
6. Ibid., p. 353.
7. Knowlton, *The Fossil Forest*, passim.
8. American Museum of Natural History (report), Vol. 30, No. 1 (1930), 71 ff.
9. Price, *The New Geology*, p. 535.
10. Ibid., p. 533.

CHAPTER XV

1. Howorth, *The Mammoth and the Flood,* pp. 48, 49.
2. In the following discussion of the mammoth I shall quote freely from Howorth directly or at times follow a summary as given by Nelson in *The Deluge Story in Stone,* pp. 119 ff.
3. Digby, *The Mammoth and Mammoth Hunting,* pp. 99 ff.

CHAPTER XVI

1. George McCready Price and Joseph McCabe, *Is Evolution True?* pp. 10 ff.
2. William B. Scott, *An Introduction to Geology,* p. 534.
3. Price, *The New Geology,* pp. 610 ff.
4. Vol. V, Sec. D.
5. Ibid., Vol. II, Sec. A.
6. Arthur I. Brown, *Evolution and the Bible,* p. 25.
7. Price, *The New Geology,* p. 626.
8. *Canadian Geological Survey Report,* Vol. V, Sec. D.
9. Price, *The New Geology,* p. 145.

CHAPTER XVII

1. F. Bettex, *Das Lied von der Schoepfung,* p. 46.
2. Quoted by Hugh Miller, *The Testimony of the Rocks,* p. 143.
3. Ibid., p. 175.
4. Origen, *De Oratione,* p. 302.
5. Carey Croneis and William Krumbein, *Down to Earth,* pp. 301 ff.
6. Ibid., p. 304.
7. Price, *Geological Hoax,* pp. 28 ff.
8. Alfred Russell Wallace, *Studies Scientific and Social,* I, 111.

CHAPTER XVIII

1. Joseph McCabe, *Ice Ages,* pp. 130 f.
2. Coleman, *The Last Million Years,* p. 7.
3. W. W. Atwood, *Physiographic Provinces of North America,* p. 270.
4. Coleman, *The Last Million Years,* p. 208.
5. Ibid., pp. 11 ff.
6. Quoted by Howorth in *The Glacial Nightmare,* II, 507, 508.
7. Ibid., p. 502.
8. Ibid., p. 510.
9. Ibid., p. 765.
10. Coleman, p. 105.
11. *Encyclopaedia Britannica,* 14th Edition, II, 19.
12. Ibid., X, 858.
13. Coleman, p. 110.

CHAPTER XIX

1. Logan Marshall, *The Story of Our National Calamity*, passim.
2. Ibid., p. 69.
3. Thomas, *Hungry Waters*, p. 226.
4. Ibid., p. 225.
5. *The National Geographic Magazine*, September 1927, p. 285.
6. Howorth, *The Glacial Nightmare*, II, 869.

CHAPTER XX

1. G. H. Betts, *The Beliefs of 700 Ministers*, p. 48.

ADDITIONAL NOTES

To p. 107: The earthquake in Alaska on March 27, 1964, lasted only 2 minutes, but the greater part of Anchorage, a city of 100,000, and many other cities were almost completely destroyed. A 2½-block section of the main street in Anchorage dropped 10 feet. The tidal wave caused by the quake reached a height of 30 feet and, traveling at a speed of 500 miles an hour, completely obliterated 29 city blocks in Crescent City, Calif., 2,000 miles away.

To p. 170: The Day of the Dead is also observed in Brazil on the same date. It is a national holiday, and people in great throngs gather at their cemeteries and place colorful flower wreaths on the tombstones or graves.

To p. 182: Near the little town of Swan Reach in South Australia, about 80 miles from the Indian Ocean, I saw an immense deposit of oyster shells of all sizes, packed together in an almost solid mass about 14 feet thick and forming a long ridge in this region. These fossil shells were being quarried and used in place of gravel to surface country roads.

To p. 187: In 1958 a farmer near Regina in South Saskatchewan, Canada, uncovered a deposit of a variety of fossils while excavating a water catchment basin for his cattle. At a depth of 12 feet he discovered tree trunks, cones and needles of fir trees, remains of birds, insects, egg shells, etc. Some grass and moss retained its original color. There are no fine forests within hundreds of miles of this region today.

To p. 201: The theory that petroleum had its origin in animal fats was confirmed by a German scientist who placed animal fats in a sealed container and exposed them to extreme heat and pressure. The result of his experiment was petroleum. *Du und der Reichtum der Erde*, par. 432.

To pp. 338—339: In 1949 a landslide on the side of Mount Rainier in Washington, caused by heavy rains, formed a dam which blocked the water from the melting glacier and thus formed a small lake. As the pressure increased from the rising water in the lake, the dam suddenly gave way and an avalanche of water rushed down the mountainside, carrying with it 50 million tons of debris, including masses of enormous boulders, and completely wiping out miles upon miles of magnificent Washington forest.

Bibliography

Allan, J. A., *Geology*, Province of Alberta, Research Council of Alberta, Report No. 34. A. Shnitka, King's Printer, Edmonton, 1943.

American Museum of National History (report), Vol. 30, 1930.

Andree, Richard, *Die Flutensagen, ethnologish betrachtet.* Viehweg und Sohn, Germany, 1891.

Anglican Theological Review, 1922—23, 1929—30.

Annual Report of the Smithsonian Institution, 1930.

Arber, E. A. N., *The Natural History of Coal.* Cambridge University Press, 1912.

Atwood, W. W., *Physiographic Provinces of North America.* Ginn and Co., New York, 1940.

Barlett, J. S., *History of Wyoming*, 3 vols. S. J. Clarke Pub. Co., Chicago, 1918.

Beecher, W. J., *The Dated Events of the Old Testament.* S. S. Times Co., Philadelphia, 1907.

Bettex, F., *Das Lied von der Schoepfung.* Verlag von J. F. Steinkopf, Stuttgart, 1922.

Betts, G. H., *The Beliefs of 700 Ministers.* The Abingdon Press, New York, 1929.

The Bible.

Bible League Quarterly, October 1931—March 1936, Nos. 129—146.

Biblical Archaeology, Transactions of the Society of, Vol. II, 1873.

Bibliotheca Sacra, 1913, Vol. 70, pp. 164—182; 1931, Vol. 88, pp. 412—427; 1932, Vol. 89, pp. 453 ff.; 1939, Vol. 96, pp. 68—86.

Bosizio, Athanasius, *Die Geologie und die Suendfluth.* Verlag von Franz Kirchheim, Mainz, 1877.

Brown, Arthur I., *Evolution and the Bible.* The Arcade Printers, Vancouver, B. C., n. d.

Buffalo Courier Express, February 22, 1942.

Bulletin of the Lutheran Academy for Scholarship, October 1943.

Burch, Guy Irving, and Elmer Pendell, *Human Breeding and Survival.* Penguin Book Co., New York, 1947.

Canadian Geological Survey Report, Vol. V, Sec. D.

Chamberlin, Thomas C., and Rollin D. Salisbury, *A College Textbook of Geology.* Henry Holt and Company, New York, 1930.

Clay, Albert T., *A Hebrew Deluge Story in Cuneiform.* Valparaiso University Press, 1922.

359

Clay, Albert T., *Amurra — the Home of the Northern Semites*. S. S. Times Co., Philadelphia, 1909.

Coleman, A. P., *The Last Million Years*. University of Toronto Press, 1941.

Croneis, Carey, and William Krumbein, *Down to Earth*. An Introduction to Geology. University of Chicago Press, 1936.

Davis, John D., *Genesis and Semitic Tradition*. Scribners, New York, 1894.

Dawson, Sir John William, *The Historical Deluge in Relation to Scientific Discovery*. Fleming H. Revell Co., Chicago, 1895.

——, *The Meeting Place of Geology and History*. Fleming H. Revell, New York, 1894.

——, *Some Salient Points in the Science of the Earth*. Harper and Brothers, New York, 1894.

Devens, R. M., *American Progress* or *The Great Events of the Greatest Century*. Hugh Heron, Chicago, 1888.

Diestel, Ludwig, *Die Sintflut in den Flutensagen des Altertums*. Verlag von Carl Habel, Berlin, 1876.

Digby, Bassett, *The Mammoth and Mammoth Hunting in Northeast Siberia*. Appleton and Co., New York, 1926.

Encyclopaedia Britannica, 14th Edition, Vols. II and X.

Frazer, James Geo., *Folklore in the Old Testament*. Macmillan, New York, 1923.

Geikie, Sir Archibald, *Textbook of Geology*, 4 vols. P. F. Collier and Son, New York, 1902.

Geikie, John Cunningham, *Hours with the Bible*, 6 vols. John B. Alden, New York, 1888.

——, *Old Testament Characters*. James Pott & Co., New York, 1885.

Gilbert, G. K., and A. P. Brigham, *High School Physical Geography*. Macmillan Co. of Canada, Ltd., Toronto, 1921.

Gray, Louis Herbert, and George Foot Moore, eds., *Mythology of All Races*, 13 vols. Marshall Jones and Co., Boston, 1916.

Hitchcock, Edward, *Religion of Geology*. William Collins, Glasgow, n. d.

Howorth, Sir Henry, *The Glacial Nightmare and the Flood*, 2 vols. Sampson, Low, Marston and Company, London, 1893.

——, *Ice or Water*, 2 vols. Longmans Green & Co., London, 1905.

——, *The Mammoth and the Flood*. Sampson, Low, Marston, Searle & Risington, London, 1887.

James, E. O., *The Social Function of Religion*. Cokesbury Press, Nashville, 1940.

Jastrow, M., *Hebrew and Babylonian Traditions*. Scribners, New York, 1914.

Journal of the Transactions of the Victoria Institute, Vols. LXII, LXI, LIX. London.

Jowett, B., tr., *The Works of Plato*, Vol. IV. Tudor Publishing Company, New York, n. d.

Kent, C. F., *The Heroes and Crises of Early Hebrew History*. Scribners, New York, 1908.

King, Leonard, *Legends of Babylon and Egypt in Relation to Hebrew Traditions*. Oxford University Press, London, 1918.

Kinns, Samuel, *Moses and Geology*. Cassell and Company, London, 1886.

Knowlton, F. H., *The Fossil Forest of Yellowstone National Park*. Government Printing Office, Washington, D. C., 1928.

Krueger, J. G., *Geschichte der Erde*. Luederwald, Halle, 1746.

Legends of Babylon and Egypt in Relation to Hebrew Tradition. The British Academy, Oxford University Press, 1918.

Lucas, Frederic A., *Animals of the Past*, 7th ed., American Museum of Natural History, Handbook Series, No. 4. New York, 1929.

Luther, Martin, *Works*, St. Louis edition, 23 vols. Concordia Publishing House, St. Louis, 1880—1910.

MacFarlane, J. M., *Fishes, the Source of Petroleum*. Macmillan Co., New York, 1923.

Marique, Pierre, *History of Christian Education*, 3 vols. Fordham University Press, 1924.

Marshall, Logan, *The Story of Our National Calamity*. L. F. Meyers, 1913.

McCabe, Joseph, *Ice Ages*. G. B. Putnam's Sons, New York, 1922.

Meyer, Adolph, *Birth Control*. William and Wilkens Co., Baltimore, 1925.

Miller, Hugh, *The Footprints of the Creator*. Robert Carter and Brothers, New York, 1881.

——, *The Testimony of the Rocks*. Hurst and Company, New York, 1857.

National Geographic Magazine, June 1902; October 1923; September 1927; August 1945.

Nelson, B. C., *After Its Kind*. Augsburg Publishing House, Minneapolis, 1927.

——, *The Deluge Story in Stone*. Augsburg Publishing House, Minneapolis, 1931.

Obermaier, Hugo, *Fossil Man in Spain*. Yale University Press, New Haven, Conn., 1924.

Origen, *De Oratione*. Library of Christian Classics, Vol. II. Westminster Press, Philadelphia, 1954.

Our Hope, 1939—1940, Vol. 46, pp. 56 ff.

Ovid, *Selected Works*, Everyman's Library. Edited by J. C. and M. J. Thornton. Dent and Sons Ltd., New York, n. d.

Peake, Harold, *The Flood in the Light of History*. Robert McBride and Company, New York, 1930.

——, *The Flood, New Light on an Old Story*. Robert McBride and Company, New York, 1930.

Pirsson, Louis V., *Rocks and Rock Minerals*. John Wiley and Sons, London, 1913.

Pirsson, Louis V., and Charles Schuchert, *Introductory Geology*. John Wiley and Sons, New York, 1924.

Price, George McCready, *Evolutionary Geology and the New Catastrophism*. Pacific Press Publishing Association, Mountain View, Calif., 1926.

——, *Geological-Ages Hoax*. Fleming H. Revell Co., Chicago, 1931.

——, *The Modern Flood Theory of Geology*. Fleming H. Revell Co., New York, 1935.

——, *The New Geology*. Pacific Press Publishing Association, Mountain View, Calif., 1923.

Price, George McCready, and Joseph McCabe, *Is Evolution True?* Watts and Co., London, 1925.

Quintillian, Marcus Fabius, *Institutio Oratoria.* The Loeb Classical Library. G. P. Putnam's Sons, 1933.

Riem, Johannes, *Neue Christoterpe,* ed. Reinhard Mumm. C. Ed. Mueller Verlag, Halle u. Bremen, 1905.

——, *Die Sintflut in Sage und Wissenschaft.* Das Rauhe Haus, Hamburg, 1925.

Rimmer, Harry, *The Harmony of Science and Scripture.* Berne Witness Co., Berne, Ind., 1939.

Roger, R. W., *Cuneiform Parallels of the Old Testament.* Eaton and Main, New York, 1912.

Scott, William B., *An Introduction to Geology.* Macmillan Co., New York, 1913.

Scrivivasachari, C. S., *A History of India.* P. Varadachary & Co., Madras, India, 1932.

Seyffart, G., *Neuere Entdeckungen.*

Smith, George, *The Chaldean Account of Genesis,* Vol. VI. Scribner Armstrong, New York, 1876.

Stearns, Harold T., *A Guide to the Craters of the Moon.* National Monument, Idaho (Reprinted from the Bulletin of the Idaho Bureau of Mines and Geology, Vol. 13, July 1928), The Caxton Printers, Caldwell, Idaho, 1936.

Sternberg, Charles, *The Life of a Fossil Hunter.* Jensen Printing Company, San Diego, Calif., 1931.

Synodal-Bericht, Suedlicher Distrikt, 1916; Oestlicher Distrikt, 1919. Concordia Publishing House, St. Louis.

Thomas, Lowell, *Hungry Waters, the Story of the Great Flood.* The John C. Winston Co., Philadelphia, 1937.

Urquhart, John, *Modern Discoveries and the Bible.* Marshall Brothers, London, 1898.

Wallace, Alfred Russell, *The Geographical Distribution of Animals,* 2 vols. Harper and Brothers, New York, 1876.

——, *Studies Scientific and Social,* 2 vols. Macmillan Co., New York, 1900.

West, Willis Mason, *A Short History of Early Peoples.* Allyn and Bacon, Boston, 1923.

Woolley, C. Leonard, *The Sumerians.* Clarendon Press, Oxford, 1928.

——, *Ur of the Chaldees.* Hazell, Watson and Viney, London, 1931.

Wormington, H. M., *Ancient Man in North America* (Colorado Museum of Natural History), Popular Series, No. 4, May 1944.

Wright, G. Fredrick, "Scientific Confirmation of Old Testament History," in *Bibliotheca Sacra* (1913), Oberlin, Ohio.

Wundt, William, *Elements of Folk Psychology.* Macmillan Company, New York, 1916.

Zeitschrift fuer die Alttestamentliche Wissenschaft und die Kunde des nachbiblischen Judentums, 1932, Heft 2/3. Pp. 117—124. Verlag von Alfred Jöpelmann in Giessen.

Index*

Adam, age of, 165
Agassiz, Louis, advocate of glacial theory, 300
Agate Springs, deposit of bones, 183, 236
Alaska, Flood tradition, 137
Alberta, coal reserves, 198
Algonquin Indians, Flood tradition, 134
Allen, J. A., geologist, in reference to fossils along the Red Deer River, 234
Alps, altitude in antediluvian days, 6
Altitude of antediluvian mountains, 122
Andaman Islands, Flood tradition, 138
Animals: cause for great destruction of, according to Darwin, 214; according to d'Orbigny, 215; evidence of great destruction of in Australia, New Zealand, and Tasmania, 215; hibernation in ark, 75; migration of, 75
Antarctica, 10; as habitable region, 4; extent of ice fields, 304
Antediluvian: Alps, 6; climate, 12; civilization, 41, 53; contour of Europe, 4; family size, 28; fauna, 13; flora, 13; genealogy of antediluvian patriarchs, 165; lack of religious articles in antediluvian graves, 53; Himalayas, 6; living space, 2; Mediterranean, 4; ocean

currents, 10; plants, 197; population distribution, 31; pottery as indicative of extent of civilization, 174; Pyrenees, 6; Rocky Mountains, 6; difference between antediluvian and post-diluvian species, 174
Appalachian Mountains, formation during the Ordovician Period, 264
Appalachian trough, 293
Aquinas, Thomas, 177
Arapaho Indians, Flood traditions, 133
Arca Noe, by Kircher, 61
Archaeology, extra-Biblical evidences of Flood, 171
Arctic regions, 10; as habitable area, 4; Arctic islands, abundant in fossils, 243
Ark: capacity, 68, 69; construction, date of, 58; description, 81, discovery of, 77–83; displacement, 60; entrance of animals, 72; entrance of Noah and family, 84; etymology of word; food supply, 75; hibernation of animals on ark, 75; Mount Ararat, 90; Phrygian pillar upon which an ark was carved, 144; provisions and supplies, 64; rooms, 81; size, in relationship to food and water supply, 67; species of animals carried, 67, 69; specifications, 58; window, 61

* This index was prepared by Mr. Victor Streufert, my student helper, for which grateful acknowledgment is hereby made.

363

Asia, lack of evidence for glaciers in, 317
Asia Minor, discovery of old civilization, 45
Assurbanipal, library of, with Babylonian Flood account, 153
Atheism, entrance into pagan world, 345
Atlantis, 5; isle involved in Greek Flood tradition, 145
Atmosphere, 97; humidity of antediluvian atmosphere, 98
Australia, single continent with Tasmania and New Zealand, 4; New Year festival, 169; evidence of catastrophe to animals, 215
Axis, of earth; degree of inclination, 9

Babylon, antediluvian kings of, 166; cubit as unit of measure, 59
Babylonian Flood account, 153; Hebrew Flood account ascribed to, 162; similarity of Hebrew Flood account, 162
Banff, Alberta, 269
Bear Island, Siberian coast, mammoth and bison bones, 243
Bering Strait, link between Asia and America, 5
Berosus, compiler of Chaldean Flood tradition, 142
Beston, Henry, 277
Bettex, F., belief in pause of Biblical narrative, between "in the beginning" and "the earth was without form and void," 281
Bible: authority of, disregarded in seats of higher learning, 345. Creation account, brevity, 276; discreditation by rationalism in biology and geology, 178. Flood account, ascribed to Babylonian account, 162; belief in by Dawson, 163; by Miller, 164; brevity, 276; discreditation by rationalism, 178; similarity to Babylonian account, 162; solution to many geological problems, 341; solution to origin of island seas, 192; and the glacial theory, lack of Biblical reference to ice age, 308;

incompatibility of Bible with glacial theories involving millions of years, 309. reference to patriarchs, 166. reliability of, 42.
Biology, Biblical account of Creation ruled out by rationalism in, 178
Bohemia, coal deposits, 196
Bones, deposits in western Kansas, 235; at Agate Springs, 183, 234; on steppes of Russia, 181; near Stuttgart, Germany, 182; bones of hippopotamus, 181
Boulders, 336; boulder transportation: ability of glaciers to transport erratics, 324, 325; movement of erratics, 300; example of, 307; problems involved, 324, 325
Brazil, knowledge of general deluge among most barbarous natives, 134
British Museum, present location of clay tablets giving Babylonian Flood account, 153
Brontosaurus, largest of sauria, 14; "thunder lizard," 224
Brunswick, Germany, bone deposit in diluvial loam, 181
Burch, Dr. Guy Irving, expert in study of population, 31

Cain, history of family, 28; descendants of, 52; construction of cities, by, 43
Cambrian period, division of Paleozoic Era, 264
Canopy theory, antediluvian climate, 12
Carboniferous Period, division of Paleozoic Era, 264; coal beds in polar regions, 8
Caribbean Sea, islands of as link between North America and South America, 5
Carnal-mindedness, 344
Cenozoic Era, most recent, subdivided into Tertiary and Quarternary, 264
Cephalopods, huge fossil forms, 20
Chalmers, Dr., statement on ability to fix antiquity of world on basis of Moses' writings, 281

Cheyenne, Wyoming, ancient shore lines discernible, 288

Chief Mountain, example of thrust fault, 273

China, atheistic Communism into, 345; destruction caused by Yellow River, 381; coal deposits, 198; gorges cut into loess deposits, 292; emperors before historic times, 168; Flood traditions, 141, 142

Christ, deity questioned or denied, 346

Christian Church, see Church

Chronology, Babylonian, 166

Chukotski Peninsula, Siberian area rich in fossil remains, 245

Church, attitude of, toward war, 349; Church in Europe and America, 345; state of Church in world today, 347; membership of, in America, 355

Civilization, in antediluvian world, 41; corruption of, 53; oldest, 45

Clay, Albert, opponent of theory that Biblical Flood account originated with the Babylonian account, 163

Clay, London clay, 261; formation of deposits, 297

Climate, antediluvian: as shown by fossils, 7; in region of Yellowstone National Park, 8; climate known to ancient world, 7; uniformity of, 9, 194; change: cause for change, 9; effects by Flood, 99; cold weather of Tertiary times, 194. canopy theory, 12

Clouds, influence of volcanic activity, 99; rate of formation to produce Flood, 98

Clyde Valley, drift deposits, 335

Coal, 193—199; coal beds: in carboniferous period, 8; features characterizing, 196; coal deposits: location of, 197; in Alberta, 198; in Bohemia, 196; in China, 198; in Nova Scotia, 198; formation of coal: vegetable matter as base, 193; three conditions requisite for, 193; water as sole possessor of

abilities for formation of, 195; plants found in 197; quantity of, 197; use of, 199

Code of Hammurabi, 46

Coleman, A. P., description of animal life once existing in Iowa, 213; inability to determine cause for ice ages, 312

Commemoration of dead, Egypt, 170

Cosmogony, 278

Cordillera, ice sheet, 314; trough, 293

Crete, old civilization discovered, 45; eastern portion submerging, 121

Critias, 5

Crowsnest Mountain, example of thrust fault, 273

Cuba, Flood tradition, 135; raised coral reef, 121

Cubit, unit of measure among Babylonians, Egyptians, and Hebrews, 59

Cuvier, Georges, reference to series of catastrophic floods, 102

Dawson, Sir William, 103; appearance of first man, 39; Canadian ice sheet, 319; on Deluge as historical fact, 163; on origin of coal, 193; on requisite conditions of coal formation, 193

Dayton flood, 1913

Debris of flood waters, 291

Deep, the great deep, all oceans of the world, 100

Delitzsch, Friedrich, 61, 64

Deluge, see Flood.

Desert belts, hindrance to postdiluvian settlement, 3

Deucalion, figure in Greek mythology describing Flood, 144, 152

Devon Valley, description of flood in, 339

Devonian limestone, conformably covered by Cretaceous beds, 269

Devonian Period, division of Paleozoic Era, 264; abundance of fish during period, 264

Digby, Bassett, *The Mammoth and Mammoth Hunting in Northeast Siberia,* 249

365

ruin, 87; upon antediluvian mountains, 292; upon balance between water and land masses, 333; upon climate, 99; upon rock formation, 287, 288; world revolution of stupendous magnitude, 286; extent, 88, 90; first impressions of, 101; Flood and geology: Flood as explanation for fissure and rubble heaps, 186; geological evidence for Flood, 177; origin of Great Lakes, 191; Flood as reasonable explanation for geological phenomena, 209; Flood and the glacial theory, 298—327; explanation for "glacial drift," 334; solution for glacial theory phenomena, 328, 342; phenomena accompanying Flood, 102; as prototype of final Judgment, 343—350; Flood waters: ability of to accomplish phenomena ascribed to glacial action, 329; amount of water, 123; power of water, 291, 337, 338; source of water, 84, 96, 97; subsiding of, 290; volcanic activities aiding cloud formation, 99

Flood, effects of flood in Winfield, Kans., 338

Flora, carboniferous, 194; superiority of antediluvian, 13; in Yellowstone National Park, 8

Forests, petrified. Origin, according to Knowlton, 216; in Yellowstone Park, 217

Fossils, animal: bison, 36; elephant, 212, 213; prehistoric reptiles, 220; seal, 213; definition of, 6, 210; human, 33; in Honan, China, 33; in Lansing, Kansas, 34; in Natchez, 34; lack of human fossils indicating early geographic distribution, 32; in glacial drifts, problems involved, 326; in mountains, 123; proof of life extant before mountain formation, 193; lack of fossils in Pre-Cambrian rock, 285; lakes, 188—192; location of findings: in every part of world as evidence for a universal

flood, 210—237; Field, British Columbia, 212; Gobi Desert, 4; Isle of Lackov, 243; Klondike region, 217; Sahara Desert, 4; South America, 213; marine: found in region of Quebec, 236; on mountaintops, 236; types, 210

Fountains of the deep, 96; definition, 100

France, fissures in, 179

Frank slide, site of mountain slide at Frank, Alberta, Canada, 292

Frazer, J. G., authority on traditions and myths, 129

Furrows, glacial, 335

Galveston, Texas, description of destructive force of water during the Galveston disaster, 331

Geikie, James, statement of Scotch geologist about coal, 196

Genealogy, Babylonian, 166; of antediluvian patriarchs, 165

Genesis and geology, 257—274; difficulties involving Genesis and geology, 275—297; reinterpretations by Bettex, Chalmers, Miller, and Kinns, 281

Geology and cosmogony, 278; and Genesis, 257—274; definition of, 258; demands of evolutionary geology, 268; problems of unsolved, 276; speculations of, 340, 177; values of, 340, 177; geology and the Flood: evidence for universal flood, 177—187; Flood as explanation of phenomena observed by geology, 209; lack of acceptance of Biblical account, 102; geology and glacial theory: general acceptance of glacial theory, 309; inability of glacial theory to solve some geological problems; geological timetable, 262—274; artificial *a priori* creation, 266; difficulties for Christian student, 264, 276; place of pre-Cambrian rock in, 285

Germany, ossiferous fissures, 179

Gibraltar, Rock of, rubble deposits in fissures, 181

Japan Current, 12

Jesus, statements on the Flood, 343, 344

Johnstown flood, 330

Jubal, father of musicians, 43

Judgment, of the world, 350

Jupiter, central figure in Roman Flood tradition, 148

Jupiter Serapis, Temple of, submerged in Bay of Naples, 121

Kames, 334; definition, 307

Kansas, remains of short-limbed rhinoceros, saber-toothed tiger, three-toed horse, 235

Keewatin ice sheet, 314; height of, 315

Kettle holes, 303

Kinns, Samuel, on significance of *yom*, 281

Kircher, Father, author of *Arca Noe*, 61

Klondike, discovery of fossils, 217

Knowlton, F. H., 8; on origin of petrified forests, 216

Kolyma, river of Siberia, 245

Kootenay Pass, example of thrust fault, 273

Krakatoa, 117, 118; description of eruption of, 119

Kurnai, Flood tradition, 139

Kurtz, Johann Heinrich, church historian, 282

Labrador ice sheet, 314, altitude of, 315; problems involved, 320—322

Lachov, Arctic island with large number of fossils, 243

Lake Agassiz, 93; former inland lake of America, 190, 191

Lake Algonquin, former inland body of water in America, present upper Great Lakes area, 190

Lake Baikal, proof of former submergence of Siberia, 189

Lake Bonneville, former inland body of water in America, 190; area of present Utah, Nevada, and Idaho, 191

Lake Iroquois, basin of Lake Ontario, 190

Lake Lahonton, former inland body of water in America, 190

Lake Nipigon, origin ascribed to volcanic action and lava flow, 192

Lake Okoboji, 306

Lake Superior, origin of, 192

Lake Winnipeg, 93

Lake Winnepegosis, 93

Lakes, as a result of great flood, 192; fossil lakes: found on every continent, 189; American fossil lakes, 190; Gobi Desert, 189; Lake Baikal, 189; Tibetan uplands, 190; glacial lakes, 307

Lamech, 44

Land, area: area of land since Flood, 3; balance between water and land masses, 333; habitable areas, 3; emergence of land: beaches in high altitudes of northern and southern hemispheres, 122; beaches of Scotland, 122; Cuban coral reef, 121; fertility of land, 3; movement of land: cause, 120; Crete, 121; submergence of land: Temple of Jupiter, Bay of Naples, 121; Egyptian coast, 121; western coast of Greenland, 121.

La Place, Pierre Simon, theory of the universe, 309

Laurentian Shield, 262

Lava flow in Rockies, 116

Lena, area of ivory hunting industry, 245

Lithuanian Flood tradition, 139

Living space in antediluvian times, 2

Locusts, fossils, 20

Loess, distribution of, 116; gorges in loess deposits of China, 292; location of deposits, 109; origin of, 108; origin of according to Howorth, 109

London clay, origin of, 261

London Daily Telegraph, sponsor of expedition by Smith to locate more tablets describing Babylonian Flood account, 154

Lord, see God

Lucas, F. A., 39

dition, 139; in one continent with Tasmania and Australia, 4

Niagara Gorge, 291

Nile Valley, old civilization found in, 45

Nineveh, 296; site of search for Babylonian Flood tablets, 154; library of Assurbanipal, 153

Nippur, fragment of Deluge story found at site of ancient Nippur by H. V. Hilprecht, 172

Noah, 57, 58; age at time of Flood, 63, 167; belief in ability to construct ark, 62; entrance into ark, 64, 68; generations of, 63; hiring workmen for construction of ark, 63; provisions taken on ark by, 64; sacrifice after Flood, 94

Normandie, Post-Dispatch account of disaster, 66

North Pole coal beds, 8

Nova Scotia coal deposits, 198

Ob, largest river of Siberia, 244

Obermaier, Prof. Hugo, 32

Ocean, destruction caused by ocean after volcanic action near sea, 117; Gulf Stream, 11; Japan Current, 12; waves originating with eruption of Krakatoa, 120; warm waters surrounding antediluvian continents, 10

Odessa deposit of bones, 181

Ohkotoks, near Sheep Creek, Alberta; location of largest glacial erratic, 307

Oil, 200—209; American production, 200; as found in fossiliferous strata, 200; first oil well in United States, 200; known use of in past, 200; modern use of, 200; reservoirs, 200; resources, 201; theories of origin, 200, 201

Okhotsk, Japan, Asian continental shelf, 5

Origen, reference to *yom* of the Creation account, 281

Orinthostoma, or Pteranodon, American representative of the Pterodactyl family, the flying reptiles, 226

Orogeny, earth's great periods of, 285

Ovid, in *Metamorphoses;* citing of Roman Flood tradition, 147

Pacific Ocean, area and average depth, 123

Paleozoic Era, 262; divisions of, 264

Papago Indians, Flood tradition among Arizona Indians, 132

Pearly Nautilus, 20

Pendell, Dr. Elmer, population expert, 31

Permian Era, division of Paleozoic Era, 264

Persia, celebration of New Year festival, 170; Flood tradition, 142

Peru, New Year festival, 169

Peru, Indiana, description of flood of, 330

Pestilence, impossibility of pestilence causing a catastrophe as great as Flood, 186

Peter, statements on Flood, 343

Petrified forests, origin, according to Knowlton, 216; large areas of in Yellowstone Park, 217

Phoenicians, generations of patriarchs, 168

Phrygia Flood tradition, 144

Plants, in antediluvian world, 197; material for coal, 21

Plato, 5

Plesiosaurs, marine reptiles, 221

Polynesia, Flood tradition, 139

Population, phenomenal growth of in modern times, 26; extent of in world at time of Noah, 26, 29; distribution of in antediluvian world, 31

Pottery, early painted pottery as representation of antediluvian civilization, 173, 174

Pre-Cambrian Era, 262

Prestwich, Professor, observation of fissures, 180; on carrying power of water, 337—338

Price, George McCready, 8, 102; on age determination of rocks, 267; on formation of coal, 195, 196

Pteranodon, or Orinthostoma, American representative of Pterodactyl family, the flying reptiles, 226

Pterodactyl, the flying reptile; Pteranodon or Orinthostoma the American representative of this family, 226

Puget Sound, drift deposits, 335

Pyramids of Egypt, 65

Pyrenees, height in antediluvian days, 6

Quebec, Canada, marine fossils, 236

Rain, duration of during Flood, 84; erosion produced by rain, 294

Radium, 260

Rainbow, 12, 94

Rationalism, in biology, leading to revival of ancient Greek theory of evolution, 178

Reason, man the measure of all things, 178

Red Deer River Valley, discoveries of dinosaur remains, 13, 224

Religion, freedom from, 345

Reproduction, length of human fertility in antediluvian world, 28; in modern world, 27

Reptiles, as dominant animal in Mesozoic Era, 264; fossil remains of prehistoric reptiles found on every continent, 220; marine reptiles, 221; Pterodactyl, the flying reptile, 226; Tyrannosaurus, largest reptile, 226

Rhine, northward flow to Orkneys, 4; Thames and Humber, as tributaries of, 4

Rhinoceros, remains of in western Kansas, 235; woolly rhinoceros contemporaneous with mammoth in northern regions of Siberia, 239

Riem, Dr. Johannes, extensive study of mythology in book Die Sintflut in Sage und Wissenschaft, 129

Rocks, age of, 261: pre-Cambrian oldest, 285; Price, reference to age determination of, 267; classes of, 258: igneous, description of, 258; sedimentary, description of, 258; metamorphic, description of,

258; formation of: account by Joseph McCabe, 259; effect of erosion on, 268; effect of flood waters on, 287; effect by floating bodies of ice, 338; process of disintegration and formation, 283 to 284; strata of: deceptive conformity of various strata, 269, 272, 287; most common stratified rock, 279; nomenclature, 267; problems caused by in attempt to harmonize geology and Genesis, 278; types of: erratics or perched, 306; rounded or smooth, 305; striated, 305, 306

Rocky Mountains, height of in antediluvian days, 6; example of thrust faults, 6

Roman Flood tradition, 147

Roskivitsky, Vladimar, discovery of ark, 77—83

Ross, Dr. E. A., authority on population studies, 30

Rubble deposits, cavern near Palermo on Sicily, 181; definition, 179; in England, 180; on Gibraltar, 181

Russia, ossiferous fissures, 179; Russian steppes, evidence of inland lakes, 190

Sahara Desert, fossils found in, 4

St. John's College, Winfield, Kansas; effects of flood, 338

St. Petersburg, exhibition of mammoth from Siberia, 253

Salt pans or salt licks, 190

Sandstone, formation of, 297

Sandusky, Ohio, examples of many striated rocks, 306

Sauria, 13; brontosaurus, 14; monasaurus in western Kansas, 14; tyrannosaurus, the tyrant lizard, 14

Scotland, elevated beaches, 122

Scottsbluff Bison Quarry, 36

Sea, see ocean

Seals, fossils found at Montreal, Canada, 213

Secularism, 344

Seth, descendants of, 52, 346

Shale, formation of, 297

Volcanoes, account of Krakatoa eruption, 117, 118; formation of clouds, 99; formation of lakes, 192; location of extinct volcanoes, 108; production of loess, 108; simultaneous with earthquakes, 108

Voyage of the Beagle, The, by Darwin, 106

Wallace, Alfred R., 4, 6, 7, 21

Water, amount of earth's surface covered by, 123, 333; as explanation for bone deposits, 334, 186; as explanation for production of coal, 195; as explanation for destruction of mammoths, 254; as explanation for phenomena ascribed to glacial action, 329, 334; bodies of water left by Flood, 91, 188; carrying power of, according to Prestwich, 337–338; disposal of Flood waters and problems associated with, 290; erosion by and examples of, 291; force of, 291; source of, 96, 290

Waves, 120

Weather erosion, 294

Welsh Flood tradition, 139

Wickedness, 344

Wind erosion, effects of, 294, 296

Windows of heaven, 97, 98

Winfield, Kansas, effects of small flood, 338

Woolley, C. Leonard, 38, 47, 48, 49

World, condition of world in beginning, 6; condition of world today, 344; corruption of, 350; postdiluvian, 296; process of evolution, 257

Worldliness, 344

Wundt, Wilhelm, expert in mythology, 129

Xisuthros, last of Chaldean antediluvian kings, 142, 167

Yellow River, destruction accomplished by flood of, 331

Yellow Sea, relationship to Asian continental shelf, 5

Yellowstone National Park, climate, 8; flora, 8; petrified forests, 217

Yenisei, river of Siberia, 244

Yom, common and first meaning of "day," 282

Zeuglodon, or yoketooth, a marine reptile, fossil remains numerous in areas adjacent to Gulf of Mexico

CPSIA information can be obtained at www.ICGtesting.com
Printed in the USA
LVOW12s0840301014

411130LV00001B/1/P

9 780570 031833